SHIFTING

SHIFTING

The Double Lives of
Black Women in
America

Charisse Jones and
Kumea Shorter-Gooden

HarperCollins*Publishers*

HarperCollins books may be purchased for educational, business, or sales promotional use. For information, please write: Special Markets Department, HarperCollins Publishers Inc., 10 East 53rd Street, New York, NY 10022.

The stories and voices that are presented in this book are derived from the African American Women's Voices Project and from Dr. Shorter-Gooden's clinical experience. However, names, places, and other details have been altered to protect the confidentiality of the individuals who are discussed. Therefore, any similarity between the names and stories of individuals described in this book and those of individuals known to readers is inadvertent and purely coincidental.

FIRST EDITION

Designed by Nancy Singer Olaguera

Printed on acid-free paper

Library of Congress Cataloging-in-Publication Data
Jones, Charisse.
    Shifting : the double lives of Black women in America / Charisse Jones and Kumea Shorter-Gooden.—1st ed.
        p.   cm
    Includes bibliographical references and index.
    ISBN: 0-06-009054-5
    1. African American women—Psychology.   2. Adjustment (Psychology)—United   States.   3.   Racism—United   States—Psychological aspects.   4.   African   American   women—Social   conditions.   5. African American women—Interviews.   I. Shorter-Gooden, Kumea. II. Title.
E185.625.J657   2003
306.7'089'96073—dc21
2003040728

03   04   05   06   07   ❖/RRD   10   9   8   7   6   5   4   3   2   1

For my mother, Jean, the beacon whenever I lose my way.
For Olive and Irene, grandmothers who paved the road.
And for Camille, a sister and a friend.
Thank you.

Charisse

In memory of my grandmothers, Ella and Rosa,
And to my mother, Margaret,
And my sister, Wendy,
And my daughter, Adia,
With love and appreciation for the gifts you have given me,
And the gift you have been to me.

Kumea

ACKNOWLEDGMENTS

It took a village to create this book. We are indebted to many colleagues, friends, and family members who helped us in various phases of this work.

We deeply appreciate those who recruited participants and collected data for the African American Women's Voices Project: Dolores Alleyne, Myrtle Anderson, Angela Banks-Johnson, Delores Bolton, Jo Ann Bradley-Jones, Gina Casey, Barbara Coles, Aja Collay, Jan Collins-Eaglin, Monique Earl-Lewis, Ayesha Edwards, Wendy Edwards, Darlene Ephriam, Shirley Flournoy, Jerine Gadsden, Sherona Garrett-Ruffin, Gail Gathings, Karen Goland, Loleti Gooden, Darlene Greene, Carnita Groves, Isabelle Gunning, Kelley Haynes, Sophia Henry, Evelyn Hospedales, Leslie C. Jackson, Irene Jackson-Brown, Ruth Johnson, Shawn Johnson, Camille Jones, Jamila LaFleur, Phyllis Mahome, Kemba Maish, Bernadette Hickman Maynard, Joy Middlebrook, Jaronda Miller, Danielle Moody, Jennifer Noble, Kimani Norrington, Nanette Oketch, Dee Sermons, Mary Shaw, Gary Shorter, Beverly Tate, Danille Taylor-Guthrie, Cassandra Washington, Carol Winn, Angela J. Wright. And a very special thanks to Shondrah Tarrezz Nash and Christina Camp.

We are grateful to Kimlin Ashing-Giwa and Joan Murray, who provided expert research and statistical consultation, and to those who served as research assistants: Adia Gooden, Keyashia Jackson, Tenika Jackson, Jennifer Noble, and Yoshi Smith.

We offer heartfelt thanks to those who reviewed portions of the manuscript and provided invaluable feedback: Valerie Coachman-Moore, Shirley Flournoy, Winston Gooden, Shelly Harrell, Kemba Maish, and Joanne Morris.

We thank the Antioch Company and Quality Artworks for their generous donations of bookmarks that were given as tokens of appreciation to the survey participants.

We are grateful for our institutions—*USA Today* and the California School of Professional Psychology of Alliant International University (AIU)—which have supported us with enthusiasm even as our attention has at times been drawn elsewhere. A special thanks to Kenneth Polite of AIU.

The feedback we received from our editor, Gail Winston, helped to push us up a steep learning curve. We thank her for her excitement about this work and for sharing her talents with us. And we appreciate Christine Walsh and all of the staff at HarperCollins who worked so diligently on this project.

Without the vision, wisdom, and rolled-up-sleeves involvement of our agent, Todd Shuster, this book simply would not be. We are deeply grateful for his seminal and central role in this work, his active championship of these important issues, his ever-wise guidance and counsel, and his faith in us.

There's no way that we could have accomplished this task without the active support and involvement, patience, and forbearance of our families, whom we love dearly and whose love for us is seemingly unparalleled. Charisse extends a special thanks to her parents, Charles and Jean Jones, who have been lifelong models of fortitude and consciousness, and to Camille and Carlton who buoyed us with their prayers and pride. And she offers much love to Jordan Reid Kinard who showed unusual patience as his mommy tapped away at her computer for hours at a time. Kumea is grateful to Winston, whose love, constancy, and wisdom help to keep her centered and reasonably sane; to Adia, whose passion for life and justice is inspirational; and to Margaret, Gary, Gretchen, Wendy, Bobby, Valerie, and Shirley, who held her hand tightly throughout the roller coaster ride.

We are deeply moved by the many women who openly, honestly, and sometimes painfully shared their lives with us and with the world. To you, we offer what can only be a very humble thanks.

CONTENTS

CONTENTS

SHIFTING

THE ROOTS OF SHIFTING

Black women are seen as "hot in the pants," tough and strong, able to withstand a lot of physical and emotional abuse, unfeeling. . . . I find this to be demeaning, degrading, and unproven. Yet I find myself constantly trying to disprove them.

CECILIA, 52, HARTFORD, CONNECTICUT

The Gifts of Black Women in America

Black women in America have learned to find humor in heartache, to see beauty in the midst of desperation and horror. They have been both caregivers and breadwinners, showing incredible strength and resilience, unflinching loyalty, boundless love and affection. They have risen above centuries of oppression so that, today, after years of dealing with society's racist and sexist misconceptions, with its brutal hostilities and unthinkable mistreatment, not only are they supporting families, they're leading corporations, major media organizations, the military, our state and federal governments. Black women have often been the champions on our nation's sports teams, breaking Olympic records, guiding the nation to victory. They have assumed a prominent place in the culture of our times both in the United States and abroad, contributing great literature, journalism, music, dance, theater, science. They have etched anew the cultural landscape with their courage and vision. Maya Angelou. Oprah Winfrey. Mae Jemison.

Venus Williams. Alfre Woodard. Judith Jamison. Faith Ringgold. Lauryn Hill. Ruby Dee. bell hooks. Carol Moseley-Braun. Anna Deavere Smith. Faye Wattleton. Toni Morrison. Johnnetta Cole. There are so many brilliantly talented, beautiful, deeply thoughtful and intelligent African American women who are shaping our world today and doing everything possible to make it a richer and better place.

Black women have so much to offer our country, so many gifts to share with all of us. And yet, as a society and as a nation, we have never quite stopped to appreciate the truth of their experience, the verity of what it feels like to be Black and female, the reality that no matter how intelligent, competent, and dazzling she may be, a Black woman in our country today still cannot count on being understood and embraced by mainstream White America.

As a society, we know very little about the psychology of Black women, a group of 19 million people—7 percent of the U.S. population.[1] The way they experience the workplace, the complexities of their romantic lives, the challenges they face as mothers and grandmothers, their spiritual and religious practices, these and so many other aspects of their lives are largely unknown to the wider community. Being ignored and poorly understood likely explains why so many Black women today still feel profoundly unhappy about their place in society. In a June 2002 Gallup poll, 61 percent of Black women said they were dissatisfied with "how Blacks are treated in society."[2] For Black men, the rate of dissatisfaction was lower—47 percent. In the same poll, 48 percent of Black women, in contrast to 26 percent of White women, said they were dissatisfied with "how women are treated in society."

Black women in America have many reasons to feel this deep sense of dissatisfaction. As painful as it may be to acknowledge, their lives are still widely governed by a set of old oppressive myths circulating in the White-dominated world. Based upon those fictions, if a Black woman is strong, she cannot be beautiful and she cannot be feminine. If she takes a menial job to put food on the table and send her children to school, she must not be intelligent. If she is able to keep her family together and see her children to success, she must be tough and unafraid. If she is able to hold her head high in spite of being sexually harassed or accosted, she must be oversexed or promiscuous. If she travels the globe, she must be ferrying drugs rather than simply trying to see the world. Fifty-year-old Melissa from Los Angeles articulates what she finds most challenging about being a Black woman in America today: "Believing what I know and not what I'm told, and beginning to understand the divide. *I am a Black woman. I am moral. I am intelligent. I am lovable. I am valuable.* But the majority of the messages I get all say that I'm not. . . . I don't know how I do it."

While most people of color, and African Americans in particular, are perceived through a distorted lens, Black women are routinely defined by a specific set of grotesque caricatures that are reductive, inaccurate, and unfair. bell hooks of the City College of New York enumerates these "gendered racist stereotypes" that include the emasculating Sapphire, the desexualized Mammy, and the scheming temptress Jezebel.[3] Today, in the twenty-first century, these and other stereotypes, so prevalent in old Hollywood movies and black-and-white television reruns, have mutated into contemporary versions of their old selves. Sapphire, for instance, can inevitably be found with just a few clicks of the remote control in an old episode of *NYPD Blue* or *Law and Order* when police make their way into a poor Black neighborhood. Sapphire is harsh, loud, uncouth, usually making the other characters seem more professional, more charming, more polished by contrast. She is a twisted take on the myth that Black women are invulnerable and indefatigable, that they always persevere and endure against great odds without being negatively affected. This is one myth that many Black women themselves embrace, and so they take on multiple roles and myriad tasks, ignoring the physical and emotional strain, fulfilling the stereotype. There is peer pressure among Black women to keep the myth alive, to keep juggling, to keep accommodating. Some women who desperately need balance in their lives, who greatly need assistance, never seek or receive it. Instead, their blood pressure soars. They overeat. They sink into depression. Some kill themselves or try. Others simply fantasize about making an escape.

Indeed, society's stubborn myths continue to do tremendous damage to Black women. They often seep into their inner psyches and become permanently internalized, battering them from within even if they're able, for a time, to wriggle free and live the truth. Stereotypes based on race, gender, and social class make it hard to trust oneself and to trust others who look or behave like you do. They set confusing parameters on who you think you are, and what you believe you should or can become. They often dictate what you expect, what seems real, and what seems possible.

The African American Women's Voices Project

Over the last two years, the two of us—Kumea, a clinical psychologist and professor at Alliant International University, Los Angeles, and Charisse, a New York–based correspondent for USA Today—have completed the African American Women's Voices Project, an extensive research project designed to explore the impact of racism and sexism on Black women in America. We set out to learn about African American women's experiences of racial and gender stereotypes, bias, and discrimination; what it feels like; and how they react and respond to it. We wanted to know about the impact of racism and sexism on different aspects of their lives, on their self-image, their relationships with men, their lives as mothers, their experiences in church, and their experiences in the work world. We wanted to hear about whether, to what extent, and in what ways Black women change how they behave in order to counter the myths and manage direct acts of discrimination. We wanted to learn about internal changes as well, the emotional responses to and consequences of prejudice, the invisible toll of bigotry on their individual lives.

Ours is the largest, most comprehensive study to date of African American women's perceptions and experiences of racism and sexism. A number of studies have focused on Black women's experiences of racial bias and discrimination, and others have focused on gender stereotypes and prejudice, but few, like ours, have looked at both areas of discrimination simultaneously and how they connect and intersect with one another. The existing research on Black women's experiences of racial or gender bias tends to be characterized by a small number of research participants, often a few dozen women; a research sample that represents a particular segment of the Black female population, for example, Black female college students or Black female managers; and samples that are geographically limited, often restricted to one or two colleges, a handful of workplaces, or one metropolitan area. As described below, our study includes a large number of women from across the country of diverse ages and backgrounds. Moreover, our research, unlike many other studies, entailed listening very closely to how Black women make sense of their lives, to the words and voices they use to evoke their experiences.

The psychology of Black women has gotten short shrift in the national discourse, mostly due to indifference and the same racial and gender prejudice that shadows Black women's lives. But it is now critical that we pay attention. The rates of hypertension, depression, and AIDS among African American women have reached crisis proportions. Understanding the pressures Black women live with, and the compromises that they make mentally, emotionally, and physically, is of utmost importance. Their lives may depend on it. Thus, the African American Women's Voices Project.

The project included a survey and in-depth interviews. With the generous and diligent assistance of research assistants located throughout the country, all of whom are Black women, we collected surveys from 333 women, ages 18 to 88, who reside in 24 states and Washington, D.C.: from large cities such as Los Angeles, Phoenix, Chicago, Dallas, New York, and Atlanta, to suburbs in New Haven County, Connecticut, and Prince George's County, Maryland; from small towns in New Jersey, Ohio, and Alabama to rural areas in Kentucky and Arkansas.[4] We were able to obtain responses from a remarkably diverse cross section of Black women in America—women of different ages, educational backgrounds, incomes, marital statuses, and sexual orientations. The survey, which has mostly open-ended questions, asks women to write briefly about their perceptions of stereotypes of Black women, their major difficulties as Black women, whether and in what ways they've experienced racial and gender discrimination, whether they feel pressured to behave differently, and what helps them to "make it." It also inquires about their joys as Black women—what they love about being Black and female. (See Appendix for more details on the survey and the findings.)

In addition to the surveys, we conducted in-depth interviews with 71 women throughout the United States.[5] The interviewees range in age from 18 to 80 and represent many walks of life.[6] Though the sample of women who were surveyed and interviewed is neither random nor representative of Black women in the United States, it provides a meaningful glimpse of the diversity of Black women across the country.

Along with the research we conducted, another source of data is Kumea's experience as a psychologist. Some examples come from clinical class.

Many of the women we interviewed commented on how deeply moving it was to be asked about areas of their lives that other people generally express little interest in and offer little understanding of. Some wept during their time with us, and told us how cathartic it felt to have the chance—sometimes for the first time ever—to talk openly about the truth of their lives as Black women.

The "Shifting" Principle and Other Key Findings of the African American Women's Voices Project

In the testimony of the women who participated in the African American Women's Voices Project, by far the most resounding theme is that Black women in America find that they still must deal with pervasive race- and gender-based myths. Of the women we surveyed, 97 percent acknowledge that they are aware of negative stereotypes of African American women and 80 percent confirm that they have been personally affected by these persistent racist and sexist assumptions.[7]

Our research shows that in response to this relentless oppression, Black women in our country have had to perfect what we call "shifting," a sort of subterfuge that African Americans have long practiced to ensure their survival in our society. Perhaps more than any other group of Americans, Black women are relentlessly pushed to serve and satisfy others and made to hide their true selves to placate White colleagues, Black men, and other segments of the community. They shift to accommodate differences in class as well as gender and ethnicity. From one moment to the next, they change their outward behavior, attitude, or tone, shifting "White," then shifting "Black" again, shifting "corporate," shifting "cool." And shifting has become such an integral part of Black women's behavior that some adopt an alternate pose or voice as easily as they blink their eyes or draw a breath—without thinking, and without realizing that the emptiness they feel and the roles they must play may be directly related.

The ways in which a Black woman shifts have of course changed over time. An enslaved woman or a Black woman living under the heel of Jim Crow would have to shift literally, casting her eyes downward, moving her body off a sidewalk or to the back of a crowded bus when a White passenger came into view. Today, shifting is more subtle and insidious—keeping silent when a White colleague sexually harasses her, for fear she will not be believed; acting eager but not aggressive at work, so as not to alienate a White boss; and then shifting again at home to appease a Black man who himself has to live with the pain and unfairness of society's prejudices and hate.

Shifting is what she does when she speaks one way in the office, another way to her girlfriends, and still another way to her elderly relatives. It is what may be going on when she enters the beauty parlor with dreadlocks and leaves with straightened hair, or when she tries on five outfits every morning looking for the best camouflage for her ample derriere.

And shifting is often internal, invisible. It's the chipping away at her sense of self, at her feelings of wholeness and centeredness—often a consequence of living amidst racial and gender bias.

To shift is to work overtime when you are exhausted to prove that you are not lazy. It is the art of learning how to ignore a comment you believe is racist or to address it in such a way that the person who said it doesn't label you threatening or aggressive. It is overpreparing for an honors class to prove that you are capable, intelligent, and hard-working or trying to convince yourself that you are really okay no matter what the broader society says about you. It is feeling embarrassed by another African American who seems to lend a stereotype truth, and then feeling ashamed that you are ashamed. And sometimes shifting is fighting back.

There are few high-achieving Black women who are not adept at shifting, and few others who, whatever their proficiency, do not find that they must shift in order to survive. But sometimes in their endless quest to prove themselves and put others at ease, many Black women break down emotionally or physically under the pressure, their lives stripped of joy. Sometimes they are unable to withstand the onslaught of negative messages. Their sense of self falters as they start to believe the falsehoods, doubting their own worth, questioning their own capabilities. They become susceptible to an array of psychological problems, including anxiety, low self-esteem, disordered eating, depression, and even outright self-hatred. They may have made others comfortable, but left themselves feeling conflicted, weary, and alone.

The devastating impact that shifting can have on a woman's psyche and soul is far more obvious today, if only because there are now statistics to document it. Our research and that of other colleagues suggests that the disconnect between who one is and who one must pretend to be can be tremendously damaging. Research consistently shows that Black women are less happy and experience more discontent than Black men, White men, or White women.[8] For example, in a National Center for Health Statistics study of more than 43,000 U.S. adults, Black women were three times as likely as White men and twice as likely as White women to have experienced distressing feelings, like boredom, restlessness, loneliness, or depression, in the past two weeks.[9] Our analysis of the survey and interview data from the African American Women's Voices Project reveals that racist and sexist attitudes and discriminatory behavior are still taking a significant toll on Black women. Specifically we found that:

- *Race discrimination against Black women persists.* Fully 90 percent of the women we surveyed say they have experienced discrimination, and 10 percent specifically remember being called a "nigger" at one point in their lives.

- *Gender discrimination against Black women is also pervasive.* Sixty-nine percent of the survey respondents report that they have experienced bias or discrimination based on gender.

- *Most Black women "shift" their behavior to accommodate others.* A majority (58 percent) of the women in our survey indicate that at times they have changed the way they act in order to fit in or be accepted by White people. Of this group, 79 percent say that to gain such acceptance, they have changed the way they speak, toned down their mannerisms, talked about what they felt White people were interested in, and avoided controversial topics.

- *Discrimination is experienced most frequently at work.* While Black women respond to racism and sexism in various arenas, it is the workplace where they encounter it most often. Sixty-nine percent of the survey respondents say that they have experienced racial or gender discrimination at work, and issues related to the workplace, including getting hired, being paid equitably and being promoted fairly, emerged as the major difficulties in being a Black woman.

- *Black women frequently submerge their talents and strengths to support Black men.* Forty percent of the women surveyed have at times downplayed their abilities or strengths with Black men. In the most extreme cases, Black women who don't feel good about themselves, who feel pressure to fulfill traditional gender roles by being passive and submissive, or who feel that they must give up parts of themselves in order to secure and keep a male partner may put themselves at risk for emotional abuse, violence, and even HIV infection.

- *Sexual abuse and harassment of Black women is all too frequent.* Many Black women suffer silently as victims of childhood sexual abuse or adult sexual harassment, sexual assault, or rape. The myths and stereotypes about Black women being promiscuous may make it more difficult for Black women to feel comfortable speaking up about their abuse experiences, and the tendency to be silent about gender abuse in the Black community makes it particularly difficult if the perpetrator is a Black male.

- *There is increasing pressure on Black women to meet conventional beauty standards.* From early childhood through adulthood, many Black women, pressured to be physically attractive and to live up to Eurocentric beauty standards, experience tremendous pain and shame related to their skin color, hair texture, body shape, or weight. The feeling of being unattractive haunts many Black women and impacts their self-esteem and relationships with men. These feelings can also put Black women at risk for eating disorders, to which they were previously thought to be immune.
- *Black mothers are acutely aware of having to train their children to cope with discrimination.* Mothering Black children involves the usual parental tasks of providing for the child's basic needs and supplying nurture and guidance, but in addition Black mothers are almost always involved in socializing their girls and boys to cope with the reality of racism, and they are often engaged in educating their girls about the dynamics of sexism. Racial/gender socialization is a central focus of many Black mothers, particularly if they are raising children in predominantly non-Black areas.
- *Black women have a disproportionately high risk for depression.* Black women are at particularly high risk for depressive symptoms and clinical depression. Yet Black women often mask their depression, submerging it in busyness, martyrdom, overeating, or overspending.
- *Black women often feel discriminated against within their churches.* Though many Black women are deeply spiritual and rely greatly on their faith to buoy them during difficult times, many feel that their gender makes them second-class citizens within traditional Christian churches.

Our findings, and the conclusions we've drawn from a review of related research conducted by other investigators, indicate that much of the physical and emotional distress that Black women in America experience today is a consequence of racism and sexism, and particularly of society's stubborn myths about who they are and can be.

America's Myths

While research reveals that Black women are misunderstood and mis-treated for a complex array of reasons, the women in our study point to five central sets of myths and stereotypes that confront them again and again.

First, Black women regularly receive the message that they are inferior to other people. Many African American women find that they must routinely struggle to disprove this untruth, often going to great lengths simply to demonstrate that they are as intelligent, com-petent, trustworthy, and reliable as their non-Black friends, associates, and coworkers.

Second, there is the myth that Black women are unshakable, that somehow they are physically and emotionally impervious to life's most challenging events and circumstances. The stereotype of the strong, tough Black woman is pervasive in American society, and many women in our study lament how hard it is for them to express and accept their own disappointments and vulnerabilities. The pressure to maintain such an image can be immense, and behind the façade, there is often tremendous sorrow.

Given the societal tendency to see masculine and feminine quali-ties as diametrical opposites, it is not surprising that Black women, deemed strong, invulnerable, and unshakable, are also stereotyped as unfeminine. Moreover, since White women presumably provide the ideal model of femininity, and because Black women don't fit the same mold, they are mythologized as domineering, demanding, emasculat-ing, and coarse. To avoid being labeled overbearing, or too assertive, a Black woman may suppress her opinions and her voice. She may mute her personality.

Fourth, there is the myth that Black women are especially prone to criminal behavior. Numerous women speak of experiences in which salespeople, police officers, security guards, and even colleagues at work falsely perceive them as dishonest and untrustworthy, as law-breaking crooks who must be watched at every moment.

Finally, Black women continue to be perceived as sexually promiscuous and irresponsible. Many Black women in America are disrespected, objectified, sexually harassed, and sexually abused. Tragically, the Black community itself often ignores the extent of this mistreatment.

For many women, dealing with these myths means stashing away their dreams. Ashley,[10] a talented actress and singer from Chicago, put off becoming a professional cabaret performer until she was in her late thirties, and hesitated even then to tell certain people that she was on stage, because she didn't want to be viewed as "one of those," a Black woman who would fulfill a stereotype by "grinning, and entertaining the White people." For years Ashley toiled in unfulfilling jobs because she was afraid of confirming the stereotype of Black people as mindless entertainers. "It made me old," she remembers of the days spent doing work that did not interest or challenge her.

Edna, a 38-year-old New Yorker, asks a poignant question: "Is there some place I can go and be seen and be heard as a human being, just as a human being? Can my humanness be heard while you're looking at a Black woman?"

The Myth of Inferiority

Lucinda gave up her house in Berkeley last year for an apartment in a luxurious high-rise building in San Francisco. She wanted to be closer to her job in a downtown brokerage firm, but she missed her old neighborhood. The folks in her co-op didn't say good morning to each other. Instead of a backyard, she had a small wrought-iron balcony dotted with petunias and impatiens. And she hadn't been living in her new building more than a few weeks before a disturbing pattern began to emerge. Her new neighbors never seemed to believe that she actually lived there.

About two months after she had moved in, Lucinda was waxing her Honda Accord behind the apartment building when a slender brunette approached her. "When you're finished," the White woman asked her, "Could you help me?" Lucinda was devastated by the woman's assumptions: "I was like, 'Excuse me?' And she was like, 'When you finish here, could you help me?' I looked at her and caught what she was saying, so I said 'Are you disabled?'"

When the woman angrily demanded whom Lucinda worked for in the building, Lucinda told her: "Nobody. I live here. And she just looked at me and said, 'Oh.'" The woman had thought Lucinda was a housekeeper.

Lucinda claims that such incidents don't weigh on her mind. "I don't give White people power and maybe that's my own prejudice. They don't have any power in my life, [over] my core, the person who I am in my being."

But unlike Lucinda, many women express how acutely painful it is to live with the myth that Black women are somehow inferior to other people. Although some of the women we interviewed claimed that they had rarely been the brunt of direct comments to this effect, nearly all of them reported how difficult it is to survive in a culture that constantly stereotypes Black women as unintelligent, lazy, unmotivated, unattractive, difficult to deal with, and unable to maintain a functional family. The message in America is that there's something very wrong with Black women.

In reality, on a number of levels—higher education, career development, professional positions—Black women in our nation are increasingly competing shoulder-to-shoulder with other Americans. According to recent statistics, 78 percent of African American women ages 25 and older have completed high school, 17 percent have completed a bachelor's degree or more,[11] and close to half a million have earned a master's degree or more.[12] The high school completion rate of 78 percent compares favorably to the graduation rate of 85 percent for White women; and while the rate has almost doubled for White women since 1960, the rate for Black women has nearly quadrupled.[13] Moreover, from 1977 through 1997, the number of Black women with bachelor's degrees increased by 77 percent and the number with master's degrees jumped by 39 percent.[14] From 1989 to 1995, the number of Black women in managerial and professional positions rose by 40 percent, which was a much greater rate of increase than that of White women.[15] And yet the general public, by and large, does not seem to be aware of these soaring rates of achievement.

Listen to Tina, a 23-year-old science major and student government officer at a university in Texas where she is one of very few Black students. Tina invests huge amounts of her time and energy trying to disprove the myth of inferiority by emphasizing to her non-Black peers and professors that she is not lazy or unintelligent but rather a talented hard-working student. She feels constant pressure to perform as the "optimum African American," and as a result, she works herself to exhaustion.

> When I walk [into a new class] that first day, . . . I feel like I come in with something to prove already, like I'm already set back by the way people are perceiving me. They're wondering why I'm here. Am I really smart enough to be in this class? . . . Last semester, there were only eight people in my biology class. After the first couple of assignments, I felt like I had to work extra hard on the professor, go to his office hours, show him I'm not in this class to sit here and coast through. In classes like English literature, where I know teachers are gonna ask questions, I go out of my way to make sure I have answers prepared for those classes. I make sure that I have stuff done for that class just so I will never look like I don't know what I'm talking about or I'm unprepared or not keeping up with assignments, even if sometimes it's making me suffer in another class.

Tina's parents warned her about the myth of Black women's inferiority. "What you have to understand, Tina, it's like you already have two strikes against you. You're Black and then you're a woman. You need to stay two steps ahead of what everybody else is doing in this world." And for Tina, this message has taken on particular salience: as a science major, she has sometimes been both the only African American and the only woman in a class. Tina feels she's "carrying the weight of not just being me, but being all Black women," and that it's tremendously difficult to please everyone all the time.

How are they going to perceive every Black woman? How are they going to perceive every woman who's in science? . . . You feel like you gotta be perfect. You gotta be fit. You gotta be smart. You gotta be strong, but not so strong that you offend everybody. You gotta be outspoken, but not too outspoken. You've got to be all these different things. You've got to be able to take crap from people and bite your tongue. . . . You feel that almost every day.

Jordan, 29, perhaps represents the extreme to which African American women can go in order to disprove the myth of inferiority. During her elementary school years, living in what she describes as "the heart of racism," she had to fight her way out of special education classes, where she was placed because it was assumed she couldn't read, even though she'd been reading since before she entered kindergarten. Outside of school, in the neighborhood, she was confronted with open Ku Klux Klan rallies. Now a nursing school graduate, she has an Afrocentric look, and she seems to feel good about herself as a Black person. Her dreadlocks dangle, and she speaks with fondness about the predominantly Black community where she spent her teenage years. Yet she's in a long-term relationship with a White man who is tattooed with Klan-related insignia. While her boyfriend disavows any current involvement in the KKK, his father is the local grand master. Jordan's aunt and uncle, who raised her, have refused to meet her boyfriend, but Jordan prides herself on not seeing color the way that they do. And she's taken on the task of educating her boyfriend's parents. The first meeting with his family, however, was brutal: They openly called her a "nigger." But Jordan persisted.

When they sat down and opened up their hearts and listened to me and saw what I was doing with their son, they kinda accepted me more. I get phone calls from them now. They just check on me. . . . I don't know what it was. I really wasn't their image of Black people or Black women. I had gone to college. I had this. I had that. I didn't need anybody. I had an intellectual background, and they saw me going to work every day. And when I talked to them, they was just like, "Maybe she is different." I don't know what it was. But it was something in them clicked. . . . They know that I'm Black, but they can talk to me. It's like, I'm with them as a person. They accept the fact I'm with their son.

We can't help but wonder what it's cost Jordan to engage in this struggle with the grand master's son and his family. It would seem that in working to disabuse them of the myth of Black inferiority, in shifting to meet them where they are, suffering their abuse and suppressing her emotions, she at times has sacrificed her own self-respect.

The reaction of the grand master and his wife to Jordan suggests another reality: disproving stereotypes does not always dispel them. Her boyfriend's parents appear to see her as an aberration. Indeed, so pervasive is the myth of inferiority that when women defy the stereotype, they are sometimes seen as suspect. Listen to Samantha, who was laid off her job, ran out of money, and then ended up being evicted from the apartment where she lived with her two young children. When Samantha, an attractive woman, clearly bright and thoughtful, sought public assistance, desperate for temporary financial support to make ends meet, the state welfare workers didn't believe her case: "They didn't see me as needing anything because of my demeanor, my ability to speak well, the fact that I can carry on a conversation and still make sense. Basically, I was told that I didn't qualify for anything even though I was homeless and even though I showed proof. I went through hell just to get what little bit I have now."

Many of the women in our study lamented that when they finally prove to others that they are hard-working, refined, and intelligent, non-Blacks often deem them to be "exceptional" or "different from" other Black people. Ironically, some may temporarily benefit from the myth of Black women's inferiority, gaining a kind of acceptance in certain circles, and a platform for success in certain careers, because they are considered "unique," "better than" other women of color.

"That's one of those games you play with yourself," says Lisa, a 33-

year-old woman who graduated with honors from MIT and was constantly praised by her professors. "Maybe I'm not that great. They're not *expecting* me to be great as a student." Lisa has dealt with such skewed expectations her entire life. She remembers tutoring a fellow student in biology when she was in the tenth grade. "He said to me, 'You know Lisa, you're really smart for a Black girl.'"

Other Black women recount that as children, they constantly had to face teachers and schoolmates who marveled at their academic prowess, at how "special" they were. And such thinking haunts these women as adults. Though they are educated, and may have come of age in homes more prosperous than their White, Latino, or Asian colleagues, outsiders still often react with surprise when Black women are well-spoken, inquisitive, or well-read. Indeed, it's a double-edged sword to hear, as many bright professional Black women do, the phrase "You're so articulate." While seemingly a compliment, the underlying message is that it is surprising to find an intelligent Black woman who speaks Standard English so well. "You don't seem Black," they are told again and again. The message is clear: When Black women are talented, professional, and competent, they're no longer really Black, because these qualities don't fit the stereotypes.

Francine, a woman in her midforties, and a high-ranking manager at a pharmaceutical company, talks about how frustrating it is not to be seen as "truly Black." "When you're Black and competent, White people see you as the exception to the rule. I can't tell you how many times a White person has told me that I'm different from most Black people. [It's] very insulting." Francine elaborates:

> I think they mean you're articulate, you can hold a conversation, you can talk about world events, you read the paper, you know how to use the computer, you have one in your house, you've got family structure, you have a sister and a brother and they're all doing well too. . . . I think they think they're complimenting me, but what they've really done is just smack you across the face. . . . I have felt ashamed that somehow I've portrayed myself in a way that makes them think I'm a better per-

son because I'm not "Black," because I've assimilated so much that I get this great pat on the back from them, and somehow I kind of divorce myself from my true being.

Being deemed exceptional can also mean bearing the burden of living up to unrealistic expectations, never easing up your workload, always conforming, staying ever mindful of your *p*'s and *q*'s to continue justifying your acceptance. Many Black women feel that they must be far better at their jobs than their White counterparts just to prove that they have a right to be where they are. They sense that the margin for error that they are offered is much smaller and narrower than the one offered to most White folks. When a White colleague falters or fails, executives seem to be relatively forgiving. But when a Black woman stumbles on the job, White executives are more inclined to see it as "proof" that she just doesn't have what it takes—that she is inferior. Black women do not believe that they have the leeway to be average, to be better at some things rather than others, simply to have a bad day. Rather, the women in our study say that they feel a strong demand to exceed people's expectations, to do everything "right."

The Myth of Unshakability

Black girls don't cry. They shake and bend and explode, but they never break. In all the black-and-white stills of Rosa Parks, arrested in Montgomery because she was tired and dared to sit, she sheds no tears. She is strong. She is unflappable. The obituaries written about Betty Shabazz, Malcolm X's widow, talked about how she got her graduate degrees and raised six daughters by herself, but not about the toll such daunting challenges must have taken on her emotionally. On television, powerful stalwart Black women have been legion—from the noble housekeeper on *I'll Fly Away* to the Black attorney on *Any Day Now*, to Jeannie, the pediatrician's assistant on *ER* who had time to forgive her philandering ex-husband and love a dying boy, even as she struggled with HIV.

Black women are told that they are tough, pushy, and in charge rather than soft, feminine, and vulnerable. The image makes her someone to be feared rather than someone to be loved. These stereotypes render Black women as caricatures instead of whole people with strengths and weaknesses, tender sides and tough edges. And ultimately they make Black women invisible because they are not seen for all that they really are.

To be deemed unshakable is not the most vile of myths. Indeed, Black women have consistently demonstrated exceptional strength and courage. And many say that it feels good to be recognized for something positive.

However, because the myth of unshakability has also become so embedded in the collective psyche of the Black community, African American women often find that they are not allowed to be vulnerable or needy, even among their own. Sharon, a 38-year-old insurance claims adjuster, in Greensboro, North Carolina, and Phyllis, a 36-year-old graphic artist from Boston, go so far as to suggest that Black women today have no right to complain, given the harsher realities their ancestors endured. "Anything past slavery is gravy," Sharon opines. Adds Phyllis, "Nothing should be driving us crazy right about now. The shit that we've overcome? Think about that. I don't care how strong we think we are. They bounce us back to slavery, you think we'd survive two weeks? I wouldn't say we were strong at all. Strong? That's funny."

Betty, 47, didn't feel the emotional weight of the loss of her mother until weeks after the funeral. She'd been the one who'd had to make the arrangements and support her father and siblings in their immediate emotional collapse. It was the typical pattern. She was always diligent and dependable. When her husband died suddenly a decade ago, Betty had at times worked three jobs to keep a roof over her family's head, support her children, and put them through college. Now, months after her mother's death, she needed someone to lean on. But even her closest girlfriends couldn't handle her grief. Her best friends would walk away from her on the rare occasions when she'd break down and cry. After all, she had always been strong, taking care of everything and everyone. Betty had to go to a psychotherapist to find someone to cry with.

Claudia, a 24-year-old single woman who grew up in a family of 10 children, had managed to get her bachelor's and master's degrees while working full-time and raising an infant son on her own. In Claudia's view: "What happens is when you're feeling independent and strong, everybody relies on you for emotional support, but nobody's willing to give it to you because they automatically think that you have it within yourself, that you don't need to have someone hug you and say, 'Everything's going to be okay' or 'Do you need any help?' People won't offer any help because they feel that you have it all under control."

But even if help were offered, some Black women would not accept it. Many who have internalized the stereotype of unshakability, when they find themselves in anguish, continue to sustain their strong Black woman persona. They are unable to turn it off, to shift from overdrive into neutral. Regina Romero, an African American psychotherapist in Washington, D.C., notes that the "paradox of strength" is such that it's often tough for these women to permit themselves to get the help they need and deserve.[16] Connie, a confident, soft-spoken woman in her late thirties and a published writer, explains how she's been crippled by the need to act strong and in control at every moment:

> The superwoman stereotype—we have embodied that. And we think that we have to be all things to everybody. And we go about doing that, but we are nothing to ourselves. . . . We are nurturing, we are taking care of our kids. Sometimes we are taking care of our sisters' kids, our brothers' kids. We're taking care of our brother, we're taking care of our sister, we're taking care of our man. We're taking care of our parents, *but not taking care of ourselves.* I think that just about every Black woman I know is doing that in some capacity, that they feel like they have to be "the all." And they are going about wearing themselves out trying to do that. . . . I really feel guilty if I do something for myself. And I think that maybe we don't think we're worth it. I think that a lot of us have been beat down by life, that even though outwardly we may be the most

sophisticated, the most together sister that there is, we're not sure we're worth the self-nurturing.

As Connie's comments suggest, strength can be an illusion. The truth, of course, is that like all other human beings, Black women are constantly trying to refill their wells of confidence and self-esteem. They struggle like everyone else to regain emotional ground lost after every broken romance, after every professional or personal setback. Sometimes they need assistance or direction. Sometimes they are sad and disappointed. Sometimes they are afraid.

To be sure, Black women are heirs to a remarkable legacy. It is hard to imagine what courage it took to go to bed each night knowing that when you rose the next morning, you would still be a slave—yet you kept on living. It is hard to discern what spiritual fortitude was required to instill pride in generations of children who were growing up in a hostile society that sought to belittle them, or worse. But the image of invincibility that has arisen out of such a history can become its own prison, an impossible standard to uphold, unrealistically raising the expectations of employers, lovers, and relatives and compelling a younger generation of Black women to judge itself too harshly.

Part and parcel of the myth that Black women are unshakable is the myth that Black people don't become depressed or commit suicide. Suzanne, 29, remembers the day that she tried. It was 1988, the year that Suzanne was in a car accident that left her partially paralyzed. She was 15 years old.

"I took an overdose," she remembers. "By the time they found out, it was too late to pump my stomach." The doctor said that she would have convulsions. "But nothing happened. So it was always a medical mystery, and I feel like that was just God intervening."

The daughter of a nurse and a construction worker and the older of two children, Suzanne was told from the time she was small that she had to set an example. And she didn't let her family down, excelling in school, doing her chores without being asked. But it was the courage she showed after the car accident that seemed to prove that nothing could ever undo her. Her relatives and friends often said that if it had been them—running free one day, struggling with a walker the next—they would not have handled it so well. But Suzanne showed her stoicism, and soon began to believe that she had to be courageous because, after all, that was what everyone expected. There was no other way to be.

"I feel like I can't be anything less than strong," she says, adding that the pressure comes in myriad ways. "I think it's because I'm a Black woman, and we're just tough. I think it's because I'm a Christian and I feel like I have to keep the good fight going, the good fight of faith—'No, woman, you can't get tired. You get up. You'd better not be weary and ill doing. . . . You've got to be a soldier, and if you're getting tired it must be because you don't believe.'"

Suzanne is close to her parents and speaks of their love and support. But she says that at times her mother's and father's words only added to the unrealistic strain that she puts on herself. Once as a teenager she had to go to the emergency room after she'd injured her arm. Suzanne writhed in pain, and her mother held her in her arms. But even then, Suzanne was told how to be. "Stop that crying," her mother would say. "You've got to be strong. Be strong. Be strong." Suzanne concludes: "I think through all those years of all those sermons about being strong, I feel like, *How dare you not be strong?* Almost like it's shameful to be anything less than strong." But that day, when she was 15, she reached her breaking point.

The Myth of Nonfemininity

If Black women in America are stereotyped as unshakable, our research shows that there is another closely linked myth that persists: that Black women are less feminine than other women and, in fact, even emasculating. The myth sprang to life in the characters of Mammy and Sapphire, then evolved into the archetype of the coarse, sassy Black girl, a ubiquitous image in popular culture. In an oft-repeated skit on *Saturday Night Live*, cast members and a rotating roster of guest hosts, including Gwyneth Paltrow and Jennifer Lopez, pose as a neck-swiveling, slang-spouting, "ghetto-fabulous" girl group in the style of Destiny's Child, drawing peals of laughter. But such warped images take an immeasurable toll on the psyche of Black women, who in their desire to be seen as ladylike, to challenge the notion that they are less feminine, may affect a way of talking or behaving that does not truly reflect who they are. Some may settle for less than fulfilling relationships because they fear, based on their own self-image, that they cannot do any better.

Of course, many Black women do have a language and style all their own, a way of communicating through gestures or a glance that is unique. Sass, they will tell you, is at times an attitude of necessity. It's what you need to be the high-jump champ on a city block. It can carry you through schoolyard confrontations or give you the last word in a political debate. It's the mask you wear to cover the hurt when a friend tells your secrets, or the armor you don when a boyfriend breaks your heart. But it is a myth that all Black women possess this quality, and that those who do are less sophisticated or less feminine.

Unfortunately, while the Black community has been remarkably adept at blocking out the negative messages of the broader society, it is perhaps inevitable that society's distortions will sometimes color African Americans' views of themselves. More than one Black male celebrity has evoked the image of the "emasculating," or "difficult" Black woman to explain why he mistreated his wife or why he is now dating a non-Black woman. Others have blamed the problems of some Black men, from chronic unemployment to incarceration, on domineering Black girlfriends, wives, or mothers who, they say, did not allow these men to take the lead or grow into responsible adults.

When asked what major difficulties she faces as a Black woman, Margo, a 41-year-old attorney in Chicago, says: "The perception of Black women as complaining, overbearing, bitchy . . . has affected my relationships with men, Black and White. For example, if I challenge my White male supervisor or coworker, I'm viewed as aggressive, and Black men view my ambition and independence as overbearing and bitchy."

"I feel that I have to walk a fine line to show assertiveness without appearing harsh," says Heather, a 31-year-old conference planner from Los Angeles. "I am always under added pressure to make certain my reactions and responses are within a predescribed window of ranges."

Too many Black women are pushed to internalize these misperceptions and accusations, their sense of self slowly corroding. Paula, a 22-year-old executive assistant, says, "By trying to disprove the whole 'attitude' stereotype, I make myself small. In other words, instead of being the strong woman that I am by voicing my opinion and saying how I feel, sometimes I back down so as not to seem like I've got an attitude, which is discouraging."

Some women say they are not approached by men from other ethnic groups because, they believe, the men don't think of them as "feminine" or "ladylike." It is a twisted testament to the pervasiveness of sexism that some Black women say that this misperception can be a good thing, sparing them from sexual harassment at the hands of non-Black men. Vera says that in medical school, her Blackness seemed to shield her from the leering advances and attention suffered by her non-Black female peers. "The reason I say it's an advantage is because I didn't have to deal with male students and male instructors on a sexual level at all," she says. "They didn't treat me as a sexual person. I was more of an 'it.' So I felt like they dealt with me with more respect than they did White women and Asian women. There were so few women that they were subject to a lot of flirtation, a lot of attention from men that was definitely of a sexual nature, and I never got that. I never felt like my professor was hitting on me. When I dealt with TAs [teaching assistants] or professors, I felt we were talking about the material."

Tammy, a 38-year-old executive secretary from Hyattsville, Maryland, believes that in order to be professionally successful, Black women have the complicated task of being both traditionally feminine and uniquely strong. "There is a constant struggle of balance between strength and femininity. In the work world, you must have exceptional strength to supersede the obstacles in your way as a minority and woman. Yet, you must be able to show the more feminine side, even in business situations."

For many of the Black women in our study, such shifting is necessary in all the realms of their lives. Anne, a 47-year-old investment adviser from Atlanta, who spends her workday in a male-dominated field and, as a single parent, handles the full gamut of parenting responsibilities, describes how "masculine" she feels at times.

> Being single and having to do absolutely everything feels very masculine. It feels hard. I need to break down for a day and just be whatever I need to be. There's hardly any space to do this. . . . Both my parents are deceased and my family is in another area, and I feel I have to be father and uncle, grandmother, grandfather. There's all these roles and sometimes it has to be very masculine. . . . Being masculine is being hard and having to be tough through the war. I can't just be the gatherer now. I got to go out and hunt, kill it, strip it down, then gather it, prepare it, cook it, feed it. I don't want to do all that. Doing all of that feels very masculine."

Still, as Anne and many others attest, one can be strong and still very much a lady. Artemis, 46, has skin the color of almonds and barely fills out a size 3. She wears her cornrows in a pageboy and is the type of woman who can go to a thrift shop, pick up an elegant gown for $40, and outshine the woman next to her who spent thousands.

She also has a smoky voice as smooth as Drambuie, and can sing the songbooks of Nancy Wilson and Peggy Lee from memory. So when she performed jazz standards at supper clubs around Cleveland, Artemis couldn't understand why, when she took the stage, she sometimes felt a chill descend upon the room. She sounded great and she looked good, so what could be the matter?

Her appearance, she soon realized, was exactly the problem.

"There's a way that people can freeze you out," Artemis says. "They can let you know without saying a word that you're not welcome. You just know it. And being Black, we're in tune to that. For example, I could be singing at a particular hotel or a corporate gig and feel it. It's subtle, but it's there. I see it in their eyes. In other words, I see their souls. . . . I see, 'What's she doing here?' And then it's, 'Who does she think she is? How dare she be here?'"

When it happens, explains Artemis, it is always women—White

women. "I have come out and the women in the audience—there's a scowl on their face. They hate me. And the musicians have seen it. I'm not making this up. The musicians have seen it. Just angry at me. Very angry."

When Artemis first saw such reactions, she felt hurt and confused, until the interracial group of men who backed her on stage explained it to her. "The musicians say, 'You're supposed to be fat. You're supposed to be real fat,'" she says. "Or I'm supposed to be loose and vulgar. I mean it sounds so silly because it is, but it's true."

Because Artemis doesn't fit the myth of the asexual Mammy or the harsh Sapphire, because she exudes femininity and is strikingly beautiful, she is rebuffed. What we find is that when Black women are stereotyped, they pay a price, and when, like Artemis, they defy the stereotypes, they may pay a price as well.

The Myth of Criminality

As challenging as it is to be seen as ignorant and incompetent, callous and unshakable, and less feminine and lovable than other women, one of the most devastating myths about Black women is that they are prone to criminal behavior. While this myth is most closely associated with Black men, Black women suffer from it as well, sometimes uniquely.[17]

It is hard to find a Black woman who cannot recall an incident in which she was treated disrespectfully by store employees who assumed she was there to steal or could not possibly afford the merchandise. And too many Black women in America can tell you stories about being mistreated by police and other law enforcement officers. Notably, in a June 2002 Gallup poll, only 29 percent of Black women said they felt that the rights of Blacks are respected in the criminal justice system.[18] According to the poll, Black women are more disenchanted with the criminal justice system than Black men, 38 percent of whom said they believed that the rights of Blacks were being respected.

In a national study conducted in 1999 by the U.S. Department of Justice, researchers found that Black women drivers are more likely to be stopped by the police than women of all other ethnicities.[19] There's also evidence that Black women are more likely to be arrested than White women for a variety of alleged offenses.[20]

So what does she do? Assert her rights to a police officer and possibly risk her life—or suppress her outrage and stay alive? Does she linger defiantly in a store where she is not welcomed—or walk out never to return? Does she protest her treatment, feeling uncomfortable in the moment but satisfied later that she stood her ground, or does she walk away and later regret that she did not do more? Such are the dilemmas that Black women often face, the questions jostling against one another as they decide which way to lean and what their decisions will cost them.

Jocelyn, 35, remembers an experience she had two years ago in a small jewelry shop in Kentucky. She just wanted to browse, but from the moment she walked through the door, she felt that every pair of eyes was on her. "I remember very vividly wanting to just hold up my hands as I was walking through the store, as if to say, 'Okay, my hands are open, you can see where my hands are the whole time I'm here, and I'm not going to steal anything.'" She stayed a few minutes, then hurriedly walked out the door.

Jocelyn says that it truly hurts every time her presence in an establishment is questioned, each time she is "randomly" selected during the searches that have intensified since the terrorist attacks of September 11, 2001. "It makes me feel unhappy . . . that we've gone through a lot of things, especially as Black women, to prove ourselves—and it doesn't mean anything," she says of such incidents. "I don't take it as a personal affront. I take it as an affront against all Black women. I don't look at myself and say, 'Gee, you're less of a person because of this.' I just look at society and say, 'You know, this is really awful that I have to feel this in my own home, in my own society.'"

Bonnie, a 42-year-old information systems manager, describes how a car dealership lost a sale because they treated her like a suspect. Bonnie had decided to purchase a high-end luxury vehicle—she had been working long hours lately and wanted to have a comfortable car in which to make the one-hour commute to and from her job. But when she went to the local dealership to purchase her dream car, a 2001 Lexus, things didn't turn out the way she had hoped. After the salesman showed her all the bells and whistles on a gorgeous showroom model, he walked away to get some additional information. Just moments after he left, a White salesman approached Bonnie and pointedly asked her, "Why are you in the car?" After letting him know that she *had* been a potential customer, Bonnie found the general manager, filed a complaint, and walked out.

Carmen, a 61-year-old teacher, shares her experience of police harassment.

> I was stopped while driving my husband home from work at approximately 2 A.M. To my knowledge, I'd been following all the proper traffic rules, so when the policeman pulled me over, approached the car with his hand on his holster, and very rudely asked for my license and registration, I inquired what I had done. I didn't have my license with me, but I was a block from my home and asked if he would permit my husband or me to go and get it. I was told no, and when I continued to ask what I had done, I was told to "shut up" or I would be "placed under arrest." Of course, this angered me. I asked on what grounds I would be arrested, and I was told to follow him to the precinct. At the station, my automobile was examined— seats pulled apart—and the officer denied saying that I would be placed under arrest. The desk sergeant explained that policemen are often placed in inner-city stations as a "punishment" and many have attitudes or have had bad experiences and so they "take it out on everyone."

So entrenched is the myth that Black women steal, that Davida, 35, recalls as a child in San Francisco playing a game that mocked such bigotry. She and her girlfriends called it the "five-and-dime."

"You ever go to Woolworth's?" she asks. "The Black girls would walk in the front, and the security would be following the Black girls, and the White girls would take all the lipstick." Later, Davida explains, the Black and White girls, all friends, would sift through the loot, brushing on fingernail polish, trying on the pilfered lipsticks.

When Davida looks back, she sees this childhood game as a way of turning the tables on those who believed that her brown skin automatically made her a criminal. But as an adult, she challenges stereotypes more directly by confronting people who mistreat her based on such lies and misperceptions. Today Davida is careful not to spend money at establishments where she has been disrespected, and she encourages her friends and relatives to do the same.

"Maybe it's an emotional defense," she says. "But they're not getting a dime of mine. I always take it there. I'm going to make sure everybody I know knows this so they don't spend their money there. We're not victims. . . . We have so much economic power. . . . We got money. And this is a capitalistic society. It's about money. And when I talk about me, I talk about all Black women. I look at us as one, and when it's an offense against me, it's an offense against all of us."

In the late 1990s, a flurry of lawsuits revealed that federal Customs officials were profiling Black women as drug couriers and subjecting them to invasive body searches more often than anyone else, even though Black women were less likely to be breaking the law.[21] Although the Customs Department announced that as of June 2001 it had overhauled its search criteria and implemented new policies to deal with the search disparities, many women continue to carry the psychological scars of their experiences. Most Black women don't have statistics to prove that they're being mistreated by local, state, or federal law enforcement officers or by security guards at their local mall. So every single day of the year, millions of Black women across America—good, honest, law-abiding women—are left to fend for themselves as they continue to live with the myth of criminality.

The Myth of Promiscuity

The last dreadful myth about Black women is that they are sexually loose. Many Black women today feel that men of other races too often see them as oversexed vixens.

During slavery and decades of segregation, the myth of sexual looseness first emerged as a twisted justification for the rapes and sexual assaults of Black women by White men.[22] While the archetype has changed slightly, the stereotype of Black women, as oversexed, care-free, and immoral remains. In the 1970s, she was the trash-talking prostitute, making cameos in films and on cop shows. In the 1980s, she took the form of the teenage mother who had multiple children with multiple lovers and paid her bills with government checks. And by the 1990s, she had become an omnipresent fixture in pop culture, the girl in the video who would bare her body for a ride in a Benz and a bottle of Cristal. Even some Black performing artists, through their compact discs and videos, have propagated the idea of Black women as sexually charged and available, as obsessed with money and men. Black female rappers Lil' Kim and Foxy Brown molded their stage personas around such images, playing insatiable divas who live for sex, diamonds, and champagne.

But our research and the work of other scholars shows that these narrow misrepresentations are especially dangerous, leaving Black women vulnerable to sexual violence and abuse. The myth that she is always interested and ready for sex forces many a Black woman to shift back and forth as she scrutinizes the motivations of non-Black men who ask her on a date, debating whether or not it is safe to go. It makes some Black women feel conflicted about their famous peers, happy that the beauty of a Black celebrity is being celebrated, but uneasy when they see her sensuality being exploited. It forces many Black women to make quick decisions about how to handle a flirtatious coworker or acquaintance who assumes that she won't be offended by lewd remarks and who, in fact, expects her to consent to sex.

The fear of being misrepresented was visible in 2002 when Halle Berry became the first African American to win an Academy Award for Best Actress. Though many were happy about the milestone vic-tory, some Black women quietly expressed disappointment that Berry had been honored for an acting part that included a graphic sex scene with White actor Billy Bob Thornton. As one woman said, "It is a dis-grace that the first Oscar to a Black woman [for best actress] had to go to a Black woman that showed her ass. It distresses me that a Black woman's work seemed to be recognized only after she stripped down and got sexual. How typical is that? I think that society already views us as sex machines. In my opinion, Halle was awarded for fulfilling a stereotype."

Of course, the truth contradicts the stereotype. In a recent review of research on sexual behavior among African Americans, Kathleen H. Sparrow of the University of Louisiana at Lafayette concluded that while the limited early research indicated that Blacks engage in premarital sex earlier and more frequently than Whites, more recent studies suggest that this pattern is changing.[23] And while the teen birth rate is higher among Black girls than White girls, research shows that the difference is primarily due to Black teens' less frequent use of contraceptives and not to substantial differences in sexual involvement.[24] Moreover, between 1991 and 1998, the birth rate for Black teenage girls dropped more precipitously than for any other ethnic group in our nation.[25]

Research indicates, too, that Black women's sexual practices are typically more conservative than those of White women. In *Stolen Women: Reclaiming Our Sexuality, Taking Back Our Lives*, Gail E. Wyatt describes the findings from her in-depth research with two representative samples of women in Los Angeles County.[26] She found that while Black women were slightly more likely than White women to have an extramarital affair, White women tended to have more sexual relationships during adolescence, were more likely to initiate sex with their partner, were more likely to engage in cunnilingus, fellatio, and anal sex, and were more likely to engage in sex with more than one person at a time. These findings are in no way presented as a criticism of White women's sexuality, but rather to point out that the stereotype of Black women as oversexed and sexually promiscuous is unfounded.

Yet this stereotype has been so much a part of the fabric of U.S. society that, according to one recent study, it has even crept into the formal assumptions of our mental health-care system. Jill Cermele, Sharon Daniels, and Kristin Anderson of Drew University in New Jersey recently analyzed the *DSM-IV Casebook* for instances of racial and gender bias.[27] The *Casebook* was developed to illustrate the *Diagnostic and Statistical Manual of Mental Disorders* (*DSM-IV*), which is the psychiatric bible for the diagnosis of mental disorders. The cases are hypothetical vignettes of people exhibiting a variety of emotional problems. Cermele and her colleagues found that the *Casebook* tended to describe women of color (in contrast to men and White women) in terms of their attractiveness and sexuality. In other words, in developing these vignettes upon which psychologists and psychiatrists throughout the country rely, the authors apparently allowed their own racist and sexist biases to creep in. Sadly, the *DSM-IV Casebook*, a tool designed to help mental health professionals identify and treat peoples' psychiatric disorders, may perpetuate stereotypes that could exacerbate such disorders.

The myth of the wanton Black woman is inescapable. It seems to come up everywhere, even in a doctor's office. "When I was getting a medical examination, the nurse didn't believe me when I told her I was a virgin," recalls 28-year-old Christine. Tiffany, 35, dealt with it during college. White men, she says, would boldly approach her and announce how curious they were about going to bed with a Black woman: "I mean generally non-Black men or foreign men have these ideas about Black women being some exotic, sexual tiger," explains Tiffany. "And I must say that 95 percent of the White men who ever approached me were looking for the sex of their lives. They'll say something to you like, 'I've never been with a Black woman.' Or 'I'd like to be with a Black woman.' They're very direct about what their intentions are. . . . Sometimes I'm shocked at how forward they are."

Stacy, a decade younger, says that it's not uncommon for non-Black men to hit on her at dance clubs in the most vulgar ways—even to assault her. "The men seem to push up on me more because they seem to think that they're going to get somewhere, and it's disrespectful, and it's obvious what they're doing. They'll just be straight out and ask you, 'Do you want to come back to my place?' And I'm like, 'I just met you.'"

For many Black women, the assumption that they're sexually available contaminates their work life too. Ten years ago Diana worked as a civilian in a law enforcement agency. She recalls how a high-ranking White man propositioned her in her first months on the job:

I had one gentleman, who was beyond officer—he'd been promoted up one level—he actually solicited me for prostitution.

He said I'd make a wonderful prostitute. It was very well established at the time that I was happily married. He just thought he and I could make a lot of money together. And I was 26. . . . I shook it off; I was graceful with it. What I should have done is run out of the office screaming and filed a major lawsuit. But I figured it would be my word against his, and there was no sense in trying to take it anywhere else. I quashed it with, 'Not my style, never anything I would consider.' It would have been the civilian against the cop, the female against the cop. I didn't even want to try and argue this because all he has to do is deny it, and I'd be the one carrying the baggage.

Though Diana would have been well within her rights to report this superior officer, she suppressed her anger, rebuffed him gently, and continued to function effectively on the job.

Like Diana, Angela, age 48, harbors painful memories involving White men's attitudes toward Black women: "There've been times when socially I've been befriended by White men and I can't get past the race," says Angela, 48. "And there've been one or two times I have kicked myself years later that I didn't. But I just couldn't. It's like, *I automatically don't trust you.* And then later on, I saw that something that they had said or done was really a gesture of kindness, of friendship. But at the time I'd been so conditioned to not become used by White men."

Angela received such lessons as a young girl in Ohio. "I must've been in elementary school, and one holiday there was a parade downtown," Angela remembers. "After the parade we got back on the bus to go home, and there was a Black girl on the bus who was in the parade. She had on a little cheerleader sort of skirt. And the bus was crowded and I remember this White man touched her or fondled her, and she said something to him. She made a lot of noise and I remember my mother telling me that we had to be careful of White men. And that stuck. So it was pretty emphatic the way my mom got it across to my sister and me. You know it wasn't Black men that we had to be afraid of. It was White men that we had to be real careful about."

Angela concludes: "If I were to meet a White man tomorrow, or a man of a race other than African American, and he wanted to have a relationship with me I think that I would consider it. But that's now. That's recent."

Transcending the Myths

Myths and stereotypes do much of their damage subconsciously. They seep into the inner psyche and take up residence, affecting how one thinks, feels, and perceives others, even while one purports to be unbiased and tolerant. Even in the most progressive and open-minded people, stereotypes often hold sway. They're insidious. They're sneaky. They have had centuries to sink in. And every day these myths and stereotypes betray our view of ourselves as decent, fair, and just and undermine our hopes and ideals.

Stereotypes are also damaging within a group. They often become internalized. Though invisible, they wield much power. They can cause the self to diminish, to shrink, or to disappear.

But fortunately, the news isn't all bad. Yvonne, 43, who lives in northeastern Ohio, is a model of how one can triumph over myths and stereotypes. When she was first asked whether she's been affected by them, like a number of our interviewees, she was quick to deny it. But later in the conversation, she talked about a conference many years ago that she and her parents had with her seventh grade math teacher, a White man whom she respected and trusted.

Yvonne had been doing poorly in the course, and his very clear message was, "You'll never have the head for math." She believes that behind this prophecy was the teacher's view of her station in life as a Black woman. "What else was I going to be anyway? I'm going to cook in somebody's house. I'm going to be a homemaker. I'm going to be a domestic, so you're not going to be doing anything having to do with math."

Dropping out of high school, she worked for many years in dead-end, low-paying jobs, but two years ago, with the support of her husband, she made the bold decision to earn her GED and then enroll at the local public university. Tearfully, she confesses that she's just recently mastered her multiplication tables. All those years, she'd been so demoralized by the teacher's words that she'd been too petrified to try her hand at numbers. "All my life thinking, *How am I going to get there?* It made me feel like I couldn't do it, I can't do it because you told me I would never have a head for math. . . . And I never did. Until now."

Yvonne had shifted her ambitions, lost faith in her own abilities, because of the negative words uttered by an admired teacher. But after many years, she was able to block out his message and find her way back to believing in herself.

Though Yvonne is now mastering math, her calling is to be a poet. She has written and performed her poems at readings, achieving celebrity on campus and in her local community. If she was haunted for almost three decades by a few words, Yvonne today has become her own wordsmith, the definer of her own reality. She has found a way to rewrite the story of Black women.

We're All in This Together

Conducting the African American Women's Voices Project, and creating this book, was not a distant or detached exercise. As Black women, the two of us have lived much of what we talk about in the following chapters. Charisse for many years believed that there was only one fight, that against racism. She didn't see sexism as her struggle and was largely blind to it. Only recently has she begun to realize that the biases she and other Black women face, and the compromises that they make because of their gender, can be just as cruel and damaging as those wrought by racial bigotry. For Kumea, a pivotal life experience was integrating a White school in the mid-1960s. Though she survived and, in fact, thrived academically, it took her many years to sort through the emotional residue of that experience and to feel fully centered in her own identity as a Black woman.

Over and over, as the two of us listened, we heard our own experiences echoed in the stories that women shared. We found our concerns about the double jeopardy of racism and sexism voiced by many other women, and in a multiplicity of ways. At times we found ourselves crying with the women with whom we talked—crying for them, for us, and perhaps for all of you who are concerned about the human condition.

Yet we were frequently buoyed by the passion of our participants. Lynn, a 43-year-old from Washington, D.C., says, "This was not an easy survey. It made you dig deep and look inside yourself and examine your soul. I applaud your efforts, because Black women have been second class for too long." Greta, a 40-year-old from southern California, encourages us with a prayer: "May God bless you in your glorious endeavors." And 58-year-old Janice from Connecticut admonishes us, when we publish, to "tell it like it really is."

The more we listen, the more committed we become to providing a platform from which Black women's experiences, perspectives, traumas, and triumphs can be seen and heard. In the coming pages, we offer a window into their worlds: how they discover their own beauty despite the distorted images society reflects back to them; how they find their own voices, even as their speech is mocked and their ideas dismissed; how they transcend bigotry and remember their own worth.

Black women will find particular resonance in these stories. Those who thought they were alone in their experiences will learn that they are not, that many of their sisters share the same truth. They will be able to put a name to all the compromising and emotional ups and downs they weather each day. And by becoming aware of how and why they shift, they can change their lives. They can examine their relationships, their health, their feelings when they look in the mirror, and determine if they have shifted too far. If they have, they can take steps to swing the pendulum back, to regain control, to honor themselves.

But there is something too for those who are not Black and female. Anyone who has ever been prejudged, put down, or overlooked will likely see parts of their own experience in these chapters. And they will realize that they can learn much from Black women.

Finally, we anticipate that all of our readers, regardless of race or gender, will gain a deepened awareness of the terrible cost of bias and discrimination. We hope and trust that by hearing these women's voices, we will all be inspired to redouble our efforts to end bigotry and to create a world that is fair and just for each and every one of us.

THE PAIN OF GENDER SILENCE

"I Am Black but Ain't I a Woman?"

Isms travel in packs.

SHERRY, 31, NEW YORK

The games of childhood are universal. Girls and boys from all walks of life play jacks together in a schoolyard corner. They pick teams to play baseball, basketball, soccer, lacrosse, and then take to the field. The playground is a rainbow. Black, White, Latino, and Asian children share games together, as differences of gender, race, and ethnicity fade away into their play.

But there is one game today that still seems the domain of Black girls. Two jump ropes fly toward each other, slicing the air, slapping the concrete a millisecond apart. The girls rock back and forth, waiting for the right moment to leap in. They jump. They skip, turn, shout. They can hardly catch their breath, soaring, singing, laughing all at the same time. Double dutch, more often than not, still belongs to America's little Black girls.

That separate game of courage and timing, that separate place with its own rules and challenges, resonates onward, into adolescence and adulthood. For so many Black women, it's a powerful memory, and a powerful metaphor, because life, they say, seems so often, perhaps too often, like that childhood game. As girls, then as adults, Black women tell us again and again that they must struggle to keep their balance as they straddle the twin identities of race and gender, shifting their step, altering their rhythm, devising a new move at a moment's notice. Many do it with grace, navigating the intricacies of two realities: *I am Black! I am woman!*

But others get caught between the two identities, tangled, confused. Sexism and racism meld together, coming at them all at once. It is too much to focus on both, so instead they focus on one. They lose their balance, stumble, and fall.

The Quiet Reality

Speak to numerous African American women across our nation, and you will learn that many share the same lament: It's been nearly 150 years since slavery was abolished, more than 80 years since women won the right to vote, and over 40 years since the March on Washington; and yet today—still, today, in the twenty-first century—Black women are constantly made susceptible to both racial and gender discrimination, and sometimes left wondering which bias is most potent in disadvantaging them. *I am Black! But ain't I a woman?* That question, asked by the great Black abolitionist Sojourner Truth during a speech before a national meeting of White suffragists in May 1851, resonates as loudly today as it did over a century ago.

Though Black women in America frequently find the confidence, and the voice, to inveigh against racism, too often these same women feel that they must stifle themselves—and bury their pain—when being female, rather than being Black, is at the core of their mistreatment. Our research indicates that in many of the situations where they are discriminated against, harassed, or assaulted as women—when they are ignored and dismissed by male colleagues, are leered at and chased down a city street by a group of White high school boys, even when they are physically assaulted by a Black boyfriend—America's Black women are often compelled to keep quiet. They stay quiet not only because of the chasm between themselves and White women, and not only because of racism's ferocity, but also because they sense that others within the Black community may shame them for speaking out. And if their oppressor is a Black man, the situation is that much harder, because there is a clear mandate, even if it is unspoken, that Black women must do everything in their power to protect their men, to be ever faithful to them in the face of society's persistent anti-Black prejudices.

In their silence, many African American women endure disrespect, sexual harassment, and physical and sexual abuse. Their silence means that emotional wounds left in the wake of childhood sexual abuse may never heal. Silence means that the sexual harassment at the office may go on and on. Silence means that when gender bias crops up in their lives, they may look it in the face but not recognize what they see.

Ethnicity and gender are the most significant aspects of Black women's identities. Yet race has a far greater salience than gender.[1] For many, it seems, gender identity is important yet implicit—they do not actively or consciously think about it. And as a result, many Black women may not be very attuned to gender bias and gender discrimination. Jessica Henderson Daniel, a psychologist and professor at Harvard Medical School, has spoken about the pervasive "gender silence" in the Black community.[2] Referring to African American women who have been traumatized by Black men, Daniel talks about the double victimization that Black women often endure—first, victimized because of their gender, and second, persuaded by community norms not to breathe a word about it.

The cultural norm in the Black community is to acknowledge race and racism only.[3] "Race is intertwined in everything in ways that sometimes sex isn't," remarks Judy, a 36-year-old woman from central Kentucky. And of course it can be difficult at times to untangle the source of bias—to determine whether it's race or gender or both. Sharon, a 28-year-old from Minneapolis, remarks: "I haven't noticed or been able to differentiate the discrimination because I'm Black and I'm a woman. The Black overshadows the woman in my opinion." Vernice, a 47-year-old teacher in Mobile, Alabama, says, "It's sometimes hard to distinguish discrimination based on gender and discrimination based on race. Which came first—the chicken or the egg?"

Notably, 69 percent of the women in our survey indicated that they had experienced bias or discrimination based on gender. But as we interviewed women, what stood out is how often those who initially said no to questions about experiences of gender discrimination found themselves, a half hour or so later, sharing a painful description of mistreatment or sexual abuse. In the telling of their lives, many African American women reveal incidents of harassment, unequal pay, and sexual violence that are clearly about gender, though they may not immediately recognize it to be so.

The sometimes subtle, sometimes overt message that many Black women in our country seem to accept is that while racial discrimination continues to be prevalent, gender bias and other forms of discrimination dim by comparison. Black women learn that addressing those other issues is a distraction, even disloyal to the race as a whole, and to Black men in particular. For some African American women, it may simply be too complicated and overwhelming to accept that they might be maligned for two reasons, devalued because of two integral parts of their selves. It may be too hard to face that they suffer what scholars have come to call "double jeopardy."[4]

The assumption that racism exceeds and overshadows any other form of bias in our society, it should be stressed, is not without merit. In the African American Women's Voices Project, almost every one of the women we interviewed, and 90 percent of the women we surveyed, acknowledge that they have experienced racial discrimination. Ten percent of the women surveyed volunteer that they recall being called a "nigger." Whether it was walking down a street, onto a county fairground, into a store, or stepping onto the school bus for the first day of kindergarten years earlier, 1 out of 10 of these women remembers being subjected to this, the most visceral and painful of racial assaults. And of that group a startlingly high number—94 percent—are 42 years or younger, born in the midst of, or long after, the civil rights movement.

Of course, when we talk about racism, we are referring not only to discriminatory behaviors directed toward Blacks by individuals, but also to broader cultural messages, institutional policies, and practices that demean and disadvantage African American people.[5] Thus, if some women do not specifically remember being called a "nigger," they offer long, painful laundry lists of racially discriminatory experiences—from not being considered for employment, to not being seen as competent, to losing out to White people in job recognition and promotions, to receiving poor service in restaurants, to being followed around in stores as if they were about to steal. For Black women in America, racist memories pour out easily.

And thus, in their daily lives, the overwhelming reality of racism pressures many Black women, often subconsciously, to suppress their concerns about gender discrimination. A Black male boss may make a sexual overture to her on the job, but she does not report him, afraid of stoking the stereotype that Black men are sexual predators (thus jeopardizing his career). Her Black boyfriend may physically abuse her, but she hesitates before calling the police, fearful that if he is taken away, he will not come back alive. She may allow sexual harassment by a White male coworker to go unchecked, thinking that she will not be believed if she tells, or that she may even be blamed, stamped with the racist stereotype that she was sexually promiscuous and probably invited the abuse.

Racism also figures in why Black women are often quiet about the inequities found within the Christian church. Even though it is clearly women who form the church's backbone—filling the pews, organizing the fundraisers, cooking the dinners, and teaching Sunday school—in a large number of churches across the country, women are barred from standing in the pulpit and attaining other positions of leadership. Still, they do not often complain, hesitant to disrupt the one place that has traditionally been a safe harbor for Black women, their refuge from racial cruelty, and the one institution where Black men have been consistently empowered and affirmed.

We have found as well that Black women avoid seizing upon gender harassment because they perceive the struggle for women's rights in America as having been led and defined mostly by White women.

Thus many Black women see sexism as a White woman's battle, and not a part of the Black experience. This view is fostered partly by cultural norms within the African American community emphasizing race, but also by the difficulty many Black women have in feeling solidarity with White women who, though they may talk about discrimination, seem to have many advantages, and to be faring far better than their Black counterparts professionally and economically.

For example, the struggle to work in meaningful jobs outside of the home—a pillar of the women's rights movement—has been one that many Black women rarely relate to since they have been forced to work from the time Africans were brought to American shores. Black women watch White women rise through the ranks of corporations, seemingly unimpeded by their gender, and find it difficult to unite with them. They stand on a street corner, hailing a cab, only to watch the taxi pass them by and pick up a blonde instead. And it is difficult to rally with White women around the issue of equal pay, when the median weekly earnings of Black women fall below that of White women as well as Black and White men.[6] When all is said and done, women could win all the rights afforded to men, but African American women would still have to deal with being Black in a color-conscious society. It is perhaps this reality that leads Doris, a 55-year-old social worker from Boston, to say, "I see sexism as a White female–invented issue."

The Intensity of Dueling Isms

Even if Black women in America are far more attuned to racism than sexism, in reality, of course, they're constantly fighting against both of these dueling isms. Sexism and racial bigotry are often so potent and so intertwined that they end up hidden within one another like pieces of sharp ice that collect in a snowball careening down a hill. They build on one another. Racist attitudes actually lead to a unique and more egregious form of sexism and sexual harassment for Black women. Psychologist Jann Adams at Morehouse College calls this the "racialization" of sexual harassment, how the stereotypes of Black women, such as the mythical perception that they are promiscuous, may influence the nature, form, and intensity of harassment.[7] Thus, because Black women are often viewed as immoral and oversexed, they may be seen as appropriate targets of sexual interest. The assumption, perhaps sub-conscious at times, is that they are desirous of the sexual contact.

When Norma was 13, she lived in a quiet all-Black neighborhood in Washington, D.C. Walking down the street one sunny July after-noon, she was beckoned by a White driver who had stopped his car in the middle of the block. She assumed he needed directions. Instead he leered, uttered lewd remarks, and finally drove away very slowly. Ten years later, again walking down the street, but this time downtown and dressed in blue jeans, athletic shoes, and a heavy pea jacket, she was propositioned as a prostitute by a White male driver. There's no ques-tion in Norma's mind that the harassment by these men was fueled by both sexism and racism.

Sexual harassment is pandemic and poses a particular threat to Black women. In a study of African American and White women in Los Angeles County, Gail Wyatt and Monika Riederle of UCLA found that 45 percent of the women had experienced sexual harassment in public or social settings, and poor, single Black women were the most vulnerable.[8] One-third of the African American women and one-half of the White women reported at least one incident of sexual harass-ment at work, yet 67 percent of the affected Black women, compared with 45 percent of White women, had been *directly* propositioned in the workplace. Put simply, because of their gender, the Black women were accosted in a way that Black men are not, and because of their race, they were sexually harassed differently from many White women.

In our study, women often speak about the unique way in which they are targeted for harassment. Marilyn, a 39-year-old woman from Austin, Texas, says that as one of very few Blacks in her high school, she remembers "fighting off the hands of White boys" on a daily basis while the White girls went virtually untouched. Adriana, a tall, bespectacled woman in her early thirties, speaks with sadness about the experience of being sexually abused as a young teen by a White male craftsman who was working at her home. She wasn't able to tell anyone or deal with the emotional aftereffects of this horrible crime until several years later. Nina, a 46-year-old from Los Angeles County, was harassed by a White male correctional officer while working at a men's prison. "I had to quit for my own safety," she says tearfully. Shelly, a 37-year-old veterinarian, recalls her White male boss attempting to rape her in a storeroom when she was a teenager and subsequent jobs that she lost because she would not sleep with the man doing the hiring. Yet, ironically, she explains, "I just think that for me sexism has never been a problem."

And then there is Veronica, a high-ranking Navy officer who joined the ROTC in the ninth grade. During her decade-long military career she saw the many sand traps of gender. She and other female officers were routinely excluded from the bike rides and drink fests enjoyed by the men and thus locked out of the networking that could lead to promotion. When she was transferred to a base in Japan, a White senior officer began to make lewd remarks whenever the two of them were alone. Veronica was young, unsure of herself, and just beginning her career. The officer was older and powerful. So not knowing what else to do, she tried to laugh off the comments. "But at some point, because I 'tee-heed' it off," Veronica says, "I guess he felt he could touch me or rub against me, which I thought was just totally over the line. . . . At that point I basically made sure I was never in a room with him again."

Veronica agonized about what more she should do, but ultimately decided not to make a complaint. She dealt with the discomfort and fear alone. "I never told anybody. . . . For me, it was easier just to escape than to deal with it. I'm not saying that was right, but at the time that was the only way I knew how to deal with it. . . . It hurt my psyche to have this person harassing me, yet I also felt like it could hurt me professionally if he became upset that I was not interested."

While racism may have played a role in her superior's actions, that incident and several others made Veronica come to believe that gender has been the biggest obstacle in her military career. But as an African American, she has found that her awareness of such sexism is unusual. When she brings up gender discrimination to other Black women in the military, they look at her incredulously. Racism is all they profess to see. "I really think it's denial," she says. "I just find it almost impossible to believe you could exist as a woman in the Navy and never be sexually harassed."

Black men, Veronica says, are even less open to hearing about her experiences. "I feel like more of the challenges in my job have been because I was a woman than because I was Black. . . . And I get Black men who are very angry with me for saying that, because they feel I'm sort of a traitor."

At times, Veronica has chosen to be silent. At other times, she has spoken out about the bias that she and other women suffer in the Armed Forces. But she has paid a steep price for it—feeling at odds with her friends and being treated as though she has betrayed her people by deciding to be honest about her experiences. Our research suggests that such negative reactions within the Black community, both real and anticipated, compel many Black women to avoid reflecting upon the ways in which sexism continues to haunt them.

Sexual Abuse by One's Own

In one split second, Celeste was forced to reflect on the messy cauldron of racism and sexism. A widow with a young adult child, Celeste, 50, had been seeing Robert for eight months. They both loved racquetball and shared an interest in foreign affairs, and as they were both in the high-tech industry, they could share "war stories" about work. Celeste was delighted that she'd found such a great companion. But as the romance evolved, Robert became increasingly irritable and moody. He would come over to Celeste's home almost every evening, and sometimes he'd talk for hours about how he'd been overlooked again for a more lucrative sales territory for the business computers that he sold. Celeste listened compassionately, but she was struck by how out of sorts Robert became. He'd bang around in the kitchen slinging pots and slamming cabinet doors. And more and more when they had disagreements, Robert moved quickly to fighting mode—raised voice, taut neck, flared nostrils—but he'd never touched her.

Then one evening, Celeste recalls, Robert came by at about 10 P.M. He'd obviously been drinking. He was palpably angry, and his voice was strident. "Where the hell have you been all evening? I've been calling since 6:30! You been seeing someone else!" Suddenly Celeste was angry too. "How dare you come in here, drunk, accusing me!" And then he struck her—in the face with the back of his hand.

Celeste ran to the bedroom and locked the door. Robert threatened from the other side. She was shocked and scared and conflicted about whether to call the police. She knew all too well how brutally cops could treat Black men. As Robert pounded on the door and yelled, Celeste was debating with herself about whose life was more at risk—hers or his?

She dialed 911. When the police arrived, "they came in with guns drawn. I was scared to death. They took him outside. It was very humiliating." Celeste had made the tough decision to protect herself.

Julie made a different choice. She had thought twice about going to work for Tariq. The two had met at a cocktail party a few years before and dated briefly. Julie had been drawn to Tariq's deep, resonant voice, his ability to talk about any subject with seeming knowledge and authority, and his strapping good looks. He always told her that she looked "just like" Nia Long. He had a way of charming her that, at first, she found irresistible.

But after a few months, Julie grew tired of Tariq's constant flirting with other women and last-minute dates. One night she prepared an elaborate meal for him with homemade bread, lobster bisque, and a complicated shrimp risotto. When Tariq failed to show up, and later admitted that he had spent the night with another woman, Julie cut off the budding romance then and there. A casual friendship ensued, although Julie kept her guard up, sensing that Tariq might not be someone she could trust, even as a friend.

About a year later, Tariq called to let Julie know that he was getting married to Becky, a woman several years his junior, whom he had met over the Internet. For a moment, Julie felt a pang of regret, but then she remembered how untrustworthy and irresponsible Tariq could be. She congratulated him as enthusiastically as she could and, from that phone call on, knew she would hear from him rarely, except for an occasional hello on her answering machine or perhaps an exchange of Christmas cards.

But Tariq, it turns out, would cross her path again, less than three years later. At that point, Julie was in her late thirties, still single, and dealing with ever-worsening financial problems. She had been a coordinator for music programs in a large Pennsylvania school district but had been recently laid off, following the school board's decision to slash its arts budget. Julie began teaching violin to a few students while searching vigorously for a full-time position.

After two months of barely making ends meet, Julie still had not found anything. Her severance was dwindling, and she was getting desperate. Then, out of the blue, Tariq called. He told her that he had become the associate director of a center dedicated to urban studies. After Julie told him about the difficulties she was having finding work, Tariq said that one of his administrators was going on maternity leave soon, and he'd love to bring Julie on board temporarily if she was interested.

Julie hesitated. She told Tariq she thought it might be awkward to work together since they had once been involved. But Tariq assured her that their relationship would be strictly professional. Besides, he said, he was a married man with a baby on the way.

Julie wasn't on the job for even a week before the harassment ensued. Tariq would call her into his office, loosen his tie, and then block the door. Or he would come over to the corner cubicle where she sat and, when no one was looking, luridly plant a foot on her desk and lean in toward her so that his crotch was only inches from her face. "Or," she remembers, "he'd call me in his office and read me statistics on birth control."

Yet Julie stayed. The job paid well and she was still unable to find a job in her field. She couldn't bring herself to complain about Tariq, even after two White women she had befriended told her he had also harassed a 22-year-old intern from Bryn Mawr who had since left the center.

"I talked to my parents about the harassment, my father in particular. . . . I wanted to let them know I was considering quitting my job. And my father told me it's going to be hard to prove, especially because you've had a past relationship with him. I thought, 'Do I really want to be exposed?'"

And there was another, even more powerful reason that kept Julie from reporting Tariq's behavior: Tariq was the highest-ranking African American at the center and the only Black male in a position of management. As disrespectful as he was, as nervous as he sometimes made her, she couldn't bear the thought of walking into the office of the White human resources director and reporting that a Black man was sexually harassing her. She still remembered the Anita Hill hearings and couldn't shake the image of Senator Hatch grilling Hill as a humiliated Clarence Thomas looked on. She thought: "I do not want to go before these White folks . . . and talk about this Black man."

Instead, Julie tried to speak to Tariq. She approached him one day and told him that he was making her uncomfortable. Tariq told her that he was just "playing around," that they were old friends having fun. "If you're so uptight," he told her, "I'll stop."

For a few weeks Tariq seemed to go out of his way to avoid her, abruptly walking out of the lunchroom when she walked in, seeming cool, almost hostile, when they bumped into each other in the hallway or parking lot. But a few weeks later, when Julie went to Tariq's office to discuss a proposal, things took a turn for the worse. When their conversation ended and Julie stood up to leave, Tariq suddenly jumped out of his chair, rushed around behind her, and shut the door so quickly that Julie almost walked into it. "It wasn't until I almost walked into that door that I became afraid," she remembers. "Before that I'd [just] been annoyed."

Julie rushed back to her office and called a woman who had recently left the center to work for another nonprofit agency. Were they hiring, she asked? Could she help Julie get an interview?

Later that week, Julie spoke to the agency's hiring director. The following Friday she went into the center, rapped on Tariq's door, and submitted her resignation. She walked out of his office, out of the building, and never returned.

"I was angry that I was willing to defend myself as a Black person but not as a Black woman," she says quietly of her decision to leave her job rather than embarrass Tariq in front of their White peers. "If he had been White I would've moved forward and I know that. . . . I'm not real proud of that."

Julie's decision to choose racial solidarity over her own concerns as a woman, to choose silence over disclosure, places her in the company of many Black women in America today. Our research shows that many African American women, when given the chance to reflect upon it, remember having been mistreated, and in some cases seriously abused, by boys and men within the Black community. Their memories sometimes conjure entire lifetimes of abuse—from the earliest days of childhood straight through adolescence and adulthood.

Childhood sexual abuse is a trauma that many African American girls must endure, and it often cripples their healthy development. In a study of a randomly selected group of women in Los Angeles County, Gail Wyatt found that, among the Black women, a startling 40 percent reported some form of sexual abuse involving body contact prior to the age of 18.[9] African American girls were most vulnerable to abuse during the preadolescent years from ages 9 to 12, and the sexual offenders were often stepfathers, mothers' boyfriends, male cousins, and uncles. Notably most of the victims had not disclosed the abuse to anyone. Thus, a significant portion of the sexual abuse of Black girls takes place at the hands of boys and men within the Black community, yet gender silence prevents the community from addressing this problem as aggressively as it might. So many Black women retreat to their families, Black churches, and other Black institutions for a sense of safety and opportunity, only to be confronted by a culture in which sexism is commonplace.

With her delicate light brown skin, high cheekbones, and clear eyes, Karen, now a grandmother, has the face of a teenager. She raised her son and daughter by herself and has always been the steady, mature hand that has guided her family. But she's never had a significant, long-term relationship with a man. When she's around men, she feels like a child again, like the little girl left alone with relatives she barely knew, a child frightened, anxious, and ashamed.

Karen vividly remembers the summer following her eighth birthday and the first time it happened. She had gone to Texas on a Greyhound bus to stay with relatives she had never met. Jeff, her jovial teenage cousin, would sneak her lemon drops and invite her into his bedroom to listen to Sam Cooke records. Karen cherished and trusted this new world in which she felt she had close friends within her own family.

Back home in San Diego, Karen attended an elementary school that was primarily White. She often felt isolated and vulnerable there. Now, she could enjoy the comfort of being surrounded by family members in a rural town whose population was largely African American. She especially adored cousin Jeff, who was warm, affectionate, and self-confident. She felt safe.

But one night, Jeff's friendliness and affection went too far. His parents, Karen's great aunt and uncle, both worked evenings, and Karen was home alone with Jeff. He asked Karen to sit on his lap, and then he began to fondle her. "You like that, don't you?" he asked her repeatedly. She didn't like it, but it continued to happen—several times a week until the summer ebbed.

"Now don't go telling nobody," Jeff insisted. "You understand?"

She never did.

Now, some 40 years later, Karen rarely has the confidence to date men. "I feel intimidated when I'm around too many men at one time," she says, "whether they're Black or non-Black." Though she's been able, on occasion, to develop a short-term relationship, and even had two children by one boyfriend, Karen's experience of childhood sexual abuse has resonated throughout her adult life.

Sadly, when one observes popular Black culture in our nation today, one quickly discovers that the sexist mistreatment of Black women is tolerated and even directly fostered. African American girls, raised in an era when women run corporations and vie to be president, are often pushed, especially within the Black community, to be impervious to or dismissive of the misogynistic messages embedded in rap lyrics or the near-pornographic video images that dance across their television screens. At colleges and universities across the nation, Black men, in keeping with this culture and the codes of the broader society, are often expected to shuttle Black women in and out of a revolving door, to pursue them based on their sexual attractiveness and willingness rather than their more personal attributes and passions. Young college women may speak to each other about their disappointments, label their ex-boyfriends "players" or "dogs," but as a society, we rarely encourage them to challenge such mistreatment or look at it in the broader context of gender. Thus, even as many of these women study by day to become independent professionals, by night they party to sexist fraternity chants, like: "We pimp the ho's, we drink the wine, come on (boys), it's party time!"[10]

Then, too, sexist messages about Black women have actually become entertainment for the whole nation. Famously, when boxer Mike Tyson was convicted in February 1992 of raping Desiree Washington, a contestant in the Miss Black America beauty pageant, some questioned why she had gone to his hotel room in the first place. When Tyson was released from prison three years later, while some Black women chose to participate in a candlelight vigil for abused women, others celebrated his freedom. As Tyson made his way through the crowds at a Harlem rally, one woman reportedly yelled to him, "I just want you to know that African American women love you."

On the televised 2001 Hip-Hop Source Awards, where the Reverend Jesse Jackson was among the presenters, "Area Codes" by Ludacris was performed and dramatized. "I've got pros [whores] in different area codes" went the refrain; and as it was recited, dozens of scantily clad women, most of them Black, pranced across the stage.

In 2002, a videotape surfaced that allegedly showed R & B crooner R. Kelly, who is in his midthirties, having sex with an adolescent girl. Kelly denied the charge, and when Chicago police launched an investigation, many Black women spoke out in Kelly's defense. His defenders who saw bootleg copies of the tape said it was easy to believe that the girl was an adult. They argued that the man in the video was not Kelly, and that even if it was, it took two to participate, so Kelly was not solely responsible. The girl was 14 years old.

Living with, and within, this culture in which sexist attitudes and actions against Black women are widely tolerated, many women have their own stories to tell. Genine, 28, from Evanston, Illinois, reflects on the challenges of her junior high school days. "What I remember about being a girl is that you had to protect yourself from boys, because they weren't safe." Genine routinely wore biker shorts under her dresses to shield herself from boys who tried to peer under them, and she was constantly maneuvering to keep her bra straps from being snapped.

Twenty-year-old Sandra from the San Francisco Bay area describes several occasions in high school when she was surrounded by seven or eight Black male students who called her names like "bitch" and "ho" and taunted her with questions like, "Are you going to suck his dick?"

"The only sense that I could make of it is that I had had a relationship with a member of their group the previous year, but he had graduated," she says.

Sandra remembers that the harassment took place even though many other students were around. When some students asked, "What are those guys doing?" the response of her peers was, "Oh, that's just the basketball team messing with the girls again." Sexual taunting was known and accepted as their sport. When Sandra finally found the courage to talk to the principal, a Black woman, she was told to talk to the dean who, in turn, advised her to go back to the principal. "They didn't want to do anything because these [boys] were their sports stars."

Sandra's only way of coping, in the end, was to steel herself so she wouldn't cry when the boys began to harass her. "Why," she still asks herself, "did this happen to me? Because I was a woman? Because I had boobs? What's the matter? What did I do?" And worst of all, Sandra explains, "Nobody did anything. And that really hurt, because you can't do anything. You can't do anything."

The Muted Tones of Sexism

Child sexual abuse, sexual harassment, and domestic violence are all clear and obvious forms of gender discrimination, and Black women often have to shift in dramatic ways to manage these assaults. They shift by trying to bury these traumatic experiences, by denying they ever took place, by fleeing school and job experiences where they've been betrayed and violated, by fighting to protect the very people who have assailed them. And sometimes they shift by pouring their energies into speaking up and fighting back.

But shifting occurs in subtler ways as well, as Black women respond to quieter, more everyday forms of gender discrimination. Sexism, like racism, occurs on a continuum from small, relatively minor events to major assaults, and, like racism, sexism encompasses not only individual behaviors, but also cultural messages and institutional policies and practices, which debase or create disadvantages for women. Subtle forms of sexism have an impact.[11] Black women still have to shift to manage them. And again, they are often reluctant to speak up about what they experience.

Pat, an assistant principal of a predominantly Black elementary school in Atlanta, who works with a Black male principal, says: "I've been told by female parents of the students at my school that they [the parents] would prefer talking to the male administrator." In Los Angeles, Linda, a television producer who left her high-powered job in the entertainment industry to seek a better work environment, shares the following: "The men liked to deal with men better. And that was really kind of an unspoken but clear thing. Black men liked to deal with either each other or White men more than they would like to deal with me. That was just subtly there."

Many women speak of being paid less than men who hold the same position and have comparable or lesser credentials. Alise, 32, from Akron, Ohio, remembers her boss's response to her request for a raise. "I was told that I didn't need a pay increase because I had a husband."

Keenly aware of the double jeopardy of racism and sexism, Tenika, a 37-year-old woman who was launching her own accounting firm, realized that to name the company Tenika Henley and Associates might make it difficult to garner new business. Few firms like hers were owned by women, fewer still by Black women, and "Tenika Henley" would be a giveaway. She reluctantly decided that for strategic reasons she'd name the firm T. Bernstein and Associates, using her first initial and her White, Jewish husband's last name. It was a shift to help ensure economic survival.

Maya, a 39-year-old director of a neighborhood development center in Chicago, recounts that when she attended her first meeting of the predominantly Black board of directors, the president, a Black man named Turner, announced: "We have two of our women here today. We wanted to get diverse, so we have two of our women in here, and I'd like the two women of ours to stand up." Maya comments that if someone had said, "'We have two Blacks here and will our two Blacks stand up," everyone would have understood how inappropriate and demeaning it was. The board would never have sat still if someone said "our Blacks." Maya was irritated, but it was difficult to respond, particularly since she knew that Mr. Turner was, as she says, a "sweet person of good intentions."

Another woman remembers how she would wince every time she got mail from her church addressed to "Mr. and Mrs. David Robinson." She and her husband were members, but he was hardly active. More importantly, she didn't think of herself as "Mrs. David Robinson." Actually she was a doctor and used her maiden name in professional settings, but she would have settled for "Ms. Mary Robinson." "Mrs. David Robinson"—who was that? But though she resented the presumptions of the sender, and found humor in the fantasy of letters addressed to "Dr. and Mr. Mary Tolbert," she never said a word about it. "It's a small thing, really. Yeah, it annoys me, but I'm sure I won't be respected for bringing it up. I'll be seen as pushing a woman's agenda and not playing by the rules."

Listen to Pat, Alise, and Tenika, listen to Maya and Mary, and listen to scores of other Black women across America, and what you hear may not be a litany of the most egregious sexual assaults, but one of constant subtle experiences of sexism that over time take their toll, wearing away the souls of many Black women. Those who have been physically violated by men within the community may be in the minority, but our research suggests that most Black women have experienced discrimination and harassment at the hands of Black and non-Black men because they are women. Beth Bonniwell Haslett and Susan Lipman of the University of Delaware talk about how challenging it can be to deal with these "micro inequities," because these events are widely perceived as being minor and forgivable, and thus many women are reluctant to complain about them.[12] And those women who do speak up may find that the payoff is nonexistent or negligible. It's easy to be deemed oversensitive. Yet these small, everyday events accumulate. One must wonder how much energy it takes for Mary and Maya to not speak up about these minor irritations, to let them go, over and over again.

Still, at least Mary and Maya are aware. Many Black women don't notice subtle sexism. Their shifting takes the form of denial. They may even unknowingly perpetuate gender bias. The benefit of denial is remaining comfortable, being protected from the nuisance of awareness. But the price is the loss of one's connection to reality, no longer being able to see clearly and participate fully in the world. And that which is not faced cannot be changed.

Scaling the Wall of Silence: Speaking Out Against Sexism

As strong as the pressure to remain silent may be, the good news is that when given the chance to focus on how racism and sexism affect them and when offered support from friends and family, many Black women find the courage to voice their grievances and seek change in their lives. By letting the perpetrators of racism and sexism know that as Black women they have had enough, that no, they will not allow themselves to be mistreated because they are Black and female, they put an end to all of the shifting that hiding such oppression inevitably entails—shifting into denial as they convince themselves that the oppression arises from something in their own behavior, shifting into silence so that Black friends and colleagues won't push them to confront a sexist White boss, shifting into submission to protect a Black man from society's racist assumptions and conclusions. Indeed, the only way, really, to free African American women from the dueling

isms is to challenge both forces of ignorance and hatred fully and vigilantly, to correct such mistreatment whenever it takes place, no matter who the perpetrators are, no matter what their race, position, or
station.

While many of the women in our study tell stories of racism and
sexism that they had buried away, stories of conflicts that they had
never discussed or resolved, a few women share stories in which they
decided to confront and transcend the painful situations in which they
were placed. For instance, Isabelle, a very thoughtful 33-year-old, talks
of how agonizing and emotionally complex it was to deal with a fellow
student's harassment.

Isabelle had been in an M.B.A. program where the students were
predominantly White. The small cadre of Black students spent a lot of
time together, socializing, studying together, and helping one another
deal with the challenges inherent in being a tiny minority within the
university.

Charles was one of the "brothers" whom all the Black women felt
connected to early on. He was chatty, warm, and easygoing, and as one
of the youngest in the group, he exuded a childlike exuberance that
was endearing. Between classes he loved to hang out and shoot the
breeze in the student lounge, and at the end of the day, he was the one
to pull together a small group to go out for pizza or Chinese food. But
Charles was as serious about academic and career success as he was
about socializing, studying long into the night and often spinning
yarns about the millions that he'd soon be making. Some students
rolled their eyes when he'd launch into another of his "I'm-going-to-
rule-the-world" fantasies, and he was dubbed, somewhat derisively,
"Mr. MBA." But everyone loved him in spite of it all.

Early in the second quarter, Charles developed a crush on Isabelle.
"Come on, baby," he would say to her after class in the hallway. "Let's
get together." But Isabelle wasn't interested in Charles. She liked him
as a friend. In fact she thought of him as a younger brother, but she just
wasn't attracted to him romantically. "I'm too busy right now," she told
him gently when he asked her, over and over again, to meet with him
after class.

Though Charles's entreaties were at first simply annoying, they soon became inappropriate, disruptive, and frightening to Isabelle. On a couple of occasions in class, when Isabelle was addressing the professor, Charles leaned over and pulled off the scrunchie that secured her braids, unleashing them onto her shoulders. It bothered her, but she felt she couldn't do anything—and no one else intervened. Isabelle began to make sure that she was always seated between other students, but Charles started taking the seat behind her, and whispering seductive comments to her throughout the class.

After more than a month of the harassment, Isabelle confronted him about his behavior, telling him that she didn't feel comfortable with it. But things only got worse.

When Isabelle completely cut off all contact with Charles, he began to corner her in the corridors at school, blocking her path. Sometimes he followed her to the women's restroom and waited outside for her to reappear. In the evenings, he called her at home, and when she refused to speak and hung up, he persisted, sometimes phoning her five or six times a day. Though she told him why she wasn't speaking to him, nothing seemed to make a difference. In the classes that she shared with him, she hid in the back of the room, rarely raising her hand.

Although Isabelle was ready to free herself of Charles's harassment, she still felt protective of him. For a while she decided she wasn't going to tell other people what he was doing to her. She had supported Charles in the past when he had difficulty getting along with a White female student who accused him of being too "aggressive." In retrospect, she remembers the inappropriate, sexualized behavior that he had displayed toward the student. "Race was more important than sex at that point," she says. "It was more important to be a part of my community and support the members than to think of myself as a woman."

But Charles's unrelenting assaults were now leading her to think more about gender. With the support of a girlfriend, Isabelle went to talk with Dr. Gallardo, a Latina faculty member. "If this is happening to you," Dr. Gallardo told her, "it's probably happening to other women." Dr. Gallardo encouraged Isabelle to file a grievance with the university's sexual harassment committee.

Isabelle felt some relief after her meeting with Dr. Gallardo, and she finally felt that she had options. But when she began to share her plan with her Black women friends, she met resistance. They made her feel as though she were exaggerating the situation, and as though she might have been inviting the abuse. "'Oh, it's nothing. Charles doesn't treat me like that. Why do you think he treats you like that?' Like it's my fault that it's happening, like maybe if I were a stronger sister, he wouldn't be messing with me. If I was loud or sassy, if I cursed or threatened him more, then it wouldn't be happening. . . . I felt totally isolated. I was questioning myself constantly."

After much reflection, Isabelle realized that if Charles had been a White man, she would have quickly garnered the support of the entire Black student community. "Everybody would have been, like, 'Oh, hell no!'"

As afraid as she was that she would lose some of her closest friends, Isabelle decided that enough was enough. One morning, she quietly went into the university administration building to file a complaint against Charles. Within two weeks, Charles was called to a hearing, where he admitted to the inappropriate behavior. He was put on academic probation and told that he must avoid all contact with Isabelle. In addition, he was required to get counseling so that he could better understand what sexual harassment is, why it's a problem, and how not to perpetuate it.

Isabelle, for her part, was immensely relieved. Most of the women in the Black community did not confront her about her decision. In fact, a few months later, a number of the women who had previously found it difficult to support her told her that their reluctance sprang from their own experiences with sexism. "They just couldn't deal with what I was saying," Isabelle says, "because they had so many [similar] things happening in their personal lives. This triggered so much stuff for them that they couldn't take it on—so they had to just push me away. All their feelings about being a Black woman and dealing with Black men and dealing with men in general, and their sexuality and their femininity and their vulnerability—they just couldn't deal with my story."

In mustering the courage to report her experience of sexual harassment by a Black man, Isabelle confronted the powerful cultural norm of gender silence. She speaks of going from a point where she did not realize the impact of gender and sexism to now being very conscious of the twin forces of racism and sexism in her life. She went from being detached from a central part of her experience to being connected and feeling whole. "In the past I found that the gender issue was so hidden," she explains. "I could talk about racism all the time with all kinds of people, but to talk about sexism was a really difficult thing. It just seems to have roots that are so, so painful for so many people. . . . It just seems like it's more entrenched in who we are as women."

By going through the experience she did with Charles and the Black community at her university, Isabelle learned that as painful as it can be, standing up and asking to be treated with complete respect is central to the progress of Black women. "We're long-suffering," she says. "We're available to men, we're open, we're receptive, we're nurturing. Sexism is part of what we deal with, and it's not questioned very often. But it should be questioned more."

Unfortunately, for African American women racism and sexism do not create an either-or proposition. They don't get to choose which one will haunt them and which one they'll be free of. They have to manage them both. And the Black community as a whole needs to find strategies to acknowledge and confront both forms of bigotry. Gender silence is crippling and corrosive. If the Black community can truly become a safe harbor for Black women, sparing them the anguish of gender discrimination, Black men and women together can then focus even more energy on fighting racial prejudice.

If you've ever jumped double dutch, you know that the key to mastering the sport is to focus on both ropes in unison. Perceiving only one rope at a time inevitably leads to stumbling. Of course, if you've jumped or if you've ever watched others deftly straddle the ropes, you know that no two jumpers do it the same way. Each finds her own way to manage the ropes while expressing her unique style and abilities. And sometimes her moves are so artful, so graceful, and so rapid-fire, you almost believe that the ropes have disappeared altogether.

THE MANY SHIFTS
OF BLACK WOMEN

Black women are the yoga masters. We're required to bend in as many different ways as possible in our daily activities. We have to be extremely flexible and people expect us to be good at it—friends, family, relatives, coworkers, society. For each different role that we perform in society, we have to bend a different way. And if we don't perform those roles well, we're perceived to be and sometimes we perceive ourselves to be, less than adequate, or failures.

SHAY, 33, CAMBRIDGE, MASSACHUSETTS

Black women in America expend substantial psychic energy on managing the threats of racial and gender bias. We still live in a country where the myths about Black women too often obscure the truth. As a nation and a society, we have yet to eradicate the prejudices and discrimination relentlessly directed toward African American women. Our research shows that in response to this unrelenting oppression, many Black women in America today find they must spend significant time, thought, and emotional energy watching every step they take, managing an array of feelings, and altering their behavior in order to cope with it all. Too many Black women in America are coping with shame, with feelings of low self-esteem, with the sense that they will never be as confident, successful or as appreciated as they wish they could be. Sometimes they're coping with crippling fear and anxiety: if they say what they think or act the way that comes naturally, they will be rejected, excluded, even hated.

And so they do what we call "shifting." African American women change the way they think of things or the expectations they have for themselves. Or they alter their outer appearance. They modify their speech. They shift in one direction at work each morning, then in another at home each night. They adjust the way they act in one context after another. They try to cover up their intelligence with one group of friends and do everything possible to prove it with another. They deny their sadness and loneliness. They shift inward, internalizing the searing pain of going out into the world day after day and hitting one wall after the next, solely because they are Black and female.

Our research shows that a large number of Black women in America feel pressured to present a face to the world that is acceptable to others even though it may be completely at odds with their true selves. Specifically, 58 percent of our survey respondents report that at times they have changed the way they acted to fit in or be accepted by White people, and 40 percent say that at times they have downplayed their abilities or strengths around Black men. The women we interviewed use a variety of images to describe the shifting process, referring to the "mask" they wear, the "chameleon" they have become, having to constantly "bend" what they do and who they are to please others. They say they must shift to conform to codes set by various segments of society, modulating their language, their behavior, even their personal appearance, to make White colleagues feel comfortable, and then shifting again to appease fellow Blacks who may feel that a woman who speaks too distinctly has forgotten who she is and is "trying to be White." And then they may shift again, because some middle-class African Americans are put off by a Black woman who uses colloquialisms, wears her hair naturally, or speaks her mind too loudly or too often.

In some cases, Black women shift in ways that are less conspicuous

to others, quietly changing the way they think or feel rather than making obvious adjustments in their outward appearance or behavior.
Some women say that they constantly mull over much of what they
say and do. They become hyperalert, endlessly on patrol, scanning the
environment for danger and ever prepared to respond. Others erect a
wall of stoicism to protect themselves from the profound emotional
pain that they would otherwise feel. Still others internalize society's
chronic discrimination and hatred, losing themselves in overwhelming
feelings of self-loathing and inadequacy. All of these are forms of what
we call "shifting."

When we talk about shifting, then, we are referring to all of the
ways African American women respond to and cope with racial and
gender stereotypes, bias, and mistreatment. Our contention is that all
Black women are forced to react or respond in some way to these challenges—and thus all Black women shift. Sometimes shifting is conscious—the person is fully aware of her reactions and is making active
decisions about her behavior. But perhaps more often, shifting is done
subconsciously, without apparent thought. She's shifting on automatic
pilot. And yet what may be virtually effortless can be costly physically,
emotionally, and spiritually, severly compromising her health and well-
being.

Shifting as Survival, Shifting as Self-Destruction

For many Black women, shifting is a matter of long-term survival. It's a
skill that African American women have mastered over centuries not
only to broaden their opportunities socially, educationally, and professionally, but to rework the prevailing image of their Black sisters and
brothers in the eyes of other Americans. Alberta, a 50-year-old dentist
in Philadelphia, says, "I've felt pressured to make certain that I am
always perfect, that my entire race is judged by my actions." Sandra, a
27-year-old graduate student in Newark, New Jersey, reports that what
she finds most difficult about being a Black woman in America is "rep-
resenting every Black woman in the world every day of my life. Any
move I make or step I take, I am never judged as an individual, I make

a statement for Black women—good or bad, whether I want to or not. My shoulders get tired of holding up this responsibility." Wilma, a 38-year-old data programmer from Dallas, Texas, reports: "The way I was brought up is, when you walk out the door, you represent our entire family. So when you act like crap, we look like crap."

Of course, all people, of all ethnicities, whether male or female, find that at times they must adapt their way of thinking or behaving to respond to particular situations and to fit in to specific environments. You avoid wearing shorts and sandals to your job in a corporate office. You speak to your grandmother from China in her native tongue so that she feels more comfortable. You cheerfully shake the hand of your tennis partner even though she just won the match. And all marginalized groups—Native Americans, Latinos, gays, lesbians, and others—are compelled to conform, to adjust, to shift, in response to bigotry. But our research suggests that because of the singular way racism and sexism converge in the lives of Black women, because of the unique status and legacy of African Americans in this society, and because of the hatred, misperceptions, and lowered expectations that bigotry evokes, Black women may have to shift more often and more consistently than most other Americans. They must endlessly compromise themselves to put other people at ease, counteract the misperceptions and stereotypes, and deflect the impact of those hostilities on their lives and the lives of their mates and children. Black women must go to greater lengths to show that they are feminine, that they are capable, that they have something important to contribute. As 47-year-old Fern from New York puts it, "I know I'm living against the stereotype at all times."

Shifting can be adaptive—it may, indeed, be a matter of survival—when it allows a woman to explore different genuine parts of herself, make connections with people who may be very different from her, and pursue opportunities in the mainstream. Some Black women are able to stay centered and keep their shifting within bounds, navigating the waters of adversity resourcefully. Moreover, the resilience and creativity of Black women who have managed to hold their heads high in the face of bigotry and remain true to themselves is legendary. Ida B. Wells, Mary McLeod Bethune, Zora Neale Hurston, Elizabeth Catlett,

Shirley Chisholm, Althea Gibson, Cicely Tyson, Audre Lorde, Nikki Giovanni, and many of their unheralded sisters are evidence of the capacity of Black women to rise above and not be defeated by racial and gender discrimination.

But shifting can also be profoundly self-destructive to a Black woman. Too often she moves from being in touch with her inner authentic experience to putting all her attention into creating an outer acceptable façade. Rather than maintaining a healthy consideration of others, she acquiesces to the tyranny of their biases, needs, and expectations. She feels frustrated, lonely, and inadequate. Or as she is pressured to bounce between divergent identities—one "Black," one "White"—experiencing what we call the yo-yo paradox, she may start to feel that she is constantly treading on shaky ground; confused, selfconscious, and conflicted. She may become psychologically or even physically ill from the stress of being all things to all people and nothing to herself. She's adrift spiritually, and the process of shifting, initially a life preserver in stormy seas, has morphed into a weighty anchor, and she's drowning.

Shifting as a Coping Strategy

Our research finding—that shifting can be emotionally as well as physically destructive—is supported by numerous prior studies by colleagues in the field showing that racism and sexism are stressful conditions that can profoundly challenge a person's mental and physical health.[1] For example, Hope Landrine of the Public Health Foundation in Los Angeles County and Elizabeth Klonoff of California State University, San Bernardino, have conducted a number of studies that provide evidence of the deleterious impact of racism and sexism on psychological well-being. In a study of 520 Black adults, including 277 women, Landrine and Klonoff found that people who reported experiencing more racism were more likely to be beset with psychiatric symptoms, such as depression and anxiety.[2] Moreover, they concluded that among Blacks, those who are most likely to fall prey to psychiatric symptoms are women who are experiencing numerous stressful life events and who are dealing with greater racial discrimination. Similarly, in two studies on the impact of sexism on women, where Black women were a minority of both samples, Landrine and Klonoff found that experiences of sexism were a powerful predictor of psychiatric symptoms. Women who reported more experiences of sexism also reported more psychological difficulties.[3]

Of course, research has shown, too, that people—given their diversity and complexity—vary in how, and to what degree, they are affected by stress and how well they are able to cope with it. Some coping styles are so effective that they prevent the stress from having a negative impact on the person altogether. Some reduce the intensity of the stress but are not entirely protective. And some coping processes fail, leaving the individual susceptible to feelings of low self-esteem, depression, substance abuse, and a plethora of other mental and physical ailments.[4] Likewise, our research shows that a particular form of shifting can be an effective coping strategy for one woman, and a useless, counterproductive, or absolutely destructive one for the next.

According to widely accepted psychological theory, coping strategies are generally either *cognitive* (requiring you to think differently) or *behavioral* (requiring you to alter how you behave). Common examples of cognitive coping strategies include denying a problem ("I'm not afraid of airplane turbulence. I'm absorbed in this magazine article"), minimizing or distancing yourself from a problem ("I'm a little concerned, but I'm not going to worry about this bumpy plane ride since driving a car on an icy road is much more risky"), or wresting a positive meaning from a negative event ("This bumpy plane ride is giving me the chance to work on my feelings of fear").[5] When people deny a problem, they unconsciously disavow awareness of it. When they minimize or distance themselves from the problem, they know that the problem exists, but they make it smaller in their minds or they think about it selectively. A Black woman may deny the presence of racial discrimination in her life, minimize it as a primary concern, or derive meaning from the experience, for example, by seeing a racist encounter as an opportunity for growth or a way that God is teaching her something valuable. When people are dealing with race- or gender-based hatred and mistreatment, cognitive processes often help them to manage and overcome the feelings of sadness, anger, betrayal, or anxiety that are all but certain to arise.

Examples of common behavioral approaches to a problem include: gathering information, confronting the perpetrator, and other direct attempts to alter the situation.[6] Whereas cognitive processes often help people to manage their feelings about a stressful situation, and are especially useful when the person cannot change it, behavioral processes are often aimed at situations that can be changed through direct action. Thus, when it comes to shifting, behavioral strategies that Black women may employ include changing how they look or present themselves, how they speak, where they work, and whom they spend time with. When they take direct steps to challenge bias—for example, by bringing a race discrimination case—they are also relying on a behavioral form of shifting.

Based on our interviews and surveys, we have identified six basic shifting strategies that Black women frequently use to cope with bigotry, each of which can incorporate cognitive and behavioral components.

1. *Battling the myths.* Black women alter their behavior in order to disprove and transcend society's misconceptions about them.
2. *Scanning, surveying, and scrutinizing the environment.* Many Black women cope by carefully monitoring how they are being perceived at every turn.
3. *Walling off the impact of discrimination.* By downplaying, ignoring, or denying the role of sexism and racism in their lives, many Black women are able to transcend the pain and suffering they would otherwise experience.
4. *Seeking spiritual and emotional support through churches, religious communities, friends and family members.* By finding a higher purpose and building emotional connections in their lives, many Black women find they can rise above the daily onslaught of sexism and racism.
5. *Retreating to the Black community and abiding by the home codes.* Black women often return to the Black community for relief and

solace, but then may be faced with pressure to abide by a different set of cultural conventions and codes.

6. *Fighting back.* They may directly challenge and work to overturn racism and sexism.

Battling the Myths

Before we interview 34-year-old Lena, we are told that she is an incredibly modest person, given her tremendous talent and success. When asked about her life experiences, she quietly recounts her numerous educational and professional accomplishments: She entered Princeton at the age of 17 and graduated summa cum laude three years later. She went on to earn both a law degree and an MBA at Harvard, then eventually moved back to her hometown, New York City. For the past three years, when not managing her duties as the marketing director of a fashion company, she has helped coordinate legal workshops in poor communities.

As uncomfortable as Lena seems to be reciting all of her accomplishments, and as humble and unassuming as she obviously is, she acknowledges that around some White people she feels she must shift into a cockier pose, reciting her credentials to put them on notice that she is as educated and talented as they are, if not more. "I have realized that with certain White crowds I need to be a bit more pretentious and full of myself than I would ordinarily be. . . . I'm not one to go around saying, 'Oh, I graduated from Harvard' unless it comes up. But I notice with White people, at times you need to put that out there just to give them pause and make them respect you."

Lena explains further: "I've watched my best friend, who's very good at throwing in 'When I was shopping in France' or 'When I went skiing in Vail.' Sometimes with White people I guess you have to play their game . . . to get their ear, to get them to open up to you, to let them know that 'she's one of those cultured Black people.'"

Lena is not alone in her strategy of going out of her way to highlight her credentials and her value to people who may otherwise stereotype her. Much of the shifting that Black women do is motivated by a wish, sometimes conscious, sometimes not, to confront, transcend, and hopefully defeat the ugly myths and stereotypes that so many in society continue to hold about them. Many women have developed ways of acting, talking, and dressing that conform to White middle-class norms of behavior and thus may help debunk and unravel discriminatory myths. Many feel pressure not just to meet White cultural codes but to exceed them. A number of women, for instance, talk about how educational achievement is a way of reversing the myth of inferiority. They say that they constantly emphasize their academic and professional achievements in order to be taken seriously by White people.

Anita, a 30-year-old graphic artist from Boston, says that earning her bachelor's degree was a way to garner credibility and respect from Whites. Susan, a 22-year-old college student from Phoenix, speaks of how consistently voicing her plans to attend law school is a way to alert Whites to her worth and promise. Indeed, for many generations, Black women, often more than Black men, were encouraged to get a good education as a way out of domestic service and to avoid being ambushed by society's race-based myths.[7] Arguably, this central coping strategy has paid off handsomely: Black women today boast remarkably high secondary school and college graduation rates.[8]

But working to defeat the myths about Black women's inferiority is hardly easy. Nancy, a 26-year-old single mother, talks about her experience as a student at a predominantly White university in Denver.

> I was the only one from my family to go to college. I had to adapt to Whites' expectations of me. I felt I had to change my external appearance—the way I talk, the way I walk, the way I carried myself, the way I wore my hair. I had to create all of this hype in order to be perceived as an intelligent Black woman. . . . I felt like Dr. Jekyll and Mr. Hyde, like I had to walk on eggshells around White people.

Janet, a woman in her late thirties from Mobile, Alabama, who has held positions in various corporate settings, also sees shifting as a difficult enterprise. "I really take it as work. It's more than just cultural. It's more than just correct English. You have to become a whole other person. It's like having a split personality. I have to step in and out of all of these shoes all day. I feel like I'm changing clothes and changing hats. It's work."

Elaine, a former corporate executive in San Francisco, California, whose dreadlocks graze her shoulders, says this.

> If I'm in a boardroom situation, I'm very cognizant that I have to change my voice. And it's funny that there'll be White folk around. Because if some of my Black friends come to the office and put their ear up to the door, they'll hear a whole different conversation. I think many of us have to be chameleons. We have to move in and out of our private lives, back into our corporate lives. And I don't think that Whites have to do that as much. When I think about it, I think it's a big deal, because it's something else that we—I—have to do. And I don't think it's natural. And I don't think it should be that way. But that's how it is. So much of being Black is "That's how it is." I have to do everything I can do to be just like them, in order to convince them. So if that's acting White, that's acting White. I have to put food on the table.

The ability of women like Janet and Elaine to take on and contradict the myths is highly valued within the African American community and actively passed down from mother to child, from mentor to student. We met Retha, 36, in her high-rise Atlanta apartment. Active in a Big Sister program for the past seven years, she has taken under her wing more than a dozen girls living in Atlanta's public housing projects, and occasionally mentored their brothers as well. In between helping them with homework and easing them through their growing pains, Retha coaches them in the art of shifting, offering them the tools that she believes can help lift them out of poverty.

> I just state to them, "Look, when you go to work you have to pull your pants up; and yes, honey, you do have to talk the king's or

queen's English. You have to speak properly. And that's a reality. If you're going to get a job, you're going to have to assimilate. That doesn't mean you have to give up who you are. And nor does it mean that you forget where you come from. But you have to be bilingual and in some cases trilingual. . . . And you can't curse out everybody because they're not going to take it. They're not going to understand that you're going through some kind of pain. They're not going to understand because they don't care. At some point you're going to have to give in—you're going to have to compromise, and at some point fall in line."

Scanning, Surveying, and Scrutinizing

Black women shift, too, by constantly assessing the biases and prejudices that they're facing and pondering the best way to respond. Their thoughts literally dart back and forth as they ask themselves, *Should I or shouldn't I?* They make split-second decisions on whether to challenge an opinion; on whether to work overtime to disprove the myth that Black women are lazy, or go home to spend time with their children. Should they wear the African robe they love to the office Christmas party or play it safe with the same DKNY pantsuit that they've worn before? They debate whether to speak up right away when they hear a racist joke at work or let it go, because sometimes the cost of speaking up is greater than the gain. They lie awake late into the night reviewing every word that was said at the meeting earlier in the day, wondering if they made their point cogently but not stridently, anguishing about how they might have done it better, and trying to discern the hidden meaning behind the responses and reactions of their colleagues. They can't turn off the thinking, and this can be exhausting.

In order to facilitate this moment-to-moment thinking process, many women become full-time researchers on their experiences in the world, forever developing hypotheses, collecting data, and revising theories in accordance with new evidence. They are exceedingly alert to their own behavior and vigilant about what's happening around them. These women find themselves emotionally revved up, looking for meaning in every syllable, inflection, gesture, and glance. They're always "on." *Did my boss say how much he liked the memo I wrote because he expected something less from a Black woman? Did he fail to give me a promotion this year because the company isn't doing well, or because he doesn't want to see a Black woman progress any further at the firm? Did I seem defensive when he suggested that I go back to school and get my master's degree? I know it's good advice, but haven't a lot of White people in the company excelled and been promoted without it?*

Other researchers have found evidence of coping styles that involve active, constant monitoring. In a review of research on how prejudice is experienced, Janet K. Swim and her colleagues at Pennsylvania State University concluded that one major strategy that oppressed groups use to deal with discrimination is to anticipate encounters in order to be better prepared to handle them.[9] And Sherman A. James of the University of Michigan has coined the term "John Henryism" to describe a coping style characterized by persistent, prolonged effort that involves the use of considerable energy. This approach to life's difficulties is named after John Henry, the nineteenth-century Black steel driver who refused to give up when competing against a mechanical steam drill.[10] John Henry won the contest but collapsed and died immediately thereafter from utter exhaustion. The lesson here is that high-effort coping can be costly, and research that James and others have conducted supports this notion. James has found evidence of a relationship between John Henryism and hypertension in Black men and women.[11] In other words, Black people who persistently engage in high-effort coping are more likely to have high blood pressure, which is a risk factor for heart disease. John Henryism appears to be a broad coping strategy that includes our notion of scanning, surveying, and scrutinizing the environment.

While being alert and aware makes some women feel more in control of situations that are often beyond their control, being tuned into everything and contemplating each and every one of their own moves means that they can't exhale, they can't relax. Selma, a 73-year-old retired school

administrator, says, "I guess I select my words differently. I may say something among my own peers that I probably wouldn't say in a mixed group.
I take more time and think about getting ready to speak because I don't
want them to put me in a stereotype group." Forty-eight-year-old Sharon,
who works as an administrative assistant in Miami, says that at work, "I
just need to watch what I say. To whom I say it." She says there is constant
pressure to monitor not only her speech but "how you carry yourself."
Michelle, a 31-year-old insurance claims adjuster in New York City, who
twice was passed over for a promotion that was given to less experienced,
less senior White colleagues, has learned to listen to Whites "in stereo," in
other words, to decipher the subtext behind the stated message.

Yolanda, a student at a predominantly White college, finds herself
carefully monitoring the reception she gets in classes. Even after the
semester is well underway, she constantly scrutinizes the environment
and her own behavior. Recently she found herself ruminating: *Why are
my classmates so aloof? Is it because this is an upper-division math course
and they're surprised that a Black person is here? Why are there always
empty seats beside me? I feel like I'm being friendly, but am I somehow pushing them away? When the professor answered my question, why did he have
that patronizing tone of voice? Am I reading too much into it? Am I participating enough in class so that he knows that I'm prepared and that I can do
the work? Am I trying too hard?* Yolanda reports that she is emotionally
drained from this unrelenting inner dialogue and feels she has become
"paranoid." She didn't appear to us to be unreasonably mistrustful but
her continual cognitive shifting has clearly taken a toll.

Olympia says that her indecision over what to wear is symbolic of
her constant rumination about how she comes across, how she's
viewed as a Black woman, and whether she'll be awarded the next
business contract. A 42-year-old married woman with two children,
Olympia decided to start her own business after spending 15 years
working in development and public relations. Three years ago she
launched a consulting firm that specializes in providing public relations and marketing services to colleges and universities. Olympia is a
font of vision and ideas and believes she works well with the graphic
artists and webmasters she hires to help her do a job.

But for Olympia, getting and maintaining the work always looks easier on the outside than it is on the inside. "People have no idea what I go through," she says. When she is building a relationship with a new college or university, Olympia scrutinizes the motives of the various university officials and particularly tries to sort out whether and to what degree they might be racist or sexist. She is also constantly wracked with self-doubt, questioning how to present herself, second-guessing decisions she's made. Oftentimes her self-scrutiny takes the form of anguishing over what to wear.

One recent weekday morning, before an important initial meeting with a college president, two trustees, and the vice president for development, she found herself in a near panic, rummaging through her jewelry box for her pearls. From the time the meeting was scheduled two weeks prior, she'd been waffling between three different outfits. She'd finally decided on a conservative, navy blue pantsuit, and her pearls, a single strand that had been a present from her great aunt on her twenty-first birthday. But on the morning of the meeting, already dressed in the suit, she couldn't find them. "I was almost going crazy. It was as if wearing the pearls would make or break the interview. Somehow the pearls, because they're conventional, because they're traditional, meant that I was ready to walk into that environment. Somehow the pearls would be a connecting point between them and me." Finally, Olympia found them—they were buried underneath the colorful beaded necklaces and bracelets that she prefers to wear. As she affixed the gold clasp at the nape of her neck, she was able to relax, if only for a moment.

Walling It Off: Blocking the Pain of Bias

Suppressing or managing the feelings of sadness, anger, disappointment, anxiety, and shame that arise from experiences of bias is often a central motif in Black women's lives. Constantly living with these feelings is painful—and dangerous. Feelings of low self-esteem are often triggered, particularly when a woman internalizes the bigoted message, blaming and beating up on herself, rather than focusing on the real, external problem. And as we discuss in more detail in Chapter 5, carrying around feelings of being inadequate and unworthy puts women at risk for depression.

Many African American women are faced with so many intensely unpleasant feelings, they simply put up their guard. Many women whom we interviewed or surveyed speak of disengaging emotionally to deal with the assaults of racism and sexism. By constructing a wall around their feelings, they are able to ignore the bias that they are experiencing.

Women who wall off racism and sexism are shifting cognitively: by screening out distressing facts, they are shielded, at least for a time, from the emotional impact of these painful experiences. The polar opposite of the scanners, surveyors, and scrutinizers, instead of being revved up and "on," the deniers are in sleep mode.

Research by other scholars supports the efficacy of a walling-off strategy. Brenda Major and Toni Schmader of the University of California, Santa Barbara, report that one approach that stigmatized groups use to manage stereotypes and discrimination is to psychologically disengage so that their feelings of self-worth are not dependent on how they are seen or treated by those who are biased against them.[12] In a study designed to learn about the general coping styles of African American women, Kathleen Smyth and Hossein Yarandi of the University of Florida found that one predominant mode of coping was to minimize the situation—in other words, to make light of the problem or detach from it.[13]

Researchers have found that, more often than not, African Americans and women tend to minimize experiences of discrimination, subconsciously denying or knowingly ignoring bias. When other people mistreat them because they are Black or female, they often find it less painful to heap blame on themselves than to acknowledge the racist or sexist animus that led to the situation. For example, in a series of laboratory experiments, Karen Ruggiero of Harvard University and her colleagues asked volunteer subjects to take a test.[14] The experimenter informed the Black research subject that one member of a panel of White judges would evaluate his or her test. The experimenter also confided that either none, some, or all of the members of the panel discriminate against Blacks. Similarly, in the gender study, women research subjects were told that one member of a panel of male judges would evaluate their test, and that either none, some, or all of the members discriminate against women. After the test had presumably been graded by one of the panelists, the test booklet was returned to the subject with the grade F. Subjects were then asked to complete measures that assess how they make sense of the feedback and how they feel about themselves.

Ruggiero and her colleagues found that although Blacks and women sometimes perceived discrimination, they were more likely to minimize discrimination and to blame themselves for their failures. A similar study with White males as the subjects had rather different findings. White males were substantially less likely to blame themselves and more likely to see discrimination as the reason for their poor performance.[15] Ruggiero and her colleagues also explored the meaning behind these results. They determined that if the Black and female research subjects had attributed their poor performance to discrimination, while they could have held onto a more positive sense of their own personal abilities, they would be faced with more negative feelings about themselves as a socially rejected group. By attributing their failure to their own abilities, Blacks and women could maintain a sense of control, the sense that they, not others, determine their fate. Ruggiero's research shows that shifting by minimizing, denying, or ignoring discrimination may serve a psychologically beneficial function for those who are faced with bias every day. In essence, if racism and sexism do not exist (or at least can be perceived as not affecting them in any significant way), then Black women can attempt to succeed based on their own talent and hard work.

Yet minimizing and denying is often costly. In a study of African American and European American women, Nancy Krieger of the Kaiser Foundation Research Institute in Oakland, California, found that Black women who accepted and kept silent about racial or gender discrimination were four times more likely to report high blood pressure than those who talked to others about it or took action.[16] Black women who reported no experiences of sexism or racism were 2.6 times more likely to be hypertensive than those who reported such experiences.

When asked whether she has ever experienced sexism, Tamar, a 37-year-old college administrator, says, "Yes, by being ignored." When encouraged to elaborate, she says she can't come up with any concrete examples, but then notes, "I think I stay in denial. I think denial has been a very effective tool for me."

Wendy, 32, works by day as an accountant, but she is also an accomplished classical and jazz flutist, who has recently begun performing at weddings and receptions on the weekends. When she arrived at the Chicago hotel where a twenty-fifth wedding anniversary party was being held, she noted in passing that the crowd appeared to be all White. Wendy was directed to an official-looking woman who was managing the affair. When Wendy began to introduce herself, the woman glanced at the flute case, and blurted out, "Oh, you're here to set up the flute for the musician?" Wendy quietly responded, "No, I *am* the musician."

Wendy didn't think any more about it until the following day when she was struck by how racist the woman's comment was. The woman had so much difficulty seeing a Black woman as the solo flutist that she'd invented a new role—the person who sets up the flute. But none of this had passed through Wendy's mind at the time. When she first approached the woman, Wendy was worried about performing and bringing just the right musical interpretation for the occasion. In hindsight, she acknowledges that her denial saved her. She would have been even more nervous if she had realized that her credibility as a flute player was being questioned.

Charlene, 42, had a traumatic experience when her family moved and she transferred from a predominantly Black high school to a barely integrated White high school outside Hartford, Connecticut. An excellent student, she trusted and felt close to her teachers, but all of that changed overnight. She remembers entering a science class that had been in session for several weeks. The teacher asked her to take a test even though, having just arrived at the school, Charlene obviously wasn't prepared. When she took the exam and got a perfect score, Charlene recalls, "The teacher was amazed—not pleased, amazed—and I felt I'd escaped a trap." Rather than praise Charlene for her excellent work, the teacher expressed his surprise, and ironically, his disappointment.

"It was very painful," Charlene tells us. "Even though I remember the teacher, the faces of the students are all blank. I was at that school from 9th through 12th grade, but I can remember the names of only three students and one teacher." Meanwhile Charlene harbors vivid memories of her Black friends and the adult advisers for the Urban League youth group with whom she spent her Saturdays. Charlene talks about living two separate lives—one on school days and the other on the weekends—and she understands her partial loss of memory as a way of coping with the overwhelming alienation that she experienced at school. In her own interpretation, her "amnesia" helped her to block out the lack of support and unfair treatment and allowed her to continue to thrive academically in spite of it all.

Laura, a 35-year-old administrative assistant for a government agency in Oakland, California, describes the daily challenge of dealing with the White people with whom she works and the way she tries to "wash off" the strain when she gets home each night.

> A lot of times I can't let my guard down when I'm in that environment. I can't relax. I have to have my guard up. I have to be as professional as I can be. I need to be as tactful as I can be. When I'm in my home, I know I don't have to be all that. But every day I walk into work I have to be that way. . . . As I told my friend, my little thing is, "I have gotta go home and wash some of this White off of me. I want to wash some of these White folks off of me. They've been on me all day. They've been around me. They've been on top of me. They've been talking to me, telling me what to do. I just need to wash that off of me."

Toni, a middle-aged woman in Houston, Texas, who has worked for years as the lone Black person in her law enforcement unit and has challenged the unfair treatment she has experienced by filing numerous grievances, talks about how her coping strategies have evolved over time. "I'm used to it now, but going through the process was difficult and emotionally draining. I don't know whether it's being 50, but there's a time when you just get real clear and you're able to express it. So now I can see things before they happen. It's a very predictable environment. It's actually quite easy, so emotionally for me, I'm very detached. I used to be very involved. You just go in and focus on the work you need to do." For Toni, separating her experiences from her emotions has been key to making her work life tolerable. The shift to disengagement has made it possible for her to continue at her job, doing work that pays well and that she finds meaningful.

Sadly, however, the wall many women create to protect their emotions in the workplace also blocks out their ability to feel elsewhere. Tina, a junior high school physical education teacher in her late thirties, talks of the toll that spending her life being defensive and guarded with Whites has had on her. "It's horrible. . . . There's a certain disconnection, a mistrust and fear that I carry around that keeps me away from any type of real connection to people, because I have to label the situation quickly. . . . I've spent a lifetime not accepting and acknowledging my flaws and then putting everybody else up against this test and not being able to really relax and be myself."

Loretta, a 42-year-old utility company executive in Lexington, Kentucky, began to build a barrier between herself and the outside world when her family moved to a predominantly White suburb the summer before she entered fourth grade. It took her almost 30 years to fully comprehend how her way of coping had numbed her emotions in all areas of her life.

Loretta recounted harrowing tales of how she would have to run home from school many afternoons as White children chased her, their racial slurs carrying on the wind. In class, though the other children would smirk and giggle when she answered a question and shuffle in their seats as she gave her book reports, Mr. Talbot, her White fourth-grade teacher, rarely did anything about it. Loretta began to monitor the way she spoke in class, copy her homework over twice to make sure it was neat, and study extra hard to maintain her A average. "You have to detach your emotions from your experiences at hand," she says. "That's the only way you can really prevent people from breaking your spirit."

Loretta carried this belief into adulthood, both in college where she was usually the only Black woman in her classes, and in the corporate arena where she tended to be the only African American in key management positions. If she was isolated, she did not focus on it. She had grown used to putting her feelings aside as she went about the tasks at hand.

"Once you're used to living in a hostile environment and you get good at it, and you understand the rules, it's hard to let down your guard," Loretta explains. "I remember for a long time, even when I was at college, it was hard for me to see White people as individuals. I saw them as this White cloud of people, this big group or cloud that I was moving through. It wasn't as if I was trying to build relationships with them. It wasn't as if I was trying to be included in what they were doing. I needed to figure out why I was there, what I needed to do to get through my thing. I just needed to survive."

Then, about three years ago, Loretta attended a seminar for managers of color. The workshop essentially instructed those in attendance to do what Loretta had always done—to separate their feelings from the situations they encountered, not to dwell on inequities. Hearing her typical coping strategy described by someone else allowed Loretta to reflect for the first time on how much damage such shifting had done to all corners of her world.

"At first it sounds kind of powerful, like 'It doesn't really matter what happens to me—what's important is how I respond.' And I remember thinking 'Oh, that's good stuff.' And then I thought 'That is so unhealthy!'. . . How painful to realize how over time I had lost my ability to feel in the moment. It's like, 'I don't have the luxury of being scared right now. I need to figure out how I'm going to get out of this situation. I can be scared later.'"

Of course, for many Black women, denying or ignoring the sexism and racism they experience is not an option. The feelings flood through. The armor, no matter how well constructed, finally cracks and falls away. Many women speak of a sadness, an anger—and sometimes a profound sense of shame—that, in spite of their best efforts, seeps into their consciousness.

Tracy struggled throughout high school where she was one of only a handful of Blacks. She had to deal with both the lowered expectations of teachers and the subtle but palpable ostracism of her peers. Fifteen years later, she worked for several years as a field representative for a White city councilman in a midsize town. After deciding to take a position as an administrator in a Black community-based health clinic, she suddenly became aware of the racism of the councilman with whom she'd worked so closely. As the wall that she'd constructed began to fall, Tracy became furious at herself for having tolerated his frequent derisive comments about Black activists and politicians in his district and throughout the city.

"My decision to leave allowed me to see," she reports. "I remember shutting down the anger, the pain, and taking all that on myself. And not wanting it to be my battle. *Not now. I'm a grownup. It's going to make my life too messy. I'm a grownup.* That's how I had reasoned. And I sat there and I felt so ashamed—ashamed of having accepted it, ashamed of having heard those comments and being silent."

When walling off racism and sexism is no longer possible and negative emotions creep in, too often Black women develop a persistent view of themselves as unworthy and undeserving. Nineteen-year-old Rita, a college student and waitress, says, "I have the hardest time accepting me, who I am as a Black woman. I am never satisfied with . . . my looks, personality, accomplishments." Renee, a 26-year-old legal secretary, confides: "They've lured me into losing sight of who I am as a Black woman and being more focused on how others view me and what is lacking in me. Negativity doesn't breed pride in oneself."

Seeking Spiritual and Emotional Support

As they face the blows of bigotry and the insidious feelings of sadness, shame, and self-doubt that are likely to arise as a result, many women turn to spirituality and religious faith and rely on the love and affirmation of relatives and friends. Seeking spiritual and emotional support can be a way of shifting away from the feelings connected to bias and prejudice, exploring alternative problem-solving strategies, and garnering a new perspective. What we heard in our study mirrors what other researchers have also found: to manage the myriad stressful situations in life, Black women often lean on religious faith and prayer,[17] and they frequently count on emotional support from an extended network of kin and friends.[18] When we asked 29-year-old Wanda from Phoenix, Arizona, what helps her make it as a Black woman, she put it simply: "God, prayer, family, and friends." This spiritual shift enables many Black women to forge ahead valiantly no matter how trying life becomes.

For many Black women a strong sense of purpose and transcendent connection is absolutely crucial to their happiness and well-being. These women have a sense of themselves and a reason for living that go beyond their own individual welfare. Many are deeply religious and find powerful meaning and genuine solace in their beliefs. In the face of life's unfairness, they rely on faith. Jill, a 22-year-old from Arkansas, copes with everyday incidents of racism—like being treated poorly by store clerks and waiters— by praying constantly that she won't react with a condescending attitude and tone. Her Pentecostal faith enables her to stay calm. Lynn, a 45-year-old woman from upstate New York, who was raised as a Methodist and later converted to Buddhism, has experienced blatant racism and sexism in two consecutive workplaces and is currently unemployed. Yet she is optimistic and lacking in bitterness. "I try to see people as individuals rather than as part of a race. There's not so much separation these days. People touch each other's lives more and they're just a little more accepting." The Buddhist emphasis on self-awareness, acceptance of others, and peace has sustained her during the worst of times. Marilyn, a 52-year-old actress in southern California, never allows the ups and downs of her profession to get her down. As a Christian, she sees whatever happens as part of "God's plan." When asked what helps her survive as a Black woman, Sofia, a 28-year-old psychotherapist from southern California, answers, "my spirituality, my connection to my roots, and my support systems. I recognize that who I am and what I do has been purposed by God." Suzanne, a 38-year-old from Monroe, Louisiana, says this about the racism and sexism she endures: "My suffering is nothing in comparison to Jesus.'"

Sometimes women's spirituality includes a powerful sense of connection to the larger Black and African community. Belinda, 35, from Silver Spring, Maryland, makes it by "remembering my connection to the past and creating a space for myself that keeps my culture at the front while embracing things from other cultures and traditions as well. I love belonging to a race that produced great women like Maya, Sojourner, and Alice, and knowing that there is a seat for me on that throne as well!"

Georgette, 42, who feels trapped in a reasonably well-paying but dead end corporate position in Dallas, celebrates her culture and heritage through intensive study of West African countries that she has visited regularly. Though she feels put down, diminished, and alienated as an African woman in America, she takes great pride in being a member of a larger world community of African people. Her American identity is painful for her, but her identity as a person of African descent empowers and ennobles her.

Many Black women rely on each other—sister circles made up of friends, mothers, siblings, and cousins—as a way of staying connected with and affirming their selves. "I think we push each other," says Donna, 41, of her large group of girlfriends in Los Angeles. And Amelia, a 30-year-old from Tuscaloosa, Alabama, reports that what is critical for her is "being able to bond with and draw strength from other sisters who have paved the way for us."

Retreating to the Black Community and Abiding by the Home Codes

Given how overwhelming dealing with bias in the larger society can be, many African American women retreat to the Black community as a safe harbor. They are glad to be able to return to a predominantly Black environment at the end of the workday, on Sunday mornings, during breaks from school. In essence, they shift by going home.

But many women stress that sometimes what is otherwise an effective coping strategy creates a new set of challenges. They often feel as though they cannot be themselves among other African Americans, that they must also shift to meet several of the complex behavioral codes that exist within their own community—what we call the "home codes"—rules of comportment within Black culture that are defined not just by race but also by gender and class. Several of these codes are a direct result of bigotry. In particular, when a community is buffeted with negative stereotypes by a more powerful, dominant group, it is inevitable that some of the biased perspectives seep in. Social scientists call this "internalized oppression."[19] Sadly, when this happens, the victimized group becomes a partner in discrimination. For example, in some circles of the Black community, Black women are expected to act "White" or "bourgie." Conversely, other segments of the Black community, in an effort to disavow anything resembling White folks, demand that she be "down home" or "ghetto." In addition, because the Black community is not immune to sexist norms, she may be pressed to be submissive and unassuming with her male partner at home. While retreating to the Black community can be restorative, managing the home codes can be daunting.

For many Black women, being upwardly mobile means suppressing their Black identity. Thus, to be accepted by those African Americans who are focused on deflecting stereotypes and fitting in with the mainstream, a Black woman may have to leave her African *kufi* in the back of the closet and take care that she isn't too animated when she speaks. Many women feel pressure to become more formal, showing certain Black peers that they can adapt to "White," upper-class behaviors. To fit in with this group, a woman may need to have the "right" credentials, attire, and decorum. Thus, she may have to adopt the same false persona for Black people that she usually reserves for her White coworkers.

Danielle, 26, has always felt more comfortable around other African Americans. She grew up in a working-class family in the Kent, Ohio, area and lived in and attended schools in racially mixed areas. She graduated from high school, worked as a secretary while enrolled in a couple of college courses, then got pregnant, and pregnant again two years later.

Her parents, struggling to raise three of their grandchildren, were unable to give her much financial support, so Danielle landed on welfare for a short period of time. But five years ago, she got another secretarial job, and since then she's been juggling single motherhood with making a living. Finances are tight, and frequently she finds herself penniless a few days before her next paycheck. Most of her friends are in the same boat, working hard to survive. But Danielle has one friend who hangs out with a "more upper-class group" of Black women.

"Sometimes I feel I have to talk more proper and take the time and pronounce all my words correctly," she says of the evenings she has joined the women for dinner or a jazz concert. "And I'm not comfortable with it. I feel I have to change who I am to be around them, to fit in with them. I have to change my whole way. I'm not real ladylike. I don't like to wear dresses, sit down legs crossed, wear makeup. And they are very proper and dressed nice. I dress in what I can afford, usually big clothes, and they dress tight. They look real nice. And sometimes they say, 'Why not dress like a woman? Put on a dress, a skirt.' It's always hard to make these changes. I don't want to have to change myself to fit in with anybody else or to change myself and be something that I don't like."

But if women like Danielle lament having to try to act "White," many women speak about the pressure to prove to other Black people that they have not sold out—that they identify first and foremost as African Americans and not with the White communities where they often live and work. Some feel they must remain mute about their ambitions when they're around less-educated relatives and alter their speech to stop others from saying that they think they are "better" or are "trying to be White."

Erin, 25, grew up constantly hearing from family members that her oldest cousin, Terrence, "thought that he was White." Throughout his childhood, Terrence was enrolled in gifted classes and he chatted about astronomical principles the way some boys discussed comic books. He was soft-spoken, and when Erin visited his mother, Aunt Patsy, and overheard Terrence talking with a friend, she used to have to run to the dictionary to decipher some of the words he used. His best buddy, William, was a White guy he had known since elementary school, and together they shared the honor of being salutatorians of their senior class. Erin secretly admired her big cousin, but she heard so often from the other relatives that he thought he was better than they were—that he thought he was White—that she began to believe it was true.

Then, when Erin was around 12 years old, she made a discovery: her cousins viewed her exactly the same way. Their criticism was hard to understand. Her closest friends were Black. And she loved the family's gatherings—how Uncle Joe yelled at the television set during the football games and her grandmother and aunts fussed endlessly about the food. But because she preferred to read while her cousins played video games, because the latest slang flowed from their lips and tripped off hers, because she couldn't dance very well and studied the violin, her cousins said she "thinks she's a White girl."

Eventually, Erin stopped talking about her school life, the awards she'd won, the grades she earned. "I'm more quiet," she says today, stressing how she continues to modify how she behaves at family weddings and dinners. "I don't bring up my achievements that much because they have said that I think I'm better."

What has troubled Erin most is the tension she feels within her immediate family, with her older brother, Robbie, and younger sister, Rose. Robbie went to community college for a year before getting a job as a trucker, while Rose was married and divorced with two children by her twenty-first birthday. Erin recalls that on the day she graduated from UC Berkeley, while her parents beamed, her siblings seemed less than enthusiastic. They made snide remarks, asking if the White classmates Erin posed with in photographs would be too scared to come to the family's home in East Oakland for the evening celebration. "Dang, Erin," Robbie commented. "Don't you know any sisters?"

Erin mourns the distance between herself and her siblings. "That's one thing that makes me feel strange about going back to graduate school, because I don't want to get too much higher than either of them. I don't want them to only have a high school education while I have all this stuff. To me that's going to push me further and further away from them, not because I'm acting differently, but just because they're going to think, 'Oh, she's this and that.' And I want us to be a family."

Another consequence of the home codes is a tendency for women to downplay their accomplishments or act submissively when involved romantically with Black men, a shift that grants their brothers the power at home that racism may deny them in the larger society. While societal messages about the roles of women impact all ethnic groups, some Black women feel a particular pressure to alter their behavior in order to counter the racial myth that they are less feminine, as well as to boost the ego of their male romantic partners.

Verna, a 26-year-old computer programmer in Washington, D.C., says, "Whenever I act needy, Black men come running. Sometimes I have to keep quiet about where I work, also about owning my own house. . . . The more successful I become, the less likely I will get married." Chanel, a 34-year-old engineer in Greensboro, North Carolina, explains, "I was dating a guy who had a job and was doing well but it seems as though I was doing better. I downplayed my accomplishments to make him feel better about himself and his accomplishments. A lot of success that I was having, I wouldn't even tell him about it." And Marlene, a 61-year-old divorced woman, says: "In marriage I would *never* accept or apply for a position that was above my husband's because he resented attention to my success."

Of course, all groups have internal codes of behavior, ways of communicating and behaving that bind them together as a community. But for African Americans—a minority group with a uniquely painful history in a society that can still be intensely hostile toward Black people—the need for community may take on additional urgency. Understandably, many Black Americans may view outsiders, and those who seem to identify with them, with a measure of suspicion. Thus the home codes become more vital.

But while abiding by the codes of the Black community, most Black women are simultaneously battling the broader society's myths and stereotypes. Changing how they look or behave to accommodate the varying codes of race, class, and gender, can be dizzying. Sadly, in shifting to satisfy so many others, or believing that they should, many

Black women find themselves teetering on the cusp of their various personas, feeling conflicted, confused, and self-conscious. The yo-yo effect has taken hold and they may begin to lose touch with their true selves.

Fighting Back

There is another central way that many Black women respond to racial and gender bias: They fight back. They seek to move beyond sole reliance on the five coping strategies described thus far. These women are often well practiced at battling the myths, scanning, denying, seeking support, and retreating to their own community. But they're no longer content to simply suppress negative emotions. They're motivated to put an end to the prejudicial demands, pressures, and pulls that kindle the feelings of anxiety, sadness, anger, and shame. They're ready to take on the task of educating and challenging others, to do everything they can to make the world a better, more just place.

There is, of course, a long and noble tradition of African American women who have refused to take it anymore, from Harriet Tubman, who led hundreds to freedom on the Underground Railroad; to Rosa Parks, whose defiance sparked the Montgomery bus boycott; to author and educator Marian Wright Edelman, who has consistently argued that we must not settle for a rich nation in which children are malnourished, undereducated, and abused. For many African Americans, fighting back is a deeply meaningful coping strategy—a proactive form of shifting. Through advocacy, and sometimes through combat, and often with prayer as an ally, Black women are able to confront racism and sexism directly and transform the world in which they live. They begin to thrive, not merely cope.[20] They challenge and overcome society's oppression, rather than just reacting to it.

"I remember in a history class, the teacher would say 'and the slaves,' and every time he said 'and the slaves,' he would stare at me," explains Jeannette, a 45-year-old nurse practitioner from Chicago. "It was demeaning, as if I were literally enslaved in that moment myself. I was really very aware of my powerlessness or what I experienced as powerlessness. I felt extreme anger, knowing something was really wrong with this story. This I took home to my parents. And my father said, 'You must go back and you must instruct the class.'"

Jeannette protested and tried to get out of it, but her father insisted. He sat her down and taught her about Fannie Lou Hamer and the Mississippi Freedom Democratic Party, and she returned to school and stood up in history class and delivered a lecture without the teacher's permission. Jeannette says that when she finished, "I sat down afterward and felt safe. And I realized how unsafe I'd felt before." The teacher never said anything to her about what she'd done.

Jeannette was ultimately victorious. She not only created space for herself and found her own voice within her history class; she also educated her teacher and classmates. Her refusal to sit there and take it, her unwillingness to lose herself in the hostile classroom modeled for others how they can speak up, challenge obstacles, and hold onto themselves.

As a child growing up in a rural Ohio town with few Blacks, Danni, a woman in her late thirties who wears her hair in short twists, experienced hatred first-hand. Every single school day, Ricky, a White boy at her school, yelled racial epithets at her. Danni recalls:

During those times I really wished that I wasn't Black. *If I wasn't Black*, I thought to myself, *I wouldn't be going through this*. Then in high school, I really discovered my Blackness. I would go to a little drugstore that we had in town. They would order for me *Essence* and *Right On!* magazine, and I would read about things. I would read *Essence* and I tried to dress the way the models did. I started wearing an afro. It was amazing for me, coming from that environment. I'd be like, "This whole book, they've got Black women in it." . . . And then something clicked for me about being proud. By that time, it had reversed, and I was very proud of who I was. And that was the first time that I had ever revolted against Ricky. I would chase him. I would call him names back.

Danni shifted from being the passive recipient of ongoing verbal abuse to becoming a fighter who could defend herself and seek justice. Her initial shift to a sense of shame and low self-esteem was eventually transformed into healthy self-love and respect, a sense of sureness about her Blackness and her womanhood. Her early racist experiences provided an arena in which she was forced to survive and ironically pushed her toward the self-discovery that today allows her to thrive.

Unlike Danni, Monica, 35, didn't have to fight against bigotry as a young person because she rarely encountered it. She was an only child and her artist parents owned a small studio in San Francisco. Her parents' circle of friends was multihued. Monica counted a Korean sculptor, a Jewish novelist, and a Cuban trumpet player among her godparents. It was only when Monica graduated from high school, started college, and began moving beyond her family's social circle that she had her first bitter taste of discrimination.

During her freshman year at San Francisco State University, Monica had a work-study job on campus, but she wanted something that would pay a little better. So when she spotted an ad in the college newspaper for hostesses at a local restaurant where her family and many of her friends ate from time to time, she decided to apply. She and a White girlfriend, Sarah, hoped they could land jobs on alternate evenings and rode the bus together to the eatery one fall afternoon.

The restaurant's co-manager asked Sarah to come into her office first, and after about 15 minutes, Sarah walked out beaming. Though she had no previous restaurant experience, the manager said she liked Sarah's "fresh, all-American look" and asked her to come back the next day when the restaurant's owner would be in. Then it was Monica's turn.

The manager, a woman in her fifties with gray-streaked hair and a formal demeanor, closed the door behind Monica, sat on her desk, and with a look of mock pity said, " 'Oh, honey, we don't take colored girls.'"

"It didn't register," Monica remembers more than a decade later. Stunned, she mumbled a reply that she no longer recalls, walked out of the office, and quietly told Sarah that they should leave. But a day later, Monica sprang into action.

"I think the next day it just hit me," she says. "I told myself, 'I'm not going to hate you, because I know what that feels like now. So what I'm going to do is just keep my money from you and tell all my friends to keep their money.'"

Monica immediately called her parents, friends of the family, and a handful of schoolmates to tell them what had happened. She asked them to call and protest, and several did, saying that they would no longer give the restaurant their business. Monica called the restaurant herself that afternoon to complain to the owner. But when she had left three messages over the course of two days and heard nothing from Mr. Daniels, she again took the bus downtown and tried to confront him face to face. Told he was busy, she stood out front, telling customers walking in that the restaurant refused to hire Black hostesses. She only left when one of the waiters said that the managers were threatening to have Monica arrested for trespassing.

Monica finally heard from Mr. Daniels after she had contacted a local newspaper reporter, who in turn called the eatery for a response. Mr. Daniels apologized for "any misunderstanding" and offered her a job. Monica refused, but a week later, she heard that there was now a young Black woman standing near the door, ushering guests to their tables.

In the years since, Monica has continued her activism, launching letter-writing campaigns to protest negative portrayals of African Americans on television and boycotting businesses that have poor track records hiring people of color. "You see, everything is economics for me now. Everything," she says.

Today, she's a successful graphic artist and Monica also volunteers her time at group homes throughout the San Francisco Bay Area, teaching young people about art and taking many of the Black children under her wing. She encourages them to acquire the education and job skills necessary to overcome the obstacles they will likely encounter because they are African American. She is fighting back by preparing a younger generation of fighters.

For Roberta, fighting back seems to be in the blood. At 52, she is the founder and director of the nonprofit Consortium of Programs for Racial Harmony, a group of community-based agencies aimed at improving race relations, enhancing intercultural communication, and fostering nonviolent conflict resolution. Although Roberta often has to work 60-hour weeks, frequently laboring after midnight on a proposal that is due the next day—and even with a son in college and a daughter who recently graduated—Roberta has passed up a number of job possibilities that would pay her twice her current salary. Her work at the consortium is the kind of work that she's been inching toward for a lifetime, work that speaks to her concern about ethnocentrism and the state of race relations in the United States, work that gives her the freedom and flexibility to make real change.

The beginning of her social change work, Roberta explains, was in August 1962, when she and her father attended a board of education hearing in the southern city that was her home. Her father was an attorney, but he spent much of his time advocating for racial justice. When the public was allowed to speak at city council meetings, he often strode to the podium and eloquently took the city fathers to task for their blatantly racist policies and actions. After one of her father's evenings with the city council, the phone rang at the Pennington home with a warning that the house would be bombed that night. The threat was alarming to Roberta, but for the most part, she and her three siblings, like their parents, refused to be fearful. "As far as I knew, challenging racial injustice is what you do. It's not a big deal. You just do it."

Roberta was the oldest, and when it was time to go to high school, her parents decided that the all-Black high school in their area was not acceptable. It was sorely underfunded, with outdated books and poorly equipped science labs. The Penningtons applied for Roberta to attend one of the White high schools—a school that had not been integrated. By law, the board of education had to consider the request, and thus Roberta and her father arrived at the meeting on a steamy summer evening. Roberta well remembers her father's words, enumerating in great detail the inequities between the White and Black schools. When he'd finished, he and Roberta were excused from the room, then ushered back in less than five minutes. The verdict: "We do not approve your request." Mr. Pennington, however, had the last word. "You may have decided no this time. But you will change this. There will be integrated schools. It's only a matter of time." That night

Roberta learned two lessons: not to be rattled by a temporary defeat and the importance of vision—seeing beyond what is to what must and can be.

Although in 1962, the battle was lost—Roberta ultimately attended the Black high school—these days she feels as though she's winning the war. Roberta has dedicated her life to challenging bigotry, hate, and injustice, to ensuring that the obstacles that beset her don't cripple anyone else. For her, shifting has often meant putting aside her feelings, forging ahead, and refusing to accept racism and sexism as daily conditions of life.

While many Black women rely on shifting strategies that help them to handle society's race- and gender-based oppression—and though we see these coping strategies as completely understandable and adaptive responses to such hatred and mistreatment—we were deeply moved by the testimony of women like Jeannette, Danni, Monica, and Roberta. These are women who have all made the courageous decision to try to sap society's oppression rather than live with it, to fight back rather than accommodate to it, to quell and rise above the pain rather than to accept and internalize it. They are paving the way for all of us, creating a world where all people can fulfill their potential and thrive.

SEEKING A VOICE

The Language and Messages of Black Women

> *You always have to explain yourself because people jump to conclusions about what you mean or what you said or your tone. Right away people are on the defensive. You have to explain yourself so that you won't be misconstrued, which sometimes gets on your nerves, because you just want to say what you mean and mean what you say, without having to break it down because "You think I mean that because I'm Black."*
>
> ERMA, 49, LOS ANGELES

Nancy, now 64, will never forget what it was like to grow up in Mississippi, when there were FOR COLORED ONLY signs on public bathrooms and smart Black children like her were deemed "a credit to their race." Each morning, Nancy and her two younger brothers walked half a mile to the local Black school, where the day started with the Pledge of Allegiance and wobbly renditions of "The Star Spangled Banner" and "Lift Ev'ry Voice and Sing." Then the children pulled out their books and sat down to learn.

The teachers, all African American, were loving but strict, determined that these children would excel. Over the years, Nancy had many excellent instructors. Mrs. Lena Jenkins, who taught her English in grades 9 and 10, was perhaps her favorite.

Mrs. Jenkins would stand in front of the students, prim in her starched blouse and low black pumps, and listen to them recite Shakespeare. She would tell the boys and girls to sit up straight, to always behave like ladies and gentlemen. And every day she emphasized the importance of speaking properly, the way White folks presumably did, with no noun-verb disagreement, or slang, or anything else that would draw attention to the speaker's Blackness. "They want to believe you're ignorant," she would say. "Don't give them the satisfaction. Prove them wrong as soon as you open your mouth."

Knowing how to speak and what to say, Nancy explains, was not only a matter of pride. For Black people down South, knowing how to express oneself—and when to be silent—could mean the difference between life and death. Nancy knew always to say "ma'am" and "sir" when she bought taffy from the elderly White couple whose candy store sat a few blocks from the elementary school. Though it made her angry, she held her tongue every time she went to the movies and was steered upstairs to the balcony while rowdy White teenagers sat below. And when she went to the bakery where her mother worked, she spoke quietly and distinctly, impressing the White owners with her manners and intelligence and making her mother beam with pride.

After high school, Nancy migrated north to Chicago, moving in with an aunt and uncle who had left Mississippi years earlier. She quickly got a job working as a secretary for the city government. But even though she had left the South behind, Nancy felt more pressure than ever to heed the lessons taught by Mrs. Jenkins and to watch every word she said. For the first time in her life, she often found herself around Whites.

Nancy felt particularly self-conscious at work where she was one of only a few African Americans. She noticed what happened when Louise, another Black secretary, spoke up because she was being given more work than the White receptionists. The White managers began to label Louise a "troublemaker" behind her back, stopped saying

"Good morning" to her at the start of each day, and did everything they could to make her feel unwanted and unimportant. When the city had a budget crunch and staff had to be laid off, Louise was the first in their office to be let go. Nancy tried to justify Louise's dismissal: Maybe Louise hadn't been diplomatic enough. Maybe she just hadn't known when to be quiet.

Nancy also observed the way her White office mates would smirk whenever Annie Mae, a Black woman who worked in the lunchroom, would come around with donuts and coffee. Also hailing from Mississippi, Annie Mae spoke loudly and laced her speech with verbs that never seemed to agree with the subject, and Southern expressions like "y'all" and "over yonder." Even though Nancy would get mad at her White coworkers for patronizing Annie Mae, she also felt anger at Annie Mae for not making an effort to speak better. *Can't she see they're laughing at her?* she would think. *She's been up north for years now. It's time to let that country stuff go.*

Nancy didn't ever want to be treated like Annie Mae or Louise. She found herself taking more and more time to formulate what she wanted to say and how to say it "properly" when dealing with her White colleagues. But again and again she found that her deliberateness often kept her from saying anything at all. By the time she'd figured out how she wanted to communicate, the conversation had moved on, the moment had passed, and her voice had gone unheard.

"I know that some of the people wondered why I was so quiet," Nancy says. "I worried sometimes that they'd think I was dumb. But better for them to wonder than for me to say the wrong thing and convince them that they were right."

After listening to Nancy and to scores of other women across the country, it's clear that deciding exactly how to express oneself—and when it's even wise or safe to say anything—is often a lifelong struggle at the very center of what it means to be Black and female in America today. It's at the heart of shifting, because what you say and how you say it is often the first and most important way that other people, Black or not, size you up, determine where you stand, and decide how to treat and deal with you. If you always speak "White," you may win respect in the conventional White world, but end up alienating your Black friends and family. If you always speak "Black," you risk being perceived as less intelligent and sophisticated than you truly are, and assimilation into the outside White world may become close to impossible. And if you flow back and forth deftly between the two forms of language, you may find a measure of acceptance from everyone, but woe unto you if you're speaking the "wrong" form of English in the wrong place.

For an African American woman, perhaps no act is as critical to successfully counteracting the myths and stereotypes that swirl around her as changing the way she speaks. The pitch of her voice (whether it is deemed too loud or just right), the rhythm of her speech (undulating like a blues or popping in a crisp staccato), and the vocabulary she uses (calling a coworker "triflin'" as opposed to "irresponsible") can mean the difference between acceptance and rejection. A phrase ("You so crazy"), an "incorrect" verb ("He be trippin'") or a simple inflection ("Say what?") can shape the listener's impression of her, often in ways she may not have chosen.

Carolyn, from San Francisco, who usually speaks Standard English in the office, remembers the time she was overheard by two White coworkers speaking to a Black friend near the water cooler. "Girl," she had said, "I am through with Charmaine. She be going out behind Michael's back, and hanging out with her ex-boyfriend. I never liked her no way." The White coworkers looked at each other and smirked. Suddenly, because of a single conversation, Carolyn was no longer seen for who she is—an intelligent, capable, sophisticated Black woman. Instead she seemed to be viewed as comical, unrefined, uncouth.

Of the women we surveyed, 58 percent said that at times they had changed the way they acted to fit in or be accepted by White people, and 79 percent of this group had changed their way of speaking, toned down their mannerisms, or talked about things they felt White people were interested in while avoiding controversial topics. Shifting one's style of expression and the content of one's message emerged as the predominant way in which Black women accommodate to the social and behavioral codes of White middle-class America.

"I think as Black women, it's so easy for us to be perceived negatively that it's something that you have to be conscious of," says Glenda, a 38-year-old business consultant in Phoenix. "Just because you're talking loud and animated doesn't mean you're arguing. But I make an effort to tone it down, not say it as pointedly as I would, add some levity to the situation, just because women are perceived as being aggressive if they speak quickly and loudly and Black women are perceived as being *negatively* aggressive if they speak quickly and loudly. For men it's a sign of strength. For us it's a negative sign. I try to keep my tone of voice light, slow down my speech, and rephrase things."

When Black women try to establish themselves within the White world, there's a cruel irony they often have to face. It's okay if White people make use of Black English to spice up their phrases and seem "cool," but if Black women want to be respected and taken seriously, they need to adhere carefully to Standard English in "White" settings. Although psycholinguists have established that Black English is a respectable and viable dialect, numerous women say that they are routinely diminished, discounted, or distrusted simply because of what they say and how they say it.

Many find that to fit in, keep the peace, and move forward, they must censor their conversations and funnel their ideas. Some engage in a constant internal dialogue, making split-second decisions, sometimes several times a day, about what to say not only on their jobs, but in their homes, in their places of worship, and even among family and friends. Such choices mean they must shift on multiple levels, literally holding their tongues when they would like to speak up, reining in their emotions when they are quietly outraged. They must alter their speech, minding their grammar, purging their conversations of any slang, to overcome racist presumptions that they are uneducated and less intelligent. And they must engage in a kind of mental gymnastics, quickly mulling over how to raise a point without stepping on someone else's toes.

The suppression or editing of one's voice can be debilitating and taxing. It can become hard to figure out where the voice of another person ends and yours begins. Many Black women make such compromises without reflection, unaware of how damaging and disconnecting such an emotional dance can be.

Some women also change the way they naturally speak to fit in among other African Americans. Depending on their socioeconomic status and their politics, one circle of Black people may reject a Black woman who does not spout the king's English whereas another will ignore or mistreat her because she is neglecting the vocabulary, intonations, and mannerisms that are unique to Black English.

Discriminating against or ostracizing a Black woman because she naturally expresses herself through dialect is profoundly unfair and potentially emotionally crippling. A woman who speaks with a uniquely African American cadence and syntax is little different from the French immigrant who slips into her native tongue at home and speaks English with a Parisian accent when she's at work. Likewise, a Black woman is not less intelligent because she speaks English differently from an upper-crust White woman born and bred in Massachusetts. Much to the contrary, those women who are able to switch between Standard English and the language or dialect spoken in their homes, have the special gift of being bilingual.

Most importantly, voice is the literal expression of one's identity, the echoing of the self. If you can't talk about what you believe, in a way that feels most natural, you can become alienated from your inner self. You're no longer able to express who you truly are.

Language and Identity: "I Speak, Therefore I Am"

While many African Americans speak Standard English, many also speak a dialect that has been variously called African American Vernacular English, Nonstandard English, Black English, and Ebonics.[1] Linguists have noted that rather than being a corrupted or ungrammatical form of English, the Black community's alternative means of expression is a dialect of English much the same as American English and Australian English are dialects of British English.[2] Black English is a rich and vibrant language variety, sophisticated in its construction and keen in its declaration. The woman who meets her friend's sorority sister over cocktails and says later, "I wasn't feelin' her," sums up her distaste for her new acquaintance far more passionately than if she had said "I didn't care for her much." And "Don't hate," an admonition not to criticize someone out of envy, gets to the point in a way "Don't be so jealous" never could.

Black women have many means of self-expression, each with its own cadence and power—the reveille of words that pours forth from U.S. Rep. Maxine Waters as she takes Republican leaders to task, the verbal whoop shared by members of Delta Sigma Theta sorority at a weekend step show, a mournful Bessie Smith blues scratched out of an old 78. Though the lingua franca of Black America has long enriched the American lexicon, perhaps there has been no other time like the present in which the viewpoints and language of Black women have been so accepted and celebrated by the society at large. Suzan-Lori Parks, a Black female playwright, took the Pulitzer Prize for her play *Topdog/Underdog* in April 2002. Dr. Maya Angelou has become the country's unofficial national poet. Oprah Winfrey proselytizes that you should "live your best life," and millions try to follow.

Black women have often used their voices to illuminate society's inequities, at times dictating the script that has set the mood of the nation. Barbara Jordan's measured eloquence was a high point during the dark days of Watergate. Toni Morrison's prose has revealed the travails and longings of freed slaves and little Black girls. And Fannie Lou Hamer, the famous civil rights activist nearly beaten to death in a Southern jail, told the world that she would not accept two token seats at the 1964 Democratic National Convention "when all of us is tired."

Whether or not their words are heard by the masses or recorded in the ledgers of history, the unique "Blackspeak" so many Black women use to express themselves is closely tied to both their personal and their cultural identity. Linguists and scholars tell us that language is a core component of culture, that one's language reflects one's heritage and ethnicity, and that the distinctiveness of one's culture is perpetuated in part through language.[3] How one sees, interprets, and communicates one's sense of the world is very much a function of one's native tongue. For example, mental health professionals have found that when speaking one's native language or dialect, people are able to be more in touch with their inner feelings, memories, and experiences. As a result, doing psychotherapy in English with a person who has become fluent in English but who grew up speaking Spanish can be limiting and problematic.[4] While many people often function quite effectively in a second language or dialect, they may still suffer a loss by not using their first language. When translating their experience into a second tongue, parts of themselves are sometimes inaccessible or inexpressible. Language is not a superficial attribute grafted onto the person simply as a tool for communication. Instead, the language one speaks is imbued with historical and cultural meaning and serves an important identity function for its speakers.

Anthropologists and linguists tell us that all languages and dialects are equally complex and sophisticated, that there are no superior or inferior, advanced or primitive language systems. Humans are hardwired to be able to speak and to develop language, and wherever humans are, complex vocabularies and grammatical systems have evolved.[5] Black English is one of thousands of examples.

Black English integrates British English, African linguistic traditions, and the creole varieties of English that emerged in the Caribbean.[6] It can be distinguished from Standard English not only by its grammar and pronunciation but also by its style, tone, and rhetorical characteristics.[7] It has its own cadence and rhythm.

In her seminal book *Talkin and Testifyin: The Language of Black America*, Geneva Smitherman, a professor at Michigan State University and perhaps the foremost scholar of Black English, provides a detailed description of the components and distinctiveness of the African American dialect.[8] There are pronunciation differences between Standard English and Black English, for example, the "th" sound is sometimes pronounced as "d" or "f," as when "then" is articulated as "den" or "with" becomes "wif." Often the first syllable of a word is stressed in the Black English vernacular, as when "police" is pronounced "PO-lice" or "Detroit" is "DEE-troit."

There are numerous grammatical and structural differences between the two dialects, many of which center on how verbs and verb forms are used. For example, in Black English "be" is often used to show that something occurs habitually, as in "They always be acting a fool" and "At the end of the workday, she be dragging." When the verb forms "is" and "was" are used, they are often utilized irrespective of whether the subject is singular or plural, as in "You ain't going downtown, is you?" and "Those kids was all over the place."

Similarly, for verbs in general, the same verb form can be used for singular or plural subjects. Examples are "She do her sister's hair" and "He have us working 'til seven." In Black English, plural nouns are not always signaled by the addition of s. Instead the context indicates whether the noun is plural, as in "Three boy ran by" and "I need a dozen egg."

Smitherman notes that any one speaker of Black English does not use all of the distinctive forms of the dialect all of the time. Instead, many African Americans utilize some grammatical and structural customs some of the time, while using Standard English at other times.

While linguists have studied the unique speech of African Americans for more than half a century, only recently has a small group of communication scholars begun to focus on what's distinctive about how African American women talk. These researchers are exploring how Black women appropriate and customize the language to meet their unique sensibilities and communication needs.[9] In a study of Black women's communication, Marsha Houston, professor and chair of the Communications Department at the University of Alabama, Tuscaloosa, asked 134 Black middle-class professional women and college students to write what "Black women's talk" was to them.[10] She found that 80 percent of her participants celebrated the speech of Black women—that is, they had strong, positive feelings about Black women's communication in spite of the negative views that others often held. From her research, Houston identified three emergent themes in Black women's speech. First, there was an emphasis on the wisdom in Black women's speech, particularly in talk about their personal and professional lives as well as in conversations about Black men. Second, Black women's speech was seen as tough, direct, and candid. Third, there was an emphasis on the warmth, sensitivity, and caring that imbues Black women's talk. Houston's research participants reveled in the sound, the meaning, the embrace, and the passion in

Black women's speech. They understood that Black women have a message for America.

Living with a Double Standard: The Denigration of Blackspeak

As much as scholars may herald the virtues of Black English, listen to the women in our study and you will agree that bias and discrimination based on this dialect are still rampant in the United States. As Rosina Lippi-Green, a professor of linguistics at the University of Michigan, puts it, denigrating people based on dialect and language is the "last back door to discrimination."[11] She sees this as one of the last publicly and socially acceptable forms of prejudice. Our review of the research literature indicates that Black English is disparaged by Whites and sometimes by African Americans as well, and society still has not fully embraced or acknowledged the many unique and varying idioms, intonations and ideas that flow specifically from African American women.

Instead, because Black women exist against a backdrop of myth and stereotype, their voices are often distorted and misunderstood. If she is opinionated, she is difficult. If she speaks with passion, she is volatile. If she explodes with laughter, she is unrefined. If she pitches her neck as she makes a point, she is streetwise and coarse. So much of what Black women say, and how they say it, pushes other people to buy into the myth that Black women are inferior, harsh, and less feminine than other women.

The lack of respect for Black vernacular as a legitimate alternate form of expression has made some African American women painfully self-conscious. Indeed, Charisse, one of the authors, remembers her own discomfort when a White female editor overheard her remarking how "fine" a certain man was, and then mimicked her Southern inflection. Though her editor probably meant no harm, Charisse realized she had spoken in a voice and language that she rarely used in the newsroom, and for a moment she felt exposed. Many women acknowledge that they assiduously monitor the way they speak in certain situations, fearful that they will "slip" and use the more relaxed voice they reserve for African Americans in the presence of Whites. They take care to put *ly* on every adverb, to articulate every syllable, to rehearse every answer.

Other women add that they change not only their speech but also their mannerisms around Whites. For example, 38-year-old Maria, a surveyor in Maryland, says, "I've had to calm my mannerisms and tone because they are always misinterpreted." Shawn, a 32-year-old social service worker in Mobile, Alabama, says, "I often feel that I must monitor my vibrancy and vigor." And, Mary, a 57-year-old office manager in Boston, puts it this way: "I speak more slowly, deliberately, and with fewer slang terms or 'African Americanisms.'"

It's not just that people prefer to hear Standard English and favor mainstream styles of communication. Many of them actually deplore the prospect that Black English might be taken seriously and acknowledged as a legitimate language variety. It's hard to forget the explosive controversy that emerged in December 1996, when the Oakland School Board decided to acknowledge Black English as a language of many of its children and to actively illuminate Ebonics in order to help students master Standard English.[12] To many people, the notion of honoring and legitimizing the dialect was absolutely counter to the long-standing American idea that there is one and only one correct way to speak English. And no doubt, the idea of validating Ebonics was particularly controversial because it is a dialect created by Black people. Research shows that there is wide resistance to giving the language such mainstream recognition. In fact, when Lisa Koch of Spokane Mental Health and her colleagues recently reviewed the existing research on how people react to Black English speakers, they found that Black English speakers are often viewed as lazy and ignorant, and that even African Americans sometimes denigrate them.[13]

Thus there is a great paradox—and a striking double standard. While African Americans are consistently looked down upon for communicating in their own dialect, American culture is steeped in Black English, and non-Black people in our country are free to speak the vivid language that is "Blackspeak" without any significant negative consequences. For example, Andrew Cuomo, in explaining to talk-show host Phil Donahue his decision to withdraw from the 2002 New York Democratic gubernatorial primary—and thereby avoid a potentially racially divisive campaign against the state's Black comptroller, H. Carl McCall—said succinctly, "I didn't want to go there." Indeed, Black English has contributed to a greater candor and lack of pretense in the vernacular of many Americans. Such expressions as "It's all good," "Don't go there," and "You go, girl," have become as ubiquitous in corporate corridors as they are in urban arcades. And when Whites use the latest Black vernacular or speak with a Southern sway, they are usually perceived as urbane and cosmopolitan. Yet, when Black people utter the same words in the same manner, they're often seen as "low-class" or "ignorant."

While mimicry has been called the sincerest form of flattery, understandably, some African American women believe that the appropriation of Black slang by non-Blacks too often devolves into mockery. "If I hear one more White woman say, 'You go girl,'" Ceci, a 30-year-old illustrator says, her sentence trailing off. "I can't stand it. It makes me cringe. But it's done so lightly, I can't stand up with my fist raised. I think they're mocking Black women."

Courtney, a 22-year-old college student and employee in a communications company, also talks about how insulting it is when White colleagues imitate Black dialect. "I'm like, 'Do you ever hear me talk like that?' So I automatically know that that is how they perceive me. . . . Don't come to me like that." Like many Black women, Courtney shifts her speech as soon as she walks through the company doors at 8 A.M. and she finds it demeaning to have her at-home speech presumed to be the way she would choose to communicate in the workplace.

Shunned at Home: Coping with the Language Codes of the Black Community

After a day of conforming to the strictures of the mainstream, many Black women feel relieved to retreat into a setting that is uniquely African American and familiar, and language, they stress, is an integral part of that comfort zone. There are ticks of the tongue, words and expressions that weave the bonds of sisterhood—colloquialisms that let other Black women know that the speaker identifies with and relates to them.

"I'm ready to get my skate on." (Let's go skating.)

"That restaurant was da' bomb." (That restaurant was excellent.)

"Y'all my peeps." (You guys are my true friends.)

"What's up, girlfriend?" (How's everything going, friend?)

"Why you put me on blast?" (Why are you telling other people my personal information?)

"Um, Um, Um." (Isn't that something?)

But while some Black women adopt this vernacular easily, others do not and are shunned by Black friends, colleagues, and family members for shifting "White" in their speech or for naturally speaking in a very distinct way. How one speaks is a pivotal component of the home codes, the rules and expectations about behavior within the Black community. And violating those codes can be very painful.

Vicky, 40, had always felt different from her brothers and sisters. Growing up in a working-class neighborhood in a small town in central Florida, her siblings didn't care much about school, whereas Vicky's nose was often in a book. And whereas they toted their Black English from home to school and back again, as the years passed, Vicky increasingly spoke the English that she learned in the classroom. Tragically, when Vicky and her siblings were young children a White policeman murdered their mother's only brother in cold blood. Years later, when Vicky was in her early teens, a White neighbor sexually assaulted her.

Naturally, when Vicky's brothers and sisters taunted her and said that she talked and sounded "White," she was deeply aggrieved. How could they accuse her of sounding like the men who had defiled their family? Vicky's use of Standard English didn't feel fake or "White" to her—it was just the way she talked. To be called White, especially given the racism that the family had endured, was the ultimate affront.

Likewise, Darlene, a 26-year-old receptionist in San Francisco, painfully recounts that "because I went to predominantly White schools, my Black friends always said I 'talked White' or wasn't 'really Black.' They would say that I was a 'Black White girl.'"

Lisa, a 49-year-old mental health specialist in Alexandria, Virginia, says, "I think Black people who are darker than me and who speak a little more of what some might say is Black English think I am trying to impress the White man, when actually I was born in Los Angeles and my father spoke Standard English very well."

Robyn, 34, grew up in a working-class, mostly Black neighborhood near Los Angeles, and her sterling pronunciation, broad vocabulary, and hushed voice made her a constant target of other children. She felt even more isolated as the only child of Belizian parents, a heritage markedly different from that of the other kids whose families had been in Los Angeles for generations or emigrated from Texas, Louisiana, and Oklahoma.

"As a Black girl who grew up being told I 'talk White,' I probably felt more of a pressure to try to change around Black people," she says, brushing her bangs out of her eyes. "I guess it probably started when I was younger, being threatened with being beat up because I 'talked too White.' And I never felt all that American. I think back then there was a way to be Black and a way not to be Black, and I was the second most of the time. I guess my conflict was I really wanted Black friends. I still feel much more comfortable around Black people, happier when there's a lot of Black people around. You know, when I'm the only one, that gets really tired."

To gain acceptance, Robyn began to put some molasses in her speech. She dragged out her words, stopped pronouncing every syllable as crisply as she had once done, and slipped in a curse word here and there. But the other children mostly laughed at her efforts to sound more relaxed, more "cool," more "Black." And her parents found nothing funny in their daughter's efforts to satisfy those particular color codes of language. They didn't see the value in code switching. They weren't going to tolerate any "bad English" in their house.

Though Robyn's parents were both college graduates and her mother's older sister was a dentist, her father was the only son in a family of four boys to earn a degree. One of her uncles had battled alcoholism all his life, drifting from odd job to odd job. Another was in and out of prison. And her youngest uncle made a good living as a carpenter, but had little interest in discussing the musings of Philip Roth or the latest novel by Tom Wolfe, subjects Robyn's father loved. He wanted his daughter to be articulate and successful, even if his nieces and nephews veered down the paths of their fathers.

The mixed messages collided inside Robyn's head. She was mocked by the other children for not using slang, then chastised by her parents whenever she did. "My mother is a stickler for grammar," Robyn says. "She used to correct my grammar and she used to correct my friends' grammar. She wouldn't correct them to their faces, but she'd flinch, and then I'd hear about every grammatical mistake they made after they left."

Robyn's father was adamant that she stick to Standard English. "I think my father had some real issues with Blacks, a lot of hatred of self, or hatred of Blackness, so he was not encouraging me to fit in that way. He used to make fun of football players, the way they spoke. He would make fun of various Black celebrities, you know Jesse Jackson or a powerful Black politician, particularly with a Southern accent."

Robyn's family moved to a more diverse neighborhood when she was in high school, and both her African American and White friends echoed her crisp speech. Today, her grammar is as polished as an English professor's, each word spoken distinctly, and Robyn is comfortable that this way of speaking is the most natural for her. She no longer shifts verbally. She speaks now with only one voice—her own.

Other women explain that speaking a certain way can lead even some African Americans to label you "ignorant" or "low-class." Eva remembers being treated terribly by other Black people because of her speech patterns. Tall and reed-thin, with almond-shaped eyes, ebony skin, and cheekbones that look as though they had been etched in teak wood, Eva was absolutely stunning. The other Black women on the modeling circuit couldn't find fault with her looks, so they picked on her South Side roots instead, mocking her B-girl colloquialisms and down-home drawl.

"At one time, my diction wasn't so good," says Eva, 41, who remembers how other African American women would refer to her as a "ghetto girl." The other women, more well-spoken, criticized Eva with open brutality. "They would make rude comments, straight out. . . . My girlfriends used to say that I was so beautiful, but when I opened my mouth, you saw something different."

Eva was featured in various print advertisements and did a little runway work. But despite her success, she needed a steadier job to supplement her modeling career. She became a hostess at an upscale restaurant on Chicago's Miracle Mile, greeting patrons and checking on them during dinner to make sure that they were enjoying themselves. She was excited about the position, but when she told one friend that she had gotten a job at the elite eatery, "my girlfriend said to me, 'How could you be a host in a restaurant? You don't even know how to speak English properly.'" Eva's voice resonates with anger as she remembers her sadness. "Yeah, it hurt my feelings. But it hurt my feelings to the point that I said I was going to show them that I could do different. . . . I just wanted to change the way I spoke so I could get in more with the elite crowd."

Eva started reading articles with an eye trained on correct grammar. She purchased books on good manners and style. And she incorporated the confident strut and poses she affected on the runway and on fashion shoots into her day-to-day life. She'll never forget the day, months later, when she ran into the woman who said Eva didn't speak well enough to be a restaurant hostess. "I sure showed her," Eva says. "The next time she saw me, a year later, she said 'I can't believe you are the same person.'"

Code Switching: The Challenge of Being Bilingual

Given their desire to fit in both with Blacks and non-Blacks, many women often "code-switch" by shifting between dialects, languages and styles of communication.[14] Code switching is a result of what we call the "yo-yo paradox," the pressure Black women feel to shift back and forth in order to meet the conflicting codes, demands, and expectations of different groups. They shift "White" at the office, in the classroom, when addressing the community board during a public forum; and they shift "Black" at church, during book club meetings, among family and friends. Many African American women learn how to code-switch from an early age. The lessons on which voice to use and when to use it are often as much a part of their tutelage as good manners and the ABCs. They learn that what is acceptable on the playground is not always acceptable at home, that what is required in the classroom could cause them problems with their teenage cousins. For some Black women, code switching is relatively effortless; sometimes it's even an opportunity to use voices that reflect different aspects of their selves.

But for others, code switching is a more arduous exercise. The multilingualism required to speak one way to a Southern grandmother, another way to youths raised on MTV, and still another way in a corporate boardroom can be as challenging as learning to juggle three balls without dropping one. It can lead to the painful "yo-yo effect," as a woman feels conflicted about shifting between two distinct voices, self-conscious about using the "wrong" voice in the wrong situation. Women who have difficulty switching may be mocked or unfairly criticized by Blacks and Whites alike. "She thinks she's White." "She tries too hard to sound Black." "She's a ghetto girl." "She's not very bright."

Rebecca, a 42-year-old hospital administrator from Boston, shares how she became a virtual quick-change artist to fit in with both her family and outsiders. "I grew up in an environment in which I was frequently the only Black person," she explains. "I became 'bilingual' to survive comfortably. I spoke properly but when I was around friends or relatives who were Black who didn't live around Whites, I was ridiculed for the way in which I naturally spoke, danced, and the type of music I liked. I learned to go both ways and to size up the situation and act accordingly, especially as an adolescent."

Sharon, 34, moved as a teenager from a mainly Black school district to a predominantly White school system in suburban Illinois. She knew that her new teachers expected little of her. Sharon had already been told by the counselor who helped her pick her classes that the straight A's she earned in her old high school would probably become C's here where the work was more rigorous. So Sharon bore down like she never had before. She went to the library on her lunch breaks and completed every extra credit assignment. When she struggled a bit in chemistry, she sought out a favorite science teacher from the old neighborhood to tutor her on the weekends.

While Sharon had been popular at her old school, active in the honor society, and liked by most of the students, she felt like an outcast here. And for the first time, Sharon became conscious of her behavior around Whites, "trying to prove that Black people were capable and intelligent people," she remembers. "I think I was very conscious of not using slang when I was answering a question in class or forming a question. I'm in this environment where I'm on the spot, so I have to make sure that I'm perfect and everything is together."

But the day came when someone caught Sharon with her guard down, glimpsing her in a moment when she had not yet shifted. It was a White history teacher, Miss Campbell, who overheard Sharon talking with a Black friend during a school carnival. The next day, the teacher embarrassed Sharon in front of the entire class.

"She made a comment, 'Oh when I saw you at the carnival, you were using slang and you don't use slang when you speak in class. What's up with that?' And she said this in front of the whole class, putting me on the spot. And I remember looking at her like, *Why are you asking me this question?*" Sharon stammered out a response. "But I remember being angry at her and just thinking, *I can't believe you're doing this to me.*"

Being put on the spot before her White peers made Sharon painfully aware of what could happen if you were caught using the "wrong" voice by the "wrong" person. She became determined never to be caught again. Miss Campbell's insensitivity showed that she neither accepted slang as a legitimate form of expression nor appreciated the talent it took for Sharon to shift back and forth verbally.

The job search can also be keenly affected by the words and mode of expression a Black woman uses. Melissa, 18, who grew up in a middle-class family in Houston, says that she realizes she needs to act and talk differently when she heads off to college and into the workforce, if she is going to succeed.

Because I'm Black and a Black woman, I feel that they automatically think that when I open my mouth, I'm going to say something ignorant or I'm going to be cussing. I have to stay on top of myself and make sure that I don't slip. Because at home you talk slang, you know, but outside I feel I have to be

professional. I have to make sure that I know what I'm talking
about, that I'm speaking clearly, so that they see that all Black
people are not ignorant and that all Black women don't belong
on those music videos.

Monique, 26, was the only African American working in the
blood bank of a major hospital in Louisiana until, at last, Jacqueline
was hired to help with the paperwork. Jacqueline, 34, had had a difficult life, losing her parents at an early age, growing up in foster homes,
and eventually dropping out of high school in the tenth grade. She
went on to earn her general equivalency diploma, got married and had
a daughter. But her world remained small, limited to her family, a few
friends, and the distant relatives she knew in the rural parishes of
Louisiana. Jacqueline often slipped into the patois of her youth and
used the slang that her adolescent daughter understood, and Monique
noticed that some of the White doctors and patients treated Jacqueline with utter condescension. They questioned her competence,
ignored her comments or cut off her questions before she finished
speaking. Slowly, Monique taught Jacqueline to be bilingual.

"I always say 'Jackie, speak easy, watch your voice,'" explains
Monique. It was a lesson that she herself had to learn. Raised in a
rough housing development, Monique grew up speaking the parlance
of the projects, and it was an older Black laboratory technician, long
since retired, who had pulled Monique to the side each time she used
incorrect grammar. "Now I make sure I pronounce all my syllables,"
she says. "I don't use 'like,' 'ain't,' 'yo.' Instead of saying 'What's up?'
I'm like, 'How are you today? Is everything okay?' But when I see
Jackie, I'm like, 'Hey, what's up, girl?' You know, we get like that. I can
switch."

Still, Monique never greets Jackie with such familiarity in front of
their White colleagues. "Never," she says emphatically. "Because I feel
they should never see that side of me. I like people to see me one way
and one way only."

Instead, explains Monique, in the middle of the day or during a
particularly stressful afternoon, she and Jacqueline will run to the

employee lounge or to a corner of the cafeteria and chat. "I'll snatch her away really quick and say let's go in the staff room and let's just talk for a little while because that's the only person that I can connect to. I can relate to her. If I want to calm down and speak slang, no matter what I say, she understands what I'm saying."

Code switching is easier and less burdensome for some women than for others. Myrtle, a 51-year-old teacher from a small town outside of Atlanta, remembers with amusement a discussion with her White department chair. "She wanted to know how we could switch. How we can be very formal when it's necessary, and when we're in the 'hood, hey, it just comes right out, you know? And she just thought that was just amazing. She said, 'How can you do that?' I said, 'Hey, it's something that you don't have to think about. It's just like breathing. It's like when you go home, you relax.' I guess sometimes it's a conscious effort, but then there are other times when it's an unconscious thing."

But unlike Myrtle, some Black women are fraught with worry about slipping up. Felicia, a college administrator in her thirties, who grew up in an ethnically diverse town in Michigan and subsequently attended a college that was overwhelmingly White, speaks of her duality. "I was brought up to wear two faces," she says in a quiet voice.

> I feel like I have to act a certain way with Whites. I'd be incredibly aware of my speech, have to be really articulate. Try not to talk about anything unless I know a lot about it. In college, I wouldn't ask questions. If I didn't know something, I'd just try to write it down and find out later. I couldn't be relaxed, 'cause the moment I relax and say something like, "Girl, ya know, blah, blah, blah," sometimes people would mimic me. It's like I'm hyperaware of myself and the way I'm coming off, even if nothing happens where I see a noticeable behavioral change in them because of my color or my race.

Felicia's code switching encompasses not only the words she uses but also her decision making about when and whether to speak up. Though she is proficient at migrating back and forth, it's clear that it's not without cost. Her hyperalertness and difficulty relaxing when interacting with Whites tell us that her behavioral shifts are accompanied by cognitive and emotional shifts as well. She's forced to think and feel in different, and rather uncomfortable ways. Thus, the code switching is burdensome on multiple levels.

Born and raised in Atlanta, 32-year-old Alice was drilled since childhood on what to reveal to Whites and what to keep to herself. Her elders instructed her not to let Whites know how much money she made, how nice her home might be, or what kind of car she drove "because they may become envious and want to take it away from you, or want to make you lose your job so you can't pay for it. The feeling is that if they think we get too high and mighty, they want to put us in our place." As an adult, Alice explained, she began mingling more with Whites, in college and then at the tax accounting firm where she went to work after getting her CPA. But rather than feeling as though she could relax and open up to her colleagues, she began to guard yet another piece of her private life— the informal voice that she used to express her passions and fears, the voice that welcomed her friends and embraced her two children. "I am too through" became "I am very annoyed." "There ain't no way I'm making it in tomorrow with this backache" became "If this backache doesn't go away, I may have to call in sick tomorrow."

She observed how quick many of her White peers were to assume that she had come from an impoverished background, even though her family had been financially comfortable. Some of her coworkers acted surprised to find out her parents had been married for more than 35 years and that Alice had backpacked across Europe and vacationed in Indonesia. So she went to great pains to continue sidestepping stereotypes, making sure that she spoke the king's English at all times, because while "I'm just having casual conversation," she says, "they're making a judgment."

She doesn't use slang at the office and vigilantly watches her contractions. But when she "slips," she replays the error in her mind and inevitably regrets that she made a mistake. "A common example would be the word 'ain't.' I hate that word," she says laughing. "I use it all the time at home." The few times she has used it at work, accidentally dropping it into a hurried answer or a casual aside to an office mate, she made a mental note to herself so that she wouldn't slip again. "I remembered it, thought about and said the sentence over to myself." Then she was able to move on.

Alice remembers once having to give a deposition in a case filed against her firm. After giving her testimony, she was told that the court reporter had noted every stutter and clearing of the throat and Alice became anxious knowing that her White supervisors would eventually read the transcript. "It makes you look illiterate," she says. "I wasn't bothered until I actually saw the dictation because I didn't realize how detailed it was. . . . I have to tell you that was probably 10 years ago, and I still remember it."

When asked what she was so afraid of, Alice says that despite her usual eloquence, her competence on the job and her college degrees, a single spoken error could render her ignorant in the eyes of her White peers. One slipup, Alice says, and "they probably can't hear the rest of what you're saying." So she constantly monitors her speech and scrutinizes her environment to determine how she is being perceived.

It is ironic that we live in a land where people like Alice, who have great communication competence—who can relate in more than one dialect—feel denigrated and are ever fearful of slipping up. The Mexican American immigrant, whose native tongue is Spanish and who struggles to communicate fluently in English and the Black person who speaks both Standard English and Black English, are seen as inferior linguistically to the Anglo speaker of Standard English only. Paradoxically, less communication competence is deemed to be more.

Chilling Effect: The Suppression of Speech

Even if they've mastered code switching and can shift effortlessly into Standard English, many Black women go to great lengths to make sure that their personal views do not upset relationships or impede their progress on the job, and they are careful that what they do say is not taken the wrong way. They feel pressure not only to change their style of speech—their vocabulary, grammar, and mannerisms—but also to alter the content of their speech, what they talk about, what they dare bring up.

It takes savvy to know when to disagree with a coworker (patiently arguing the merits of a young Black intern whom your colleague has just unfairly criticized, for instance) and when to keep your mouth shut and simply listen (avoiding a heated discussion about the 2000 presidential election). It takes instinct to know how to challenge a police officer (calmly asking him why he pulled you over) and when to be quiet (not mentioning that you will be calling his sergeant to complain that he just gave you a $300 ticket and threatened to arrest you).

Leslie, a 38-year-old computer programmer from New Haven, Connecticut, says that one of the major difficulties she faces as a Black woman is "pointing out inequities to the White, male world without being dismissed as arrogant, aggressive, and having an attitude."

Marva, a 23-year-old college student and geology major in southern Florida, exemplifies just how shut down some Black women become. Along with her backpack, she carries to campus every day a concern about being seen as unintelligent or inadequate. At school, she's always self-conscious and anxious, and she ends up feeling like two different people:

"One of my biggest adjustments is that when I'm around other Black people, I think I'm the most outgoing, most outspoken. But at school, I don't feel as free to just voice my opinions right away. I feel like I have to think about what I'm going to say before I just say it. I'm not as outgoing. I seem so much more reserved, almost on the brink of being painfully shy. . . . This semester I have a chemistry lab. I'm the only Black person in there, right? Well, typically, I don't have a problem in saying what I've gotta say. Speak up, you know? But I almost feel my voice just shrink when I'm in that class."

Marva reports that her ability to speak up had been so compromised that the teacher's assistant had to ask her to talk louder when she finally did pose a question. At that point she realized how bad the problem had gotten, and how terribly split she was between the fun-loving, chatty, extrovert who hung out with her buddies and the hypervigilant and inhibited woman who hid in chemistry class.

Some women avoid the kind of consternation that Marva suffered because they make a conscious decision in certain settings to never express what they are really feeling or thinking. They may be circumspect. Or they may say nothing at all. Having been steeped in a culture that has historically been hostile toward African Americans, they have learned silence can be key to survival. Joyce, a 56-year-old principal at a school in the Cleveland suburbs, puts it succinctly: "I never reveal my true feelings to Whites."

Audrey, a 53-year-old telemarketing supervisor in Dallas, Texas, says, "Recently I've been chastised because I was approached improperly by my superior, which was fine with them. But I replied in a way they felt was disrespectful and was royally chewed out. Now I feel that my best bet is just to say yes, no, or I don't know. I feel I cannot have any type of dialogue for fear it will be misconstrued."

Margaret, a 35-year-old fashion designer in Los Angeles, says there are whole topics she will not talk about with her White coworkers. "If I'm in a work setting, I usually always keep it very professional, very non-confrontational, no deep discussions on anything," she says. "No taboo subjects—politics, religion, sex, drugs, alcohol, race. And I think that the key in those situations is you don't have to get in and agree with them if they're saying something that you don't agree with, but at the same time you don't necessarily have to tell them your beliefs. In other words, you just stay politely silent."

Some women say that when they do go ahead and voice their opinions, they suffer the consequences. Stella, 48, remembers a not-so-long-ago day when the price, in the end, was worth paying.

A staff meeting had been called a few days after the terrorist bombings of September 11, 2001. Company business soon gave way to emotional discussion about Osama bin Laden and incredulity about how terrorists could have so much hatred for people whom they never met. "And part of me said, *Don't say nothing. You don't have to respond to everything that's said,* which was a lesson my father tried to teach me," says Stella, a thin, round-faced woman with a wide smile. "And I knew if I just didn't say anything, of course they wouldn't know what I was thinking, or they'd assume I agreed with them and that probably would have been a good thing, because some of these people I didn't know, or I had just met that day, at that meeting. And some I'd known since I'd been with the company, and I felt I had good working relationships with them. But since everyone was being so candid and reacting to what had just happened, I was like, *You know, I get to say something too*.

"And I did. I expressed myself. 'He didn't necessarily do it, and how you gonna prove that he did it, and what do you mean why do they hate us?' I said. 'Why do White people hate Black people? People ain't never seen a Black person in their lives, and they hate Black people, but all of a sudden this is some evil empire over there because they hate us?'"

Quiet fell over the room. In the days and weeks to come, Stella noticed that a White colleague named Deborah who had always been friendly and even spoke of inviting Stella to her weekend home, suddenly became cool and stopped offering invitations. But Stella didn't care. She was glad she had spoken up. She feels that for once she was true to herself, to her feelings, even among strangers.

Words of Passion, Songs of Celebration

During a time of unbridled patriotism in the wake of September 11, 2001, Representative Barbara Lee, an African American woman, was the lone voice in the U.S. Congress to vote against legislation that gave President George W. Bush broad, largely unchecked powers to respond to terrorism. Actress and playwright Anna Deavere Smith has offered biting commentary on the state of race relations and the role of the media in the national discourse by using her voice to mimic and interpret the voices of others. Poets and songstresses such as Jessica Care Moore, Erykah Badu, and India.Arie use music and the spoken word to spin tales of passion, affirmation, and the need to be true to yourself.

It is often a gradual process, finding comfort with your own voice. Sharon, who was embarrassed by her White history teacher all those years ago, has undergone such an evolution and she speaks of its complexity. When she shifted into different voices in the past, Sharon explains that she was not misrepresenting herself so much as expressing tiny pieces of who she was, the parts she felt comfortable allowing strangers to see and that she believed others would find acceptable.

"I think it's pretty much that whole duality thing where you kind of switch on and off," she says. "I think there are ranges of how much you let people see you."

Eventually, Sharon found it relatively easy to express herself differently depending on the situation. These days she chooses different voices to reflect her own opinions and mood more than to satisfy the conventions of others.

"As I've become comfortable with who I am, and like who I am, this is me in my own skin," she says. "There's less changing from group to group to group. . . . The personality, the person you see is the same even though some aspects of that may be a little different."

The ease with which Sharon and other Black women bridge differences and overcome barriers through language is a model for other Americans. Ideally, everyone, no matter what gender or race or background, will become multilingual, developing mastery in more than one language while feeling free to switch between them according to their own predilections rather than out of shame or obligation. Our society has always borrowed phrases and words from various cultures to create a uniquely American way of speaking. And for this reason Black English, already spoken by so many, should be fully embraced.

As a nation, we have the opportunity to value diversity in the use of language rather than seeing one language as superior, or ranking types of grammar and usage as somewhere between "good" and "bad" or "smart" and "stupid." When we hear differences in accent, when we hear dialect or slang, rather than automatically if subconsciously judging the speaker, we can expand our personal styles instead, borrowing idioms, inflections, and expressions that suit the context we're in, our mood, our sense of self. There is a wonderful beauty to language, to regionalisms, vernacular and patois, and embracing language in whatever form can enrich all of our lives.

Then, too, for a nation so uniquely diverse, it is vitally important for us to take advantage of the melting pot of ideas and messages. We can all benefit by embracing the creativity and vision of African American women, be it Lani Guinier's insights on electoral representation, Dr. Joycelen Elder's proposals on how to expand sexual education, or the grassroots proposals of a poor mother in an urban housing project. Iyanla Vanzant, the former talk-show host whose personal story and words of inspiration have sold millions of self-help books, has messages about love and self-respect that resonate far beyond the lives of Black women. And as some have pointed out, the perspectives of women—and African American women in particular—could well have enlightened the debate and calmed the rhetoric that preceded the United States' war on Iraq. A medley of voices is crucial to expanding the national dialogue and bringing about necessary and innovative change.

THE SISTERELLA COMPLEX

Black Women and Depression

I think any time you cannot think good about yourself, that's going to be depressing, whether you know you're depressed or not. Because if you're questioning, doubting everything that you do, always wondering if what you're doing is okay or if you're going to be accepted, then there's a part of you that's depressed because that's not a reality and space you want to live in.

LYNNETTE, 56, BOSTON

"I can't take it anymore," says 46-year-old Diane, tears clouding her deep brown eyes. "I'm tired of taking care of everyone else. . . . I'm absolutely exhausted." A deputy program director at a large social service agency just outside Detroit, Diane has spent decades of her adult life shifting between various personas, doing everything possible to please others, constantly laboring to put friends, family members, and work colleagues at ease, always rushing to attend to their needs before her own.

Diane's childhood story helps reveal the root of her emotional struggles as an adult. Always pushed to excel by her parents, it was tremendously difficult, Diane says, to move away from the rural Georgia town where she was born to attend an elite private university in Massachusetts. Her parents were both devout Baptists, the great-grandchildren of slaves, who never graduated from high school. Both her mom and her dad spent their entire lives working long hours in menial housekeeping and farming jobs. Diane was expected to transcend these circumstances. She was expected to leave the modest Southern town she had grown up in, get a college education, and flourish in a meaningful career. As one of the best girls' basketball players in Georgia, and with straight A's in high school, Diane felt fortunate to receive a full university scholarship. Difficult as it was to move so far away from home, at age 18, Diane boarded a Greyhound bus and headed off to New England.

Throughout college, Diane questioned whether she had what it took to survive academically and to fit in socially. As it turned out, though the coursework was manageable, she struggled to integrate her very religious, working-class Black roots with the carefree sexuality, heavy drinking, and drug use of many of her upper-crust White peers. By the middle of her freshman year, she often found herself shifting to seem more like them—drinking one too many glasses of Cherry Kijafa or Boone's Farm wine at a Friday night party, sleeping in on a Sunday morning instead of going to church, allowing a popular football jock to fondle her to win his admiration and approval. She regretted many of these choices because they departed radically from her personal values. She realized she had made them to please her peers rather than herself. She remembers feeling guilty, conflicted, and desperately lonely.

Diane also remembers feeling awkward and ill at ease among many of the African American students at the school. In her freshman year both of her roommates were Black. One was from Manhattan with doctor/lawyer parents who resembled the Huxtables on *The Cosby Show*, and the other was from San Francisco and had grown up with her mother, a high-powered regional executive for the YWCA. To Diane these young women were urbane, sophisticated, and wealthy. They seemed to exist in a world far different from her own.

By her sophomore year, Diane developed a sense of not fitting in anywhere. When she went home to visit her parents, she felt she had outgrown their simple, traditional lives. When she returned to school, she felt increasingly alienated from the status-conscious culture that dominated both the Black and White communities there.

After college, Diane spent several years working at day-care centers, but somehow always felt adrift, blue, uncertain about what she really wanted to do, and even less sure of herself than when she'd started college. Then, about a decade later, she met Kent, a wonderful Black man who shared her deeply held Christian values. Kent had a clear vision of his own career and future and wanted to share it with Diane. They married, and Diane felt like her life was on the upswing. They relocated to Detroit so that Kent could attend graduate school. Diane plunged optimistically into the traditional role of wife and homemaker and secured a full-time job working in a counseling program for runaway youth. She and Kent had three children in seven years: Jermaine, Latasha, and Monica.

But Diane's excitement about her new life waned rapidly. Her job at the social service agency was exhausting. Although she smiled to put her coworkers at ease, she was disenchanted with the agency, which, though it served mostly Hispanic and Black communities, was managed almost entirely by White people. After learning that one of her White colleagues, who had much less experience than she did, had been promoted above her, Diane began to wake up every morning at about 4 A.M. Unable to fall back to sleep, she found herself ruminating about problems at the agency and dreading having to get ready for work. When 6:30 rolled around, she could barely summon the energy to pull herself out of bed, awaken the children, and launch into the day. She felt more and more lethargic and isolated as the days ground on.

When she got home most evenings, Diane was tired and weary, increasingly unprepared to deal with motherhood. Having three children had seemed like a way to fill her life with meaning, and while she loved her children dearly, their needs were unrelenting. When Diane called up her own mother in Georgia to get some sympathy, she found her mother warm but unhelpful. "Why don't you just stay at home for a while?" she asked her daughter.

To make matters worse, Diane felt more and more distant from her husband. Kent seemed to be in his own world, focused almost obsessively on pursuing his doctoral degree and developing new professional connections. Diane felt that she had very little voice in the relationship, and that her needs were always addressed last. Many nights when Diane came home, Kent immediately went into his basement office to surf the Web, leaving Diane alone to prepare dinner and deal with the children. She found herself snapping angrily at the two older ones, Jermaine and Latasha, for little cause, betraying everything she had always said about the kind of mother she hoped to be.

To add to the tension between them, Kent began overspending, particularly on computer upgrades, auxiliary equipment, and software, which he insisted were necessary for his scholarly and academic work. Though Diane was the primary breadwinner, and though money was tight, Kent seemed intent on "keeping up" with the other upwardly mobile Black folks in their suburban Detroit neighborhood. Diane felt abandoned, unsure of whether she could sustain herself by continuing to live through her husband's dreams.

Diane had been shifting at work to act like the cheerful, confident, accepting Black woman who didn't mind a White person being promoted above her. She had been shifting at home to seem like the perfect all-accommodating mom, the sort of mother who would always be there for her children's needs and desires. And she had been shifting in her romantic life with her increasingly self-involved husband, masking her anger at him for expecting her to carry the burden of nearly all the household drudgery and base all of her self-worth on his aspirations and accomplishments. "I was tired of this life," she says. "Tired of doing huge amounts of work to keep everyone else happy, but just about nothing to go after the things I had always dreamed of for myself."

At the urging of a friend, Diane finally dragged herself to a therapist. There she learned that she was not just tired, irritable, or unhappy. Diane, it turns out, had major depressive disorder, one of the most severe and debilitating forms of depression.[1]

The Sisterella Complex: The Constellation of Depression in America's Black Women

Diane and many other African American women like her—wonderfully talented, hard-working, selfless women—often shift and suppress their own needs for so long that they are pushed insidiously, unwittingly, often invisibly, toward depression. They suffer from what we call the Sisterella complex, a manifestation of depression that is all too common in Black American women today. Much like the classic Cinderella character, Sisterella is the Black woman who honors others but denies herself. She achieves in her own right—indeed, she may overachieve—yet she works tirelessly, sometimes masochistically, to promote, protect, and appease others. She is trying so hard to be what others want and need that she has lost control of the shifting process. It's overtaken her. Sisterella has had to give too much to others. Or she's given up too much of herself. She has so internalized society's messages that say she is less capable, less valuable, that she has stopped trying to prove otherwise. She has lost sight of her own gifts as well as her own needs. Her identity is confused, her personal goals are deeply buried, and she shrinks inwardly. She becomes depressed, sometimes severely so.

Although the Sisterella complex is not a clinical term, it describes a phenomenon among African American women that has been too often disregarded. The very selflessness that characterizes Sisterella may lead clinicians and researchers to overlook the prevalence of depression in Black women. The term *depression* refers to a wide range of phenomena, from the temporary blue moods that everyone experiences from time to time; to a constellation of symptoms, including chronic sadness, hopelessness, difficulty sleeping, loss of interest in people and activities, and low energy; to a diagnosable condition or clinical depression, when a specified number of symptoms persist over a period of time. In our view, the Sisterella complex is manifest in all three forms of depression in Black women.

Depression is a significant social problem. It is estimated that within any year, 9.5 percent of adults in the United States have a diagnosable clinical depression. For women the rate is about 12 percent, nearly twice that of men, who hover at 6.6 percent.[2] In general, women are more likely to have depressive symptoms or to be clinically depressed than men; poor people are more at risk than the wealthy; and African Americans are more vulnerable than Whites.[3]

Being clinically depressed can have serious consequences for one's ability to function day-to-day in relationships and at work. Even worse, substance abuse and addiction—as well as suicide—are significantly more likely to occur in people who are clinically depressed than in those who are not.[4] Clinical depression is often caused by a combination of biological, social, and psychological factors.[5] Genetic, hormonal, and biochemical factors are part of the "biology" of depression. Our focus, however, is on the social and psychological factors, and specifically on how shifting, in particular the cognitive and emotional reactions that Black women have to racism and sexism, can yield to depression. We have found that the act of shifting—which impacts the woman's feelings and beliefs about herself and the world—sparks a range of effects that contribute uniquely to the experience of depression among many African American women.

Sisterella suffers quietly. More often than not, she doesn't make waves. She doesn't create firestorms. She turns in rather than acting out. She may feel angry, but she beats up on herself rather than the world. She experiences excessive guilt; she feels worthless and unworthy; she puts herself down. She takes on the expectations and demands of her family, her job, and the larger society but doesn't push in turn for the support, nurturance, and caring that she needs. She may turn to quick-fix remedies, like alcohol or drugs, to soothe her troubled feelings.

These are all classic expressions of depression, not unique to Black women, yet Sisterella's melancholy often has a somewhat distinctive look. If you're trying to identify depression in Black women, one of the first things to look for is a woman who is working very hard and seems disconnected from her own needs. She may be busy around the clock, constantly on the go, unable to relax, and often compromising her sleep for household, child-care, and job tasks that she feels impelled to take care of. Not taking the time to tend to herself makes her more vulnerable to depression. Or her busyness may be a way to keep her mind off the feelings of sadness that have already arisen. In many cases Sisterella is an emotional overeater. She uses food as a way to fill the emptiness inside, as a strategy to garner the comfort and solace that seem unachievable through relationships, work, and other pursuits. Alternatively, Sisterella may attend almost obsessively to her outward physical appearance, worrying incessantly about her hair and her clothing, and she may spend an inordinate amount of her time and resources shopping—trying to distract herself from the depression by focusing on remaking herself. Finally, we also look for signs that Sisterella has allowed her depression to become "somaticized," to be manifested in her body through headaches, stomachaches, and other physical symptoms.

Tragically, because many women like Diane may take a long time to see and accept that they're suffering from depression—and because many well-intentioned mental health workers, based on their own biases, may fail to notice or understand the symptoms of depression in Black women—many Sisterellas may go unseen and unheard. They may suffer silently and alone. The mental health literature confirms a pattern of underdiagnosis of depression in African Americans, meaning that even when Blacks who are depressed are evaluated by a psychologist or clinical social worker, they are often not deemed to be so.[6] Yet research shows that Black women have a high risk of experiencing the traditional symptoms of depression and that their risk is generally greater than that of Black men or White men and women.[7] Sisterella is often invisible.

Sisterella, the Stoic Overachiever: Why Depression Is Camouflaged in Black Women

Long ago Rita decided it would be too "narcissistic" to focus on her own gradually increasing sadness and sense of alienation. She was the family star—the only person in her large and closely knit extended family to finish college, much less go on to professional school. Her mother, siblings, aunts, uncles, and cousins back in Los Angeles were surely proud of her, but as she began medical school in New York, she felt a growing disconnection from them. On the surface, they were supportive, but they asked little about her experiences and seemed bored when she'd talk about her courses and classmates. Her life at medical school was completely unlike the one they knew, and Rita began to feel that she could no longer get the concrete support that had buoyed her through high school and her early college years.

Her family didn't understand how much of her time and energy would need to be devoted to her studies, and they had little empathy for her unavailability. When she stayed in New York over Thanksgiving to study for an upcoming anatomy exam, her mother called her to say how "selfish" Rita had become. And perhaps the biggest problem for Rita was her awareness that some of her siblings and cousins were deeply envious of her. Her sister Anne accidentally copied her on an email in which one of her cousins wrote, "I guess Dr. Big Apple won't be jetting down for Christmas this year." Rather than disclosing her sense of sadness and isolation, Rita found herself sharing less and less with her family about her life and how it was changing. She was concerned that she would only exacerbate their sense that somehow she felt she was better than them.

In the spring of her third year at medical school, Rita went through a particularly tough period of preparing for exams. She felt certain she was going to flunk out. Only days into her intense study period, Rita received a call from Anne begging her to return home to help deal with her mother's sudden hospitalization following a minor heart attack. Rita rushed home, her books in tow, and sat vigil with Anne until her mother regained her health. Though her mother recovered quickly, Rita's world began to spiral downward.

As the days of studying dragged on, Rita had an increasing recognition of how sad, lonely, and alienated from her family she felt. Even when she found time to sleep, it was difficult to rest. Rita's mind was constantly racing with anxious thoughts—*I'm gonna fail! Mom's going to die when I'm taking my exams! Nobody likes me, not even my family!*—and many nights she went sleepless. A voice inside told her she was depressed, but she felt she couldn't honor what her gut was telling her. That would be too self-indulgent. After all, compared to her family members, a number of whom were struggling just to keep a roof over their heads, she was privileged. Rita pressed on until her year-end exams arrived. She went through exam week on automatic pilot, and then a week later, learned that she had failed two courses. Finally she was forced to face the fact that she was depressed. After a number of conversations with a sympathetic dean, she was able to get support for retaking the exams and extending her program from four to five years so that she could take better care of herself. And she got into psychotherapy.

Rita's story of depression, which is similar to other stories we have heard, demonstrates one of the main reasons why our society may routinely fail to detect a large number of depressed Black women. We believe that many of these women go unseen because on the outside they do not clearly manifest the traditional symptoms of depression, such as fatigue, lethargy, or gloominess. Far from seeming depressed, Sisterella may actually appear to be full of power, confidence, and toughness. And like Rita, Sisterella is frequently a workaholic and often an overachiever. Most Black women have been socialized to accept the myth of unshakability. Rather than seeing themselves as needy and suffering, they see themselves as necessarily strong and stoic. Cheryl Thompson, a psychoanalyst and professor at Seton Hall University in New Jersey, has theorized about the "masochism" that many Black women have been socialized to enact.[8] Thompson defines masochism as "excessive personal sacrifice that assumes pathological proportions" and explains that it tends to blind a woman to the need every human has, when faced with life's challenges and complexities, to express her fear, sadness, and anxiety, and to reach out for help from others.

Along similar lines, Daudi Azibo of Florida A&M University and Patricia Dixon of Georgia State University point out that looking and feeling depressed is widely perceived as being incompatible with African American culture, whereas being tough, capable, and apparently invulnerable is seen as culturally consonant.[9]

Black women may also cover up their depression because they simply don't feel that they have the right to complain about any aspect of their lives. At the center of Sisterella's depression is often a Black woman's diminished self-esteem, a shame and disappointment she feels because she senses either that she is not accomplishing enough in this life or, to the contrary, that she is accomplishing too much for herself at the expense of her family. Jeanne Spurlock talks about the "survival guilt" that many upwardly mobile African Americans experience.[10] To get educated and to be successful, they shift their personalities and their pursuits to fit into mainstream America. They may leave their families behind. They transcend the legacy of slavery and discrimination with which so many of their ancestors had to contend. But in taking these courageous steps, many African Americans end up feeling a deep sense of guilt and shame. "Who do I think I am?" asks 33-year-old Ellen, a biologist in Santa Monica. "I may feel sad and depressed, but what I'm dealing with is nothing compared to what Mama had to go through as a little girl back in Birmingham."

This denial of need—a form of cognitive shifting—is often at the core of depression in African American women. The woman shifts by giving up parts of herself, losing touch with her authentic core, and suppressing who she is. These chronic, often incremental moves can lead to a loss of a sense of self, and depression is often the outcome. Classically, psychologists and psychiatrists think of depression as being precipitated by an external loss—the loss of a person, a relationship, a job, or a significant role. Based on our research and years of clinical experience, it is clear that for many Black women in America, depression is often the result of a loss of self. Dana Crowley Jack, a psychologist and professor at Western Washington University, agrees that for depressed women, the central loss is that of a sense of self—a shrinking or diminishment of the woman's center or identity. She terms this process, "silencing the self."[11]

When it comes to Sisterella, silencing the self can be a response to outright racial and gender assaults as well as to the burdens of too many demands, too many roles, and often, too few financial and other resources—circumstances that are often directly or indirectly linked to prejudice. Kevin Allison of Virginia Commonwealth University points out that members of oppressed groups experience discrimination not only through specific, discrete events, like being sexually harassed while walking down the street or being turned down for a job because of one's race, but also through indirect contextual factors, for example, being poor, residing in a crime-ridden neighborhood, or being expected as a woman to fulfill certain circumscribed social roles.[12] Notably, in a study designed to learn about the stress that Black women experience, Darielle Watts-Jones, formerly of Duke University, found that chronic, contextual stressors, like inadequate resources, working in a racist environment, and being overburdened as a mother, played a major role in Black women's experience of stress.[13] In other words, it wasn't just the specific events and incidents that were deeply affecting; it was the women's overall life circumstances, which were often tinged by bigotry. Notably, Watts-Jones found that the more chronic and acute stress Black women experienced, the more depressed they were.

Black women may need to shift between being both caretaker and breadwinner, and perhaps even work two jobs, because of the diminished opportunities and lower pay offered to Black men and women. She may suppress her aspirations and her voice in her own home while assuming nearly all the responsibilities, because she has internalized the notion that women are supposed to selflessly take care of home and children and follow their husband's lead—even if she is also a wage earner. She may juggle too many personas or tasks because she has internalized the myth that Black women are invulnerable and can handle myriad burdens, or because she is trying to prove her capabilities and humanity to a society plagued with racist and sexist notions of her inferiority. The expectations that Black women will be available to nurture and take care of others while subsuming their own needs and wants, the lack of affirmation or mirroring by the larger society, the multiple demands, the multiplicity of roles, the curtailed opportunities—all of these factors, which fuel shifting, can contribute to chronic feelings of emotional exhaustion, hopelessness, and despair.

But, as we've emphasized, Sisterella may not appear to be depressed. In fact, it's often important to her self-image not to. She may not complain, and if you ask her if she's depressed, you may get the sense that she doesn't fully understand the question. When African American women come in to see Kumea, one of the authors of this book and a therapist, they may report that they are "stressed" or "experiencing marital conflict." When Kumea asks if they are depressed, the reaction is often astonishment, as if it's a concept that they'd never dreamed of applying to themselves. A survey by the National Mental Health Association revealed that 54 percent of all survey respondents—and 63 percent of Blacks—saw depression as a "personal weakness." Only 31 percent of Blacks saw depression as a health problem.[14] Thus, the stigma associated with being depressed may make it even harder for Black women to acknowledge their emotional pain.

This presents yet another dilemma. Just as depression is seen as a weakness, professional treatment is widely frowned upon in the Black community. A major national study of the utilization of mental health services by Black, Hispanic, and White insured women found that even when differences in education and salary were controlled, White women were more likely to use outpatient mental health services than Black and Hispanic women.[15] While there is anecdotal evidence that an increasing number of African Americans are seeking professional counseling, therapy is still too often thought to be a crutch for Whites and others who are unstable or "crazy."[16] When they are overwhelmed, Black woman are pushed instead to rely on prayer, friends, and family. "Just pray on it!" they're told again and again. And while prayer and leaning on friends can be therapeutic and uplifting, they're not always enough.

In other words, even when Sisterella's depression is finally detected by friends and family members, or by Sisterella herself, she is unlikely either to be professionally diagnosed or to seek the psychological or psychiatric treatment she may require.

Filling the Emptiness with Food

Sisterella often uses food in an attempt to meet emotional needs. She overeats as a way of comforting herself, as a way of assuaging her anguish and despair. Statistics indicate that 66 percent of African American adult women are overweight and 33 percent are obese—higher percentages than those for White, Hispanic, or Asian/Pacific Islander women.[17] And for Black women being overweight is associated with symptoms of depression.[18] Binge eating, defined as eating a large amount of food and losing control over the eating episode,[19] appears to be a particular problem for depressed Black women. In a large community-based study, Ruth Striegel-Moore of Wesleyan University and her colleagues found that recurrent binge eating was almost twice as prevalent in Black than in White women.[20] Moreover, those who were more involved in binge eating were more likely to be overweight and to experience depression and anxiety. Of course women who are overweight are at greater risk for diabetes and cardiovascular disease, thus potentially compounding their difficulties. We spoke with a number of African American women whose primary symptom of depression was excessive overeating.

Cindy, a loan officer in her early thirties, has struggled throughout her life with obesity and depression. Early in life overeating became a way of managing her troubles, particularly the ongoing tension and verbal jousting between her parents, as well as her sense, as long as she could remember, of never quite fitting in with her peers. She was overweight by the time she was a young teen, and the overeating only got worse when she moved 150 miles away to the state university. She moved into the dorms with great hope and anticipation, but there, in a predominantly White school, she felt alienated and ill at ease. She felt pressure to educate her well-meaning but unknowingly racist classmates and to "defend Blackness."

Gradually becoming more and more depressed, she found herself loading up on the unlimited carbohydrates offered in the cafeteria. She really didn't mind the extra pounds. She'd grown tired of awkward and frustrating encounters with men her age and was sure they would lose interest in her the more weight she gained. Adding extra pounds was like adding a layer of protection—allowing her to avoid the social and sexual scene altogether. She was taking herself out of the game.

It was many years later that she was able to acknowledge that she'd been using food to try to soothe her depression. After years of psychotherapy and involvement in a self-help group as well, she's now finding herself beneath the layers of fat. She's much less depressed, and she's even lost most of the extra pounds.

Christine, by contrast, still contends with obesity. Having grown up with an emotionally abusive and unsupportive father, Christine fled, as soon as she was 18, to create an adult life of her own. She worked minimum-wage jobs, got married, and had two children. When the couple's youngest child was still in diapers, her husband Michael suddenly walked out with no advance warning, little explanation, and no offer to continue his financial support.

Christine was devastated but felt she had to keep going, to maintain a home for her children despite Michael's departure. After long days of difficult yet low-paying work, she would come home to a cramped apartment and the demands of single parenting. She was living far away from her family and she had a very limited support system. The best part of her day was the silence in the evening once the kids were in bed. "This was my time to read, to listen to music, and to bake my butt off," she says.

Christine not only baked but she ate, and eventually she found herself waking up in the middle of the night and eating again. Christine's shifting had begun at a young age. She had to deal with constant put-downs and disparagement from her father, who alternatively told her that she was "dumb" and "ugly." "Ain't no man ever going to want you," he would often say. When Michael left, it was like hearing her father's message again. In addition, she had to support a family on a single salary that barely covered rent, food, and child-care expenses, and she had to parent two children alone. The depression was perhaps inevitable, and food seemed to soften the blow.

Annette, like Christine and Cindy, also struggled with depression and overeating, but came to these issues from quite a different standpoint. The second of four children, Annette played the role of dutiful daughter, looking out for her mother, earning straight A's, graduating summa cum laude from a state university, and eventually earning her doctorate in American history.

Despite her beauty and intelligence, she often put herself down, noting the talents of her friends and relatives but rarely her own. She endured several unfulfilling relationships in which she invested time and energy, emotionally boosting men who seldom reciprocated and sometimes even became abusive.

Annette's tendencies toward self-sacrifice shifted into overdrive when she returned home from graduate school and found her parents on the brink of separation. Annette's mother soon filed for divorce and crisis followed crisis. Her father suffered a stroke that left him virtually immobilized. Her ailing grandfather finally had to be moved into an assisted-living facility, and her mother discovered that she had ovarian cancer.

Annette bore the emotional burdens of the entire family, stepping into roles left vacant by her siblings and parents. When her brothers and sister, angry at how their father had treated their mother, refused to visit him after his stroke, Annette trekked alone to the hospital, suppressing her own rage in order to provide him some solace. When Annette's mother stopped going to the nursing home because she could not bear the guilt of having put her father there, Annette drove to the facility and spent afternoons with "Papa Frank." While her siblings lived on their own and went about their lives, Annette moved back home to watch over their mother. She was exhibiting masochistic behavior, doing for everyone else, never for herself. And while she sometimes resented her brothers and sister for not doing more to help, Annette was usually too exhausted to dwell on it.

On top of her myriad family responsibilities, Annette was a history teacher at a local community college, counseling students, grading papers, and dealing with college administrators. To see her in action, promptly arriving each morning in a stylish pantsuit, patiently listening to her students' questions, smiling at everyone she passed in the halls, you would never suspect how overburdened she truly was. But during the little time she had for herself, she ate. She hoarded food, buying one bagel for now, and two more for later, and gaining weight so rapidly that she could hardly keep up with her rising dress size.

"I had no sense of myself," she now says. "At school I had all these kids depending on me. 'I need this, I need that, I need to talk to you. I need, I need, I need.' And my job reinforced what I was doing at home. So the weight thing got way out of hand. I didn't see it happening. I just checked out."

One day she saw a photograph taken at a wedding of a striking woman. Her dress was beautiful, her face was lovely, and she was obese.

Annette wondered who she was. Then she realized that she was looking at a picture of herself.

Recognizing that she needed to find healthier ways to cope with her emotions and overwhelming responsibilities, Annette began to get counseling. When she spoke about her escalating weight, her therapist suggested that she try Weight Watchers. Eventually Annette lost 45 pounds, and over time, she has become more and more reflective, able to see what she had been giving up by always subsuming her own needs to fulfill those of others.

When asked about this pattern of self-sacrifice, Annette explains: "I think in some ways it has kept me from growing up and moving forward and in some ways it has made me older than I should be."

The Makeover Solution

While many Black women try to dampen depressive feelings by overeating, others cope by spending valuable time and resources trying to improve their physical appearance and by shopping, shopping, shopping. Statistics reveal that Black women spend inordinate amounts of money on cosmetics and beauty care products, in fact more than any other group of women in America.[21] Many of them seem to sense that by creating an outward guise of beauty, comfort, and financial security, they will be able to camouflage the profound pain and insecurity they feel inside.

The connection between depression and an overemphasis on one's outward appearance is twofold. In addition to overspending on one's looks to mask and ease depression that may have set in for any number of reasons, Regan Lester and Trent A. Petrie of the University of North Texas have found that Black women who internalize mainstream societal beauty ideals are more likely to be depressed and dissatisfied with their body size and shape than those women who are able to ignore such ideals.[22] This, of course, supports our premise that an important part of what pushes Black women to become depressed is society's pressure on them to look and act in specific ways, to fulfill the codes of womanhood as defined by White Americans, to shift to please others.

In a related area of research, Azibo and Dixon found a relationship between depressive feelings and what they call "materialistic depression," a condition among Black women where the possession of material goods becomes the criterion for their self-worth.[23] Many Black women may buy things—clothes, jewelry, household goods—not only to muster a sense of accomplishment or to provide themselves with a temporary pick-me-up but also to create a life that appears fulfilling even if, in reality, they feel that it is not. To cover up or soothe her depression, Sisterella may go shopping.

Erica has experienced just this sort of materialistic depression. Her sadness and frustration translated into lavish overspending as well as overeating and constant fretting about her appearance. A married woman in her forties with two teenage children, Erica landed in therapy when she'd reached her limit on the job. For 15 years, she had worked for the same Fortune 500 insurance company in a series of increasingly responsible clerical positions. She was an exceptionally bright and very witty woman who could have been an English professor or a great writer. But her life had conspired against her.

Erica grew up in an inner-city neighborhood, the eldest in a single-parent family with a mother who was enterprising and hard-working. She attended a local community college for a semester or two and then felt compelled to get a job to help her mother, who had begun to have health problems—arthritis, diabetes, heart disease—and was only able to work part-time. Soon after that, Erica married and her husband moved into the family home, while her younger siblings moved out and developed families and lives of their own.

Erica and her mother had both been obese for most of their lives. Together they binged on chips and sweets. It was entertainment as well as a way to feel comforted. Erica's mother carried with her great bitterness about her husband's untimely death when Erica was only 6 years old. She believed that the racism he experienced from his longshoreman coworkers killed him. His blood pressure had always been elevated, and at age 38 he had a massive heart attack. Since then, Erica and her mom seemed to carry the sorrow for the family.

When Erica entered therapy, her underlying chronic depression had become acute. She was having difficulty getting out of bed in the morning and she was bingeing more than ever. She was listless and unmotivated and increasingly agitated about her life at work, where a new White boss whom she dubbed "an insecure wannabe hotshot" told her that she was "less productive than the other 'girls.'" She had never fit in well at her company. Her obesity, her colorful outfits, and her complicated hairstyles didn't play well in the conservative corporate culture. Erica put herself down for not having been able to work the system more effectively. She felt like a failure.

Erica also handled her depression by shopping for new clothing and shoes, new appliances and gadgets, maxing out credit cards along the way. She could pick herself up emotionally, at least for a few hours, through a purchase. All the stuff made her feel like a more successful person, like a person who'd made it in the world.

And Erica overspent on her hair. She changed her hairstyle nearly every other week—first, long and straightened, then cropped short and natural, then braided with extensions, then long with an added weave. Color was streaked here and there, with blonde and red her favorite shades. She was constantly searching for the "do" that would deem her attractive. Though her therapist thought she was quite pretty, Erica didn't see it, and much of the larger society seemed to share her view. After all, she was an obese, dark-skinned, wide-nosed, thick-lipped woman. She saw herself as ugly, and the cruel long-ago words of elementary school classmates who'd teased her about being Black and fat were embedded in her psyche. Her husband saw her beauty, but his love couldn't counter the assaults that she had experienced all her life.

Erica had had a lifetime of shifting and the result was a clinical depression—feelings of worthlessness and despair temporarily soothed by emotional overeating, compulsive shopping, and a new look. She'd had to accommodate over and over again. She'd had to give up her dreams, hopes, and needs in order to respond to others. She rarely felt comfortable or at ease in her own skin. She felt she was too Black, too fat, too ugly. And though she'd worn the rainbow-colored clothes that she loved to her corporate job and the dramatic hairstyles that gave her a temporary emotional lift, she'd paid a price for looking different.

Erica's therapist worked with her on finding a way to love herself—

on treasuring who she was, on appreciating her physical beauty and on celebrating her various talents. The aim was to help her to say no as well as to say yes. To say no judiciously to her mother, who, as she aged, came to rely exclusively on Erica for companionship and support. And to say yes to her own needs, particularly learning to ask for help and support from her husband.

Indeed, if there is one thing, and one thing only that Sisterella can learn about how to pull herself out of depression and place herself back on the road to health and fulfillment, it is to say to her friends, family members, colleagues, and loved ones: "I need your love, support, and affirmation as much as you need these things from me. I need to be able to be myself, to stop having to shift to please you. My life is valuable, and I deserve to be happy, healthy, and fulfilled."

When the Bough Breaks: Somataform Depression, Substance Abuse, and Suicidality in Black Women

If many Black women cope with depression through stoic overachievement, overeating, overspending, or obsessing on their physical appearance, there are some Sisterellas whose emotional suffering is so acute that it causes them to experience physical pain and ailments, to abuse their bodies with alcohol or drugs or, in some cases, to contemplate or attempt suicide.

Rosemary, Serita, and Pamela, whose stories follow, all struggled with severe manifestations of the Sisterella complex. None of them established the kind of emotional connection with a caregiver that is optimal for development, and they all encountered devastating losses as they got older. These experiences contributed to a sense of themselves as not good enough and to feelings of great sadness. And layered on top were societal messages that reinforced a view of themselves as inadequate and unworthy as well as societal pressures, wrought by racism and sexism, to take on more responsibility than they could bear, to submerge themselves in order to lift up a romantic partner. All three women were poor to working class with few opportunities for advanced schooling or career development. Yet all three carried the burden of being the sole breadwinner and parent. They had little to hope for, and little support in realizing their dreams. And so they shifted to try and manage their feelings and reactions, shifted to appease others, and they shifted again to manage the depression that ensued.

Rosemary walked into the community counseling clinic after months of hesitation. She was 48 and she had spent most of the last five years intensely sick, with a variety of ailments that her doctors couldn't quite explain. She'd always been somewhat fragile, missing more days from school and work than her peers because of stomachaches, colds, or flu. But recently she was beset with dizziness, fatigue, migraines, a gastric stomach that she couldn't tame, and an ever-present buzzing sound in her right ear. She'd consulted physicians and been referred to neurologists, and on a couple of occasions, she'd been hospitalized for tests, but little had been found. She took Zantac for her stomach, and Tylenol with codeine for the migraines, but she was still suffering. For years she'd been encouraged by her sister and her primary-care physician to get some counseling, but Rosemary refused, convinced that therapy was for "crazy White girls." By the time Rosemary slumped into the seat across from the intake therapist, she was able to offer, "I think it might be psychosomatic."

Rosemary had been raised by parents who, though loving and consistent with food, clothing, and shelter, were overburdened financially and overwhelmed by the demands of raising seven children who were born in a span of 16 years. They'd been unable to provide close-up support and guidance, and, as the fourth child, Rosemary was lost somewhere in the middle. She dropped out of high school, worked here and there, married her childhood sweetheart at age 20, and had three children by the time she was 26. Her husband drove cross-country rigs and was away for days at a time. Rosemary studied for her GED and worked part-time as a library aide.

And then one day, while playing in front of the house, her 7-year-old daughter was hit by a car and died. It was devastating for Rosemary, her husband Luke, and their marriage. They both simultaneously blamed themselves and each other for what happened, and more and more they turned away from each other for solace. Rosemary began to look forward to Luke's time on the road, and while he was gone, she became the super devoted, super involved mother, as if to compensate for her oldest child's death. Her two younger children became her sole passion, and when her husband packed his bags and moved in with a fellow trucker, it was hardly noticed.

Almost a decade later, when Luke had severe kidney failure and was incapacitated, Rosemary decided that he should move back in with the family. After all, they were still married, and he didn't have anyone else to care for him. It was about then that she began having migraines. And a couple of months later, she found to her surprise that she was pregnant, not by Luke—they hadn't been involved sexually for years—but by Gerry, her boyfriend at the time. It was a mess. Luke was angry, embarrassed, yet dependent on Rosemary for care, and Rosemary felt he was trying to turn her now-adolescent children against her. Gerry, upset about Luke's presence, wanted little to do with Rosemary anymore. Rosemary felt trapped. She was definitely going to have the baby. For religious reasons, abortion was not an option.

After she delivered, myriad physical symptoms took up residence in her body. The dizziness and fatigue sharpened, the migraines increased in frequency, and more and more, she found herself unable to work and in bed. When she was first hospitalized for tests, she realized that she could no longer take care of Luke, and he moved in with his sister. When Rosemary came to the clinic, she was living with her three children, ages 6, 22, and 24, and feeling that her older two were taking advantage of her. "They won't seem to grow up and leave!" she expressed. It seemed clear to the therapist that in many ways Rosemary's symptoms, though quite real, served some function for her. When she was sickly and in bed, her older son and daughter were forced to do their own laundry, cook their own meals, and wash a dish or two—tasks which Rosemary didn't demand when she was well. Fortunately, her sister would often pitch in with the 6-year-old, taking him over to her house to spend evenings and often entire weekends with his cousins. Rosemary's physical symptoms garnered her some sympathy, some attention, and some relief from the daily drudgery of caring for the home and for others.

It was also clear to the therapist that Rosemary was depressed, and that the depressive symptoms had likely preceded the physical ones. She reported that well before Luke moved back in, she had had difficulty sleeping through the night. She had gradually isolated herself from many friends, and stopped singing in the choir and attending church. Years ago she'd given up crocheting and doing crafts and decorating projects, which, since her teenage days, had been her therapy. Already attuned to society's notion that mothers are the parent that must sacrifice most for their children, Rosemary had toiled even harder after the loss of her oldest child to assuage her guilt and sense of responsibility. In grief over her 7-year-old's tragic death, Rosemary had hidden her depression behind a supermom façade and later even became a mother to her estranged husband, when he needed constant care. She'd inadvertently created young adult children who felt entitled to her constant catering, who expressed little gratitude, and who seemed to be stuck in early adolescence.

She had transferred her feelings of melancholy to her body and carried them there. She was physically ill and clinically depressed. She had a somatoform disorder: a mental disorder where there are physical symptoms that are not fully explained by a diagnosable medical condition, where something psychological appears as something physical.[24] She was suffering on multiple fronts. And finally after admitting to herself that the physicians had done the best they could, and after beginning to think about some of the connections between the events in her life and her body's reactions, an ailing Sisterella entered counseling.

Somatization, the process that underlies somatoform disorders, is the unconscious channeling of emotional distress into physical ailments. Somatization is another way that Black women mask depression. A major epidemiologic study of more than 19,000 people in five cities in the U.S. revealed that Black women have significantly higher rates of somatization than non-Black women or men of all ethnicities.[25] For Black women who have been socialized to be unshakable and who have come to believe that depression is a sign of personal weakness, physical illness may be a more acceptable way of expressing their pain.

Unlike Rosemary, who was able to finally bring herself to a therapist, Serita, 32, was referred to a mental health center by a state crimi-nal court. Angry about the lack of basic repairs to her rapidly deterio-rating apartment, she had physically assaulted the landlord's brother when he came by to collect the rent. Typically Serita wouldn't have responded that way, but that day the cocaine was calling the shots. By the time she saw the state-funded therapist several weeks later, she was sober and clearly depressed. "I'm on the way down," she reported. "My head feels empty." The therapist soon learned that Serita had been on the way down for quite some time.

Born in rural central Texas, she was reared by her mother and a stepfather whom she never liked and who was physically and verbally abusive. Often when he was irritable and angry, he would rant and rave about a toy or book that Serita had left on the floor, and in his rage, he'd sometimes slap her as well. Because he had difficulty keeping a job, the family moved numerous times in her early years, and they finally landed in San Francisco. She started kindergarten, and her strongest memory is of being made fun of because of her Southern drawl. When she ran home and told her mother, her mother laughed. Serita never felt that her mother was emotionally available to her.

Serita married at age 18 as a "ticket away from home." She had a child, but the relationship with her husband never really developed. He was a "ladies' man," and it was only a matter of time before they separated. After he moved, on the surface Serita seemed to manage fairly well, working as a checker at the supermarket and taking care of her young son. But she had few friends and little social network, and she was still anxious to win her mother's attention.

Previously a social drinker who would occasionally sip a glass of wine with her husband or friends, Serita began to drink at home—alone and a lot. She remained functional and fairly responsible—she wouldn't, for example, drink while driving. But she'd stumbled upon a way to medicate herself and to deal with her mounting feelings of loneliness, hopelessness, and despair.

When she was 28, Serita was in a terrible car accident that left her face scarred and disfigured and saddled her with chronic back pain. A handful of surgeries on her face and her back helped, but only to an extent. Serita found herself working less and less and drinking more and more, to ease the pain as well as to escape. She eventually graduated to cocaine after getting romantically involved with a user. She admitted to the therapist that for several years she'd abused tranquilizers, sleeping pills, alcohol, and street drugs.

The emotional abandonment by her mother, the active abuse by her stepfather, the premature marriage to a man who didn't love her—all of these events left her at risk for depression. Then, saddled with the burdens of being a single parent, Serita had no time or energy to even remember her dreams, let alone pursue them. She plunged into depression. The trauma of the car accident deepened her woundedness, literally and figuratively. When she looked in the mirror at her scarred, reconstructed face, she felt ugly and unlovable, just as she had as a daughter and a wife. Her descent into depression hastened.

Her strategy when she was "on the way down" was to ingest something, to switch from acknowledging her pain to enjoying the momentary relief of experiencing the world through a syrupy haze. But of course, coping in this way never provided a real solution to her difficulties. Instead it only magnified them. Still, Serita had found a way to hide from her depression. She became her own physician and pharmacist.

Pamela, 28, was referred to the outpatient clinic in Philadelphia after being hospitalized for what was considered a fairly serious suicide attempt: she had ingested several handfuls of Tylenol pills. The situation that led to the attempt was the end of her relationship with her husband Mark. The relationship had been on and off for years, but the latest breakup seemed final. He'd moved in with a woman whom he'd been seeing throughout the years when he and Pamela weren't together. Pamela was devastated and distraught.

Pamela had grown up in a family of four children. As the oldest she was the surrogate mom when her parents were off at work or running errands. She resented her mother, who she felt expected too much of her and she still carried anger about punishments that she received when her siblings did something they weren't supposed to. With her father, on the other hand, she had a close, warm relationship. Her parents separated when she was 14, and her father moved out.

Pamela felt the loss intensely, and secretly blamed herself, as children often do, for her parents' difficulties. The fact that she was able to spend every other weekend with him only eased the pain a little. And then, when she was 17, her father suddenly died.

After drifting through four years of high school, Pamela got a job as a receptionist in a hospital. She'd wanted to be a medical lab technician, but didn't feel any support from her mother to continue her education. What's more, she was desperate to move out of the house and knew that she needed an income if that was to happen.

Pamela met Mark and fell quickly in love. He was a strapping 6 feet tall, charming, and playful, and he wanted to marry Pamela. But his family didn't feel her working-class roots and deep brown complexion were good enough for their son. They wanted him to marry his light-skinned childhood sweetheart who was pursuing a college degree. Mark had dropped out after a couple of years of college and was working in computer sales.

The relationship with Mark soon became nightmarish. He was an alcoholic who was physically abusive when drunk, and it wasn't long after they were married that his violence was directed at Pamela. She had fantasies of retaliating, of even killing him, but initially she was too emotionally attached to either hurt him or leave him. In between his bouts of violence, he was effusive, remorseful, and seemingly devoted. With the constant seesaw, it took several years and a few bruised lips and black eyes for Pamela to move herself and their daughter out of the house and in with her mother. But even then, the drama didn't end. She and Mark began to see each other again, reconciled, moved back together, only to break up, and repeat the pattern again. The final straw was when Michael moved in with his girlfriend, telling Pamela, "she's pregnant."

For almost a week Pamela lay in bed, feeling unable to brush her teeth or put on her clothes. She barely ate. Then one day she got up and got dressed, left her daughter with her mother, drove to a mini-mart, bought water and a bottle of Tylenol, and downed them both. Fortunately, she wasn't successful.

Pamela's depression was severe, and she'd been suffering with it since adolescence. The lack of emotional connection to her mother, the loss of her father when her parents separated, and his subsequent death marked the beginning. It had seemed that Mark could offer the love and nurturance that she so sorely needed, but it came at a very high price—physical abuse. She tried desperately to accommodate Mark's drinking binges and outbursts, to placate him, to apologize for him to others, to tiptoe around him, to fool herself into thinking that it wouldn't happen again. She'd never felt worthy of much, and when he wasn't drinking, Mark seemed quite a catch. The shifting seemed worth it. But rather than lifting her depression, the constant ups and downs of their relationship only deepened it. When Mark appeared to be gone forever, Pamela decided there was no reason to live. She made a suicide attempt, Sisterella's ultimate shift toward self-negation.

Unlike the classic tale of Cinderella, being rescued by Prince Charming was not the solution for these women. Sisterella rarely is saved this way. Instead she survives by getting support from partners, family, and friends, and sometimes a therapist, in learning to attend to herself, to love herself, and to find balance in her life.

Toward a New Model of Depression: Helping Sisterella Transcend Her Pain

As difficult as it can be for Black women to contend with society's codes and expectations and ask for what they need to transcend these pressures—and as much as these struggles may push many of them toward depression—there is a lot we can all do to help Black women reduce and avoid the agony of the Sisterella complex. The starting place is for society to accept that the traditional psychological assumptions about how and why people become depressed may not always be sufficient when it comes to understanding the experiences of African American women. The traditional model of depression, for example, focuses on the quality of the early childhood relationship between the person who becomes depressed and their parents or parental figures. Sisterella, as we've seen, may have this plus much much more to deal with.

A more contemporary view of the origin of depression helps us to widen the lens.[26] Depression is a by-product of unmet needs. It is a result of the failure to meet the needs that every child has for affirmation and for models of whom she can become. Black women need to be loved, told that they are good, mentored and given resources for success, and freed from the shackles of other people's prejudices and rigid race- and gender-based expectations. They need parents who encourage them. They need lovers who will allow them to be at once strong and vulnerable, proud of what they are capable of, and they must be forthright about where they need help. And they need the larger community and society to bolster them with support and affirmation. It is especially critical that all of us, everyone who loves and cares about Black women, do everything we can to understand the Sisterella complex, to be aware of when a woman we know could be experiencing its symptoms, and make sure that we give her every opportunity to share what she is going through and receive the expert psychological and psychiatric attention that she may need.

It is also important to remember that while Black women may exhibit symptoms that are somewhat distinct, they are not immune from visibly suffering the listlessness, sadness, poor concentration, and other characteristics that are more commonly associated with depression. We should be on the lookout for those symptoms as well. And if she does put up a stoic façade, we cannot simply assume that she is fine. By not buying into the myth that Black women are unshakable, by taking the time to consider that there might be great pain beneath her mask, we can remind her that she is only human, and reassure her that it is all right to need guidance and help beyond the realm of prayer.

We firmly believe that if as a society we can create these interlocking circles of strength, there will be far fewer Sisterellas, far fewer Black women unnecessarily whispering, singing, or shouting the blues.

DOING DOUBLE DUTY

Black Women in the World of Work

The stress [at work] comes because you're a woman and you're Black. Being a woman can be enough stress right there. But being an African American woman causes another problem. You want to succeed. And you put too much stress on yourself. And you have to deal with Tom, Dick, and Harry, and they're all White. And Jane—she's White. And there you are—poor little African American girl. You're not even a woman now. You're a girl.

BETTINA, 38, AUSTIN, TEXAS

As Black women at my office often say, "The real me isn't in yet."

ALLISON, 34, PASADENA, CALIFORNIA

A physical trainer at an upscale gym in Los Angeles, 23-year-old Ginny wears her jet black hair short and spiky and keeps her nails manicured, painted a pale shade of mauve. Decked out in expensive workout gear, she confides that the woman we are looking at is a far cry from the person who started at this fitness center three years ago, passing out towels and checking membership cards at the front desk. And she is a far different woman from the one who three hours later will wearily tote her gym bag home to a small ranch house in a working-class corner of the San Fernando Valley.

She feels so split that she has given each of her personas a name. There is "Ginny," the girl who grew up in Watts, raised by a grand-mother who sent her only granddaughter to private school with the wages she earned as a nurse, and "Jennifer," the well-coiffed, well-spoken physical trainer.

"When I'm at home I'm Ginny, and when I'm at work I have to be Jennifer," she explains in a weary voice. "Everything has to change. Before I walk in the door I have to prep myself to be someone else. And when I come home I'm so stressed out. . . . Jennifer is quiet. It's such a mask. I'm more uptight. It's such a front. I become a whole different person because I know that if I act the way that I act at home I won't be accepted. So now I have to act like the other girls. I have to be like this all day. I have to be on my guard."

Ginny takes care to speak quietly and works overtime without complaint. "I feel like I have two things against me," she says "I'm Black and then I'm a woman. So now I have to work extra hard to prove myself. I work a lot of hours that I don't want to work because I'm afraid of being called lazy. I put up with a lot of crap that I don't have to go through because I don't want them to think that I'm too aggressive or I'm ignorant or I like to street-fight all the time."

At first, Ginny tried to rationalize the inequities she experienced. She knew that she was asked to get to the gym earlier than the other trainers, and was often told to work the floor and teach classes while other instructors were given the more lucrative sessions with private clients. But when she thought she was being taken advantage of, she would quickly tell herself that she was one of the newer instructors, and the gym's manager, Rebecca, had always been friendly and supportive, giving Ginny a chance to teach when others said it was too soon.

Ginny also tried to ignore the racism and sexism that she suffered at the gym, from the White men who leered and told her that they'd love to touch her beautiful copper skin and the White women who always seemed surprised that she'd attended college and was slim and health-conscious.

"They look at me like, 'Black women eat fat greasy food, why is she so slim? You don't eat fried chicken and collard greens every night?' You know it's like that. And some White women, they're always telling me, 'Wow, you seem very smart. What school did you go to?' 'Oh, you grew up in Watts? Really? Wow.' It's like, 'You grew up in the ghetto and you work here?' And I feel like, 'Am I a science experiment?'"

Occasionally the bias is more blatant. When Ginny is teaching a step or spinning class, she has seen some White people come to the door, glance at her, and walk away. Others have refused to allow her to be their personal trainer, saying they'd prefer someone else. Once a client told her how sorry she was for Black women, having to put up with "rotten" Black men.

About two years ago, a few months after she became a full-time trainer, Ginny realized that she was suffocating beneath the mask she donned each day for work. The anxiety about what she would face each day, the weariness from being overworked, the anger at the condescending comments and sexual overtures from clients, and all the agonizing about how and whether to respond was slowly making her very ill. She began to have trouble sleeping. She would stare at the ceiling each night, the clock ticking, her stomach in knots. Sometimes she'd wake up her husband Carlos to share her worries. When she would finally drift off, she'd grind her teeth and mumble in her sleep. "And I suffer from a little bit of depression," she says. "You know, I cry for no reason."

A year ago Ginny noticed that at the end of her workday, when she was settling into her Nissan Sentra for the drive home, her stomach would sometimes hurt so badly that she'd nearly double over in pain. When she finally went to her doctor, Ginny found out that she had an ulcer. "It's from stress," she says simply. "It's so bad that right now I can't get up in the morning. I set my alarm for 5:00, 5:30, and I'll lay in the bed until 6:00 when I'm supposed to be leaving at 6:15, hitting the snooze button because I don't want to go to work. But the only thing that makes me go is because I know we have bills and we're trying to build, and I need to go to work so we can make the money. If I didn't have that on my shoulders, I would never go back. I just feel like I'm not being fair to myself sometimes because I have to bottle up all of the anger that I feel when I'm at work."

On the rare occasion when she has complained to a couple of coworkers about the unfair treatment she feels she is receiving, they act as though "I'm being mean, I'm not trying to help the gym, I'm not being a team player, I'm complaining. I feel like if I was White, would this happen to me?"

And somewhere between Watts and west L.A., she believes that she lost Ginny. The persona that she shifts into to get along with her coworkers and clients seems to be overtaking what was once her true self. "Sometimes I think I'm turning into Jennifer," she says. "Sometimes I feel like I've totally left Ginny on the back burner. I'm a totally different person. I think Jennifer was always a piece of me, but working at the gym really brought her out. You adapt to your environment. So now I've adapted."

For Black women, the daily migration from home to office can contain all the fears, doubts, and challenges of leaving one's country for a foreign land. The workplace is where Black women feel they must shift most often, engaging in a grown-up game of pretend as they change their voices, attitudes, and postures to meet the cultural codes of workaday America as well as the broader societal codes of gender, race, and class. Work is where they are most likely to confront all the myths about Black women head on, and the stage upon which they may utilize every shifting strategy in their arsenal.

Many women testify to spending several hours a day feeling profoundly disconnected from who they truly are, a loneliness that may remain long past quitting time, when the dishes are washed and the children are in bed. Some come to feel so fragmented that they end up believing there is nowhere they truly fit in.

Given the uniquely painful legacy of slavery and segregation, Black women have always had to labor extraordinarily hard—and continue to do so—leaving their homes each day to support their families in a society that still greatly limits opportunities for African Americans. In the year 2000, 66 percent of Black women, compared to 60 percent of White women and 59 percent of Hispanic women, ages 20 and older were in the labor force.[1] Moreover, of those who were working, 83 percent of Black women, compared to 77 percent of Hispanic women and 71 percent of White women, toiled full-time.[2] Still, despite all of the evidence to the contrary, Black women are routinely stereotyped as lazy, welfare-dependent, and incompetent. This myth persists even though statistics tell us that in reality most of the people on welfare are White.[3]

The job opportunities for Black women in America are now greater than ever before. For example, from the mid-1980s to the mid-1990s, there was a 79 percent increase in the number of Black women in professional and managerial occupations.[4] Yet gross inequities in the career world are still painfully real. Black women are disproportionately in low-paying, menial, part-time jobs that offer few or no benefits, and their income is significantly less than that of White men and women and that of Black men. In 2001 the median weekly earnings of a full-time Black woman worker was $451, compared to $518 for Black men, $521 for White women, and $694 for White men.[5] While one-fifth of Black women have broken into the ranks of professionals, managers, and executives, they are less represented in management than White, Asian, or Hispanic women. Moreover, Black women managers earn 58 cents for every $1 earned by White male managers.[6]

Though often underpaid, Black women must take on, along with all of their obvious job-related duties, the additional task of shifting. With their White peers, they must shift to shatter the stereotypes of the lazy welfare mother who would rather not work at all, and the unqualified "token" who only has her job because of affirmative action. With their Black male colleagues, they shift to show their sisterly allegiance and to topple the idea held by some that their progress up the organizational ladder comes at the expense of Black men. Some shift by ignoring the codes of sisterhood that normally bond many Black women, instead striking up a more distant, neutral stance that strains those relationships yet puts their White colleagues at ease. And still others shift by downplaying their success at work. They feel guilty about their achievements and worry that other African Americans will think they have shunned their own community to make it in the mainstream.

This constant shifting, many women say, has made work a place of alienation. Having to overcome the myths; to shift their language and behavior according to every conversation, meeting, and task at hand; and to endure outright inequities all take a great toll, and their careers, personal lives, and health suffer tremendously as a result.

When we asked our survey respondents what are the major difficulties that they face as Black women, 39 percent pointed to problems related to work—struggling to be hired, having to work harder than others, being paid less than their colleagues for comparable work, and being passed over for promotions. Over two-thirds (69 percent) had experienced some form of bias or discrimination at work; 41 percent indicated they had experienced racial discrimination and 34 percent said they had experienced gender discrimination while on the job. Work emerges as the arena in which Black women are most challenged to shift.

Our findings echo those of other scholars. In an in-depth study of 825 Black and White women managers, Ella Edmondson Bell of the Tuck School of Business and Stella Nkomo of the University of South Africa conclude that for Black women racial and gender biases and barriers intersect and make it particularly difficult for them to advance.[7] In a smaller study of African American women who were professionals or managers, Lynn Weber of the University of South Carolina and Elizabeth Higginbotham of the University of Memphis found that 74 percent of these women believed that in their workplace women were treated differently than men; 68 percent felt that Blacks were treated differently than Whites.[8] Diane Hughes and Mark A. Dodge of New York University found that Black women's perceptions of workplace bias were more important predictors of job quality than other stressors, like heavy workloads and poor supervision.[9]

Strikingly, in a 1997 study of 1,562 women of color, most of whom were in professional, technical, or managerial positions, the Center for Women Policy Studies found that 42 percent of the African American women believed that they must play down their race or ethnicity, and 27 percent believed they must play down their gender in order to be successful at work.[10] Similarly, in a study of 1,735 professional and managerial women of color, more than half of whom were African American, Catalyst, a nonprofit research and advisory organization, found that 56 percent of Black women were aware of stereotypes about Black women in their companies and 36 percent believed they needed to adjust their style to fit their work environment.[11] Downplaying one's race or gender and adjusting one's style are, of course, common behavioral manifestations of shifting.

For far too many Black women, work is draining and stultifying. Often it is like handling two jobs. As Patricia, a 43-year-old executive in the entertainment industry, exclaims, "When you go into work, you have to weed through all the racism and stuff; and then, only then, do you get to do your job."

Getting in the Door: The Challenges of Being Hired

For many Black women, just getting in the door generates tremendous anxiety, since they rarely know ahead of time whether the potential employer, and specifically the person hiring them, will consider them fairly, free of racist and sexist biases.

Black women often first experience the challenge of getting in the door at an early age. When Cynthia, now 21, was 18, she called about an advertised position for an assistant at a notary's office in downtown Miami. Ms. Tate handled the call and asked Cynthia questions about where she lived, what school she attended, and whether she spoke a language other than English. Ms. Tate let her know that the new employee would work directly for her, and she seemed eager to get Cynthia in for an interview that afternoon. When Cynthia arrived in a brand new tan suit from Express, for which she'd depleted her meager savings, Ms. Tate looked up from her desk, hesitated a moment, then told Cynthia that the position was already filled.

DaShawn, a 35-year-old from Chicago, was once told directly that a woman would be inappropriate for a position in finance because "Women are not capable of critical thinking; we're too emotional."

Kelly, a 33-year-old from Atlanta, speaks of an experience "that still haunts me," and how she has used it and other trials to motivate herself. She explains, "I went on a job interview and because I have a name that is a popular Caucasian name, I knew that the interviewer assumed that I was White. I will never forget the look on her face when she saw me. It was a look of surprise mixed with disappointment." Kelly didn't get the job, and initially she felt angry and frustrated. But now, employed as a real estate broker, Kelly shared what has kept her going in spite of such disappointments. "The main thing that helps me make it is others' view that I can't," she says. "Every time I feel like giving up, this fuels me."

Colleen, a 33-year-old financial analyst, describes her last experience looking for a job. She knew what was expected. "There is always a silent requirement that if you are Black, they have to be comfortable with you. So you have to try hard to find commonalities that override racial differences. If you can't do that, interviews at search firms and job opportunities are not there."

Colleen continues: "I had a killer résumé when the search firm called and spoke with me, but when I showed up for the preliminary interview, I was treated like a fraud, as if none of the accomplishments could possibly have been mine." She has managed to weather storms like these because, "I had this grandpa who spoke so much truth you got sick of hearing it. He made you know who you were, so no one could kill your spirit."

Yvette was able to get in the door, but just barely. And once there, she had to disengage emotionally to deal with the inequities. A 30-year-old living in New Orleans, she was offered a position as a sales assistant, "even though I'd had seven years of sales experience." She adds, "White males and even Black males with no experience were offered a sales position." Yet she took the job, willing herself each day to not focus on those associates who were given better positions right from the start. Eventually, after eight months, she was promoted.

Gladys, a 38-year-old from Phoenix, has had a tougher time than Yvette, Colleen, and Kelly. On welfare most of her adult life, she has been trying, in keeping with the 1996 federal initiative, to transition from welfare to work. But Gladys is aware of receiving very mixed messages. On the one hand, she's encouraged by her caseworker to get trained and find a job, and in fact she's taken numerous clerical and computer courses. But then when it comes to securing a position, she's been stymied again and again. Gladys struggles each day to shore up her crumbling self-esteem. She confides: "They didn't want to give me a chance because of the way I looked. They never said, 'Come on board. We want to give you a chance. We're going to train you.' I wanted to hear, 'Come on in.' I was never welcomed."

The experiences of Gladys, Kelly, Colleen, and others help to explain the high unemployment rate of African American women. Even though Black women are heavily represented in the workforce, many of their sisters languish among the unemployed. In 2001, the official unemployment rate for Black women was 8.1 percent, compared to 4.3 percent for White men, 4.1 percent for White women, and 9.3 percent for Black men.[12] Phillip Bowman's research on joblessness cautions us that the *actual* unemployment rate includes both the "officially unemployed," who are actively looking for work, and the hidden unemployed, who want a job but are not actively looking.[13] Many of the hidden unemployed have given up job-seeking because they've become discouraged. For Blacks, and especially for Black women, Bowman has found a very high hidden unemployment rate. Put simply, there are far too many Gladyses, too many African American women for whom finding an opportunity to work feels, or is indeed, impossible.

Salient Objects: When Visibility Begets Invisibility

For those Black women who make it through the door, there is often the challenge of their visibility. Many Black women, particularly if they are professionals or managers, become the only Black person or one of very few in their department or company. And so they stand out. Not surprisingly, in a study of Black women's experiences of occupational stressors, Diane Hughes and Mark A. Dodge of New York University found that African American women at work sites with few Blacks reported more racial prejudice and discrimination than those in predominantly Black or more integrated workplaces.[14]

Bernardo Carducci of Indiana University Southeast has coined the notion of "salient objects" to denote the significance of feeling scrutinized in various environments.[15] Carducci has found that it's human nature for people to closely examine and be especially critical of the most noticeable person in the room. Salient objects, Carducci says, often capture our negative attention. Likewise, in a review of research on the consequences of workplace race and gender composition, Barbara Reskin, a sociologist at Harvard University, and her colleagues conclude that being a "token," being one of only a few Black workers or one of only a handful of women employees and thus highly visible, leads to heightened pressure to perform in a stellar fashion.[16] There is greater performance pressure on tokens and they are evaluated more harshly.

What the research tells us is that if you are a Black woman working in settings with few Blacks or few women, you take on an additional risk. It's likely that you'll feel unduly pressured to perform and prove yourself, and that your emotional and physical well-being may be compromised as a result. You may grapple with the yo-yo effect, feeling emotionally conflicted as you hurriedly switch personas, crossing a cultural divide every time you segue between a meeting with your boss and a quick telephone conversation with your closest friend. To "prove" your worth, you may take on myriad tasks and myriad roles, lose your sense of self and end up mired in depression, engulfed by the Sisterella complex.

What's ironic is how this painful visibility, with which so many working Black women in America must contend, also begets *invisibility*. Their minority status, glaring as it may be, at times actually makes it easier for them to be discounted and ignored. "Now that we see you," the White workplace seems to tell them, "we're going to try not to notice that you're there."

Psychologist and professor A. J. Franklin of the City University of New York has developed the notion of an invisibility syndrome, which Black men in particular contend with and which can be emotionally crippling.[17] Franklin reminds us of Ralph Ellison's 1952 classic *The Invisible Man*, which chronicles a young African American man's journey from the South to New York City and his growing awareness of his invisibility in the White-dominant world.

Our research reveals that 50 years later these issues are still prevalent and that Black women are faced with them as well. Many women speak about how such invisibility leads coworkers to be openly racist, insensitive, and hurtful. Bridget, a 35-year-old social worker in Buffalo, New York, talks about how at work she is often assumed to be a client rather than a professional. She experiences this "all the time when dealing with certain lawyers at juvenile court. I am mistaken for a client until I am able to speak, dispelling all preconceived notions."

Nicole, 36, has been a police officer in a large metropolitan district for close to eight years. Many of her colleagues seem to ignore her presence and allow their racism to pour out easily. "There's a lot of invisibility," she says. "At a crime scene, sometimes detectives get in there and they start saying things you wouldn't believe—racist comments, racist stereotypes about suspects, racist stereotypes about African American people, and I want to say, 'Excuse me, I'm over here.'"

Ketisa, a 41-year-old market researcher at a large food corporation in Los Angeles, observes: "Sometimes I believe that when you're very competent and you're really good at what you do, and you become homogenized to some degree, people almost forget that you're Black, and they forget who they're talking to. As dark skinned as I might be, because I work so much in a White world, and they become so very comfortable with me, they have tended to say things that were offensive."

Ketisa tells of a time when the team of market researchers was considering a Black male as a new hire. "A staff member from human resources commented, 'We hired a Black man once and he didn't do well, that's why we don't want to take that chance.' And I looked at her, kind of like, 'What did you say?' and she caught herself because she saw my eyes, and I said, 'We've hired a lot of Whites who've been absolutely horrible, and we're still hiring Whites.' And she was like, 'That's not what I meant.' I think she just forgot I was there."

Being invisible, for some women in our study, means being relegated to narrow, limiting, unimportant tasks that offer few opportunities for growth and advancement or being assigned to a "racial job" that pushes them into a Black ghetto within the White workplace. For example, Mary Ann, a 27-year-old publicist and account executive from Manhattan, talks of the racism in "getting all the Black clients at my firm and not being able to grow in any 'non-Black' areas of business." Lorraine, a 32-year-old assistant dean at a southern California university, shares her major difficulty as a Black woman: "I'm not taken seriously by Whites on my job. I'm only seen as an expert with minority issues. My opinion tends not to count anywhere else."

Even when they are not given a "racial job," Black women are sometimes consigned to a corner and given few opportunities to learn or progress. Irene, a 38-year-old from Austin, Texas, who is now a human resources director, tells of a former boss who gave her busy work instead of the substantive tasks she gave to Whites. And Ina, a 50-year-old government clerk from Inglewood, California, talks about how awful it felt to be given less work than her White and Asian coworkers: "It made me feel less adequate. It made me question my abilities."

The Cleanup Woman: Lots of Work, Little Recognition

There's a saying in the Black community that you have to work twice as hard as Whites to be seen as equal, and many women testify to its veracity. Often the way Black women counter the sense of invisibility and prove their credibility is to do more than their fair share of the work. Juggling varying responsibilities and roles often reflects the shifting strategy of battling the myths—as many women overextend themselves to prove they are not lazy or incompetent. But this same shifting strategy may foster the masochism that so often contributes to depression in Black women.

Bryce, a 29-year-old health administrator from Kent, Ohio, says, "As a Black woman, I constantly have to prove myself in the workplace—I have to be twice as smart and twice as savvy." A 42-year-old clerk-typist, Kirsten, from Denver, reports, "I have to dress better, act better, do my job better, and more efficiently just to be deemed equal to a Caucasian coworker at the same level." Helene, a 37-year-old executive director from Washington, D.C., doesn't hesitate to reveal her reality: "I have to work a hundred times harder than my male counterparts to be noticed and brought to the table."

Marjorie, a 50-year-old woman in Philadelphia, tells of a conversation she had with a friend about how Black women are the "mules" of the world. She is approached time and time again to be the "cleanup woman" at her job co-directing a nonprofit foundation; to be the one who takes care of the mess left behind by her co-directors or bosses. After a job well done, her reward is never a promotion or a raise. It is a compliment at best—and more work.

"I'm always feeling I'm proving myself every single day, that my past successes don't really count," Marjorie says with a sigh in her voice. "Or that they count enough for me to be here, but that just got me in the door. I feel that others don't have to be as accountable as I do, that other people get breaks that we don't get. And I see where, if allowed, I'd have all the responsibility for the work and none of the recognition and none of the pay."

Marjorie's metaphor of the cleanup woman is a painful reminder of the long history of Black women as slaves and servants, who for centuries have been overworked and given little credit, even as they maintained White households and raised White children. Although no longer confined to servitude or domestic work, many women complain of still having to take on multiple tasks for little reward, watching others who may be less qualified get promoted, and sometimes even training the people who eventually become their supervisors. As Tanya, from Miami, who's now a small business owner, puts it, "I was always good enough to train the managers but not good enough to be one." Some women say that if they complain or don't do every task equally well, it is as if they have never done anything right. They are given little margin for error, not allowed to be merely competent, to be human.

Leah, a 52-year-old legal secretary, who has worked in Boston for a large, multioffice legal firm for 15 years, talks with great pain about the inequities in her office:

> The White folks at work still get preferential treatment, and it may be things like making more money, like getting away with more—they can do more and still stay hired. Black folks are the last hired and the first fired. The differences are pretty obvious, at least to Black folks. It's amazing—the White folks can come to work late; they can just not work; they can sit at

their desk and read books. The Black secretaries are always the ones who seem to have more folks to work for. I've got four people that I'm working for now and the White girl who sits next to me is working for two folks, who basically generate a lot less work.

Leah becomes more animated as she continues: "There's this little girl whom they just hired—a cute young White girl. She has no skills as a secretary. These White folks are hired with skills that are so far below what is required to do the job, but they're brought in making more money. She's tried to pick my brain, but she's unable to do her job."

Leah feels "drained" and "depressed." She's tired of being expected to "train" attractive, but incompetent, more highly paid White secretaries. Yet compared to many other Black women, she has a good income, and she knows her options are limited: "If I leave the law firm, chances are I'm going to go into another setting that's just the same. And if I went out and found something that I really wanted to do, I wouldn't make half of what I make now. You do what you have to do."

Like most workers in the United States, Black women often have an official job description, but like Leah and Marjorie, they too often have an additional set of work expectations, an undocumented job that's based on assumptions about who they are and what they ought to do as Black women. Theresa, 43, a human resources administrator in Chicago, is one of many women who speaks of having to function as a "translator," explaining everything from Black hair textures to aspects of Black culture to White coworkers. Lucille, 66, a retired elementary school teacher in Camden, Arkansas, recalls that she once agreed to be transferred to a different school, only to learn that she and the one other Black teacher were given all of the "problem children." The unspoken expectation was that the two of them would fulfill all the usual responsibilities of teaching in addition to managing the most troubled and disturbed children. Alma, an administrator in a health clinic in Minneapolis, laments the burden of "being expected to speak for the entire race because I'm the only person of color in my workplace."

Maria, 38, who is an executive at a small printing company in the San Francisco Bay area, believes that other people expect her to switch easily between being a nurturing, Mammy-like presence who will be sympathetic and easy to manipulate, and a tough, domineering boss who can fire people without a second thought.

> Because of my position and because I'm a Black woman, they think, "Okay, let's ask her to do it because she can be mean, she can be hard." I feel like if I was a different person in the same position, I wouldn't be asked to be so many different things. I think they would look at me and say, "Okay, her talent is here, her strength is here," and that's it. I definitely feel that pull on a daily basis where people want me to be understanding, sympathetic, "I can cry your tears, I can feel your pain," but on the other hand, they want me to be the person who is saying, "I'm going to tell you off if you don't do it right."

Is It Me or Is It Bias?

Sometimes African American women are clear that they are being treated badly because of their race, their gender, or the combination of the two. But at other times, it's more subtle. It's not always easy to unravel the reasons behind a lower salary or a mediocre evaluation. And the constant wondering is in itself stressful. It doesn't help that oftentimes Black women are made to question their own feelings and capabilities, told by a non-Black and sometimes even an African American colleague, that she is being too sensitive or that there might have been a dozen reasons why her supervisor came down so hard on her that had nothing to do with race. She is left to wonder whether she failed to get the promotion because she ran up against the same web of politics encountered by some of her White colleagues, or is she hindered by something more? Is she being treated unfairly, or is her supervisor correct that she is not up to the job?

She may still ask why, long after an incident occurred, her confusion leading to sleepless nights, mounting self-doubt, resentment, and anger. She is tormented trying to figure out if there is something she can improve, or whether no matter what she does, there will always be another hurdle to overcome because she is Black and female.

"I know it's not all race, but I don't know how to separate it," says 45-year-old Frances, who has waffled between questioning her own competence and believing she is the victim of bigotry when she has been passed over for a promotion or raise. "And I don't know that anyone else knows how either."

Renita, a 38-year-old department store executive in Cleveland, speaks of the "angst you go through trying to determine if something is performance-based or racially motivated and totally outside of your control. . . . Within the corporate arena, I think there are a lot of dynamics in place. I think there's the whole systemic racism problem. I think there is the dynamic of the person you work for, and if you're fortunate enough to have a mentor or a champion who believes in you. Or let's say you have an enlightened White person as your supervisor versus a hostile White person that's your supervisor. So I think there are a number of different factors that come into play and it's not as simple as, 'these are the 10 rules to get ahead in corporate America.'"

Lisa, a 35-year-old marketing consultant in Chicago, goes back and forth constantly. In explaining a job that she was denied while a White colleague got the nod, Lisa first says that the playing field is simply not level for Black women. But a few minutes later she seems to want to justify her supervisor's actions, saying that there are expectations in corporate America that everyone must meet regardless of gender or color, and that it is understandable that you might want to promote those with whom you feel most comfortable. Finally she concludes that it isn't worth it to complain anyway, because, "If you say, 'That's because I'm a female and I'm Black,' people will just say, 'Well, look at your record, you don't have the record.' How do you put [something more subtle] in writing? How do you quantify that? How do you explain it at promotion time?"

Research shows that the uncertainty that Lisa feels about whether she's being treated differentially can actually be dangerous. There's evidence that subtle mistreatment may be more harmful than outright discrimination. In a study of the relationship between cardiovascular reactivity (i.e., changes in blood pressure in reaction to stress) and perceptions of discrimination, Max Guyll and his colleagues at the University of Pittsburgh found that for African American women, subtle, not overt, mistreatment was related to spikes in blood pressure, potentially leaving the victims of covert bias at risk for cardiovascular disease.[18] The researchers propose that because subtle discrimination is ambiguous and more difficult to pinpoint, it can be harder than blatant prejudice for Black women to identify and mobilize against.

When Shirley, 36, felt she was being treated unfairly, she didn't spend days trying to figure out the reason why. Instead, she decided rather quickly to go and talk to her boss. Shirley knew that Aubrey, a White man recently hired to help her run the municipal payroll department in a southern California city, didn't have anything on her when it came to credentials. She had master's degrees in public administration and accounting, along with 11 years' experience working for local government. So she was mystified when she walked over to the office printer one morning and saw a confidential letter stating Aubrey's salary. Even though she had been with the city for several years, gotten an excellent performance review and a good raise a few weeks before, she found out that Aubrey made $5,000 a year more than she did.

"There's part of you that really wonders, couldn't they have pushed for another $5,000?" she says. "Then you wonder, is it a woman thing? Is it my age because I'm much younger than him? Is it because I don't have a wife and kids to support that they think they can get away with this stuff? Is it because I'm single and I don't have a husband? I think we do spend a lot of time trying to figure out what people's motives are."

Shirley confronted her supervisor. "I think he was kind of taken aback that I addressed it directly," she says. He told Shirley that there was a limit to how much they could give her in one pay hike and that they had upgraded her title as a reward for her good work. Her supervisor also noted that Aubrey had relocated from the Midwest to take the job and salary had been an incentive. Though Shirley still had her doubts, she did believe that her boss had gone to bat for her, and she felt empowered that she had at least had the courage to confront him. But she was left with a nagging feeling about the department and how she was being treated. It was a feeling she could live with, but it was there. It was always there.

Karen, 34, worked at a utility company in central North Carolina. As the most senior team leader on her shift and the second most senior at the company, she expected that when a manager position arose that she'd be promoted. She wasn't. Karen says, "I was like, okay, maybe it was just me and I do need to put in the extra 115 percent to show them what I can do—you know, run the shifts, keep up with the paperwork, and everything that comes with running the office and running the shift, and of course managing the people as well." Karen dug in and worked even harder, but it didn't help.

She continues: "The second time I was passed up for promotion, there was no doubt in my mind it was because I was Black. The person who was given the position was someone else who had been there less time than me, had less experience in that kind of business, in customer service. I know it was not because I was a woman. There were other women working in positions equal to or higher than mine; therefore, it could only have been because I was Black."

Karen elaborates: "My numbers were up—my team's output was up to or above budget. They'd dropped shifts in my lap. They'd dropped people in my lap with no direction, with no instructions, and I'd pulled it off without a hitch. I was doing anything extra that was asked of me, and yet still someone else who was less qualified and less experienced got the position over me." Karen stewed over the decision for a couple of days, then sought out her boss.

She told Ms. Wallace that the decision was unfair, that her proven performance and seniority merited the promotion. Ms. Wallace seemed ill at ease and offered little by way of explanation. "I don't think there was anything they could have told me that would make me understand why this other person was more qualified than me," Karen remembers.

She considered filing a grievance with the company's human resources department, but then decided it wasn't worth it. Instead she bided her time while pursuing a job with another company. When she secured a position as a manager with a furniture manufacturer, she quit. Karen had figured out that "It isn't me."

Dodging the Barbs of Racism

Though many Black women search for the answer to that question, others have no need to ask it. The bigotry is in their face—unconcealed, blatant, and egregious. Vanessa, a 34-year-old elementary school teacher in Los Angeles, vividly remembers the first time that she was smacked in the face with racism. Working her way through college, she applied for a job as a receptionist for a local union. She liked Paul, the young White man who ran the office and interviewed her for the position, and he seemed impressed with her. Two days after they spoke, he offered her the position. But Vanessa got the first glimpse of what she was stepping into the following Monday, when she showed up early for work and Paul took her to a coffee house for a little chat.

"He sits me down and says, 'I just want to tell you this is not a very good environment,'" she remembers. "'It's all White males and when you came in to interview and left, [one of the officials] came up and said you can hire anybody but don't hire any niggers.' So he hired me just as a slap in their face and I felt, 'How dare you use me in that way.' But his thing was, you were the best candidate. This was in 1986. There were a lot of really very racist, sexist, bigoted—you name every kind of ism—men that were there. And I remember in my first three months there, a lot of people wouldn't talk to me. And I was the receptionist. I would put messages in the mailbox. You know they'd come by and just kind of give me this curt look and keep walking."

Vanessa didn't feel she could quit. The money was excellent and she needed it to pay for textbooks and college tuition. Besides, the hours were very flexible, fitting perfectly with her school schedule. She also believed herself to be a fixer of things, and she resolved that she was going to educate these men, showing through her professionalism and kindness that Black women—and Black people—were as good, as worthy, as they were.

Still, each morning, as she got out of bed, headed for the shower, and pulled on her clothes, she had to engage in a mental dialogue to bolster herself for whatever she might face that day. She would repeat a mantra: "I'm just going to do my job. I'm just going to do my job. Paul needs me, and I'm just going to do my job."

When some of the union officials refused to speak to her, she remembers, "It kind of made me feel cold, empty, angry, and determined to show them." But sometimes she was also afraid, especially on the days when Paul wasn't in and she was working in the front lobby alone. Or when she walked down the long, drafty hallway to the ladies' room on the other side of the building. She would crack jokes with the union members to break the tension, to make them believe that they were not getting to her. But they were.

"It was scary," she says. Yet Vanessa's overriding emotion was determination. The younger people in the office had always been friendly and sympathetic. And gradually, over time, many of the older men became friendlier. "I would just say, 'Hi, hello. I hope you have a good evening. Oh, so nice to see you.' And then they eventually came around. But it took months."

Years later, she told her parents what she had endured. They were angry and said that she was crazy to have stayed there for a day, let alone a year and a half. "I said, 'Ma, they loved me when I left and they hired more Black folks. If Paul hadn't brought me in, it would have stayed the same. It would have stayed White.'"

Vanessa endured emotional turmoil at that job but put up with it because she felt that she had a mission to present a more accurate picture of Black women, and thus to educate the White bigots with whom she worked. On some level she seemed to succeed, and the short-term fear and anxiety that she had endured seemed worth it for the feeling of vindication she felt in the end. But not all Black women are able to cope so well with such hostile situations. Nor should they have to.

Two for the Price of One: Fighting Gender Bias

As hard as it is to be Black in the workplace, having to also deal with gender bias makes work that much more oppressive. Popular misconceptions to the contrary, work life is as hard for Black women as it is for Black men, if not harder. Yet many people believe that Black women have an easier time in the work world *because* of their gender. And there's a widespread myth that Black women are doubly advantaged because they are a "double minority"—Black and female—and thus "ideal" for meeting organizational diversity goals. Though this myth has circulated extensively, and even though some Black women themselves have been persuaded by it, the data don't support it.[19] Rather, studies show that a large sector of Black women are stuck in the lowest-paying jobs that typically are relegated to women. And even though Black women's high school and college graduation rates exceed those of Black men, a greater percentage of Black men are in the labor force, and Black men earn more money for their work than Black women.[20-21] The truth is that Black women are faced with two forms of bigotry that jostle against each other. But since, as we've discussed, the Black community is often silent about discrimination based on gender, many Black women may not immediately recognize workplace gender bias or feel comfortable speaking up about it.

As is true with racism, sexism in the workplace falls along a continuum, from demeaning and denigrating comments that get under the skin to verbal sexual harassment to outright sexual or physical assault. Valerie, a 27-year-old career counselor in Torrance, California, completed her master's degree six months ago and began working for a small firm that specializes in providing career placement services for companies that are downsizing. She's long been sensitized to racial issues and racial slights, but her awareness of gender bias is just developing. She talks about the small but grating day-to-day annoyances. "The men are very much catered to. They don't answer the phones as much. When they have clients coming, they always ask the women if we'll put together the file folders, put together all the forms and things, and type out the labels. . . . When we have cake for somebody's birthday, the men will never clean up."

Laurette, a 53-year-old teacher from Prince George's County, Maryland, writes that women's proposals are given less consideration than those of their male counterparts. "When you deal with men and you have an idea that you wish to further, I have found that if you can get another man to voice that same idea to the man you are trying to influence, that idea will usually be accepted."

Early on Charlotte, 52, learned of the double standard. A professor of sociology, she recalls the pressure that she felt from male colleagues at a private university in Pennsylvania where she first taught:

> It was so male at that time that I had students who had never had a female professor. They all expected me to be maternal. At the end of the term, I had one student whose mother called me and pleaded with me to change his grade. And then my male colleagues started calling me up to put pressure on me. And I am sure that, had I not been female, they would not have dared to call another male colleague and try to interfere.

Like Charlotte, Frida, age 41, encountered sexism in the academy, but for Frida it was at a historically Black college. Frida grew up in a small town in the Midwest where the African American population was so small that if a new Black family moved in, the entire Black community knew by nightfall. After earning her doctoral degree in Spanish literature, she was thrilled to secure a full-time faculty appointment in the foreign language department at a Black college. She excelled as a faculty member, was named professor of the year, and was appointed coordinator of a study-abroad program her second year. But after Frida secured a grant to support the program, she was asked by her department chairperson to use a portion of the funds for a completely different endeavor, which would have been a violation of the grant guidelines.

Frida recalls: "I realized then that my chairperson was trying to manipulate me. I think that he felt that if he had a woman, he could more easily do what he wanted. I think it was a gender thing."

When Frida stood firm and refused to compromise her ethics, her chairperson mounted a campaign to discredit her. At a faculty meeting, he publicly accused her of mishandling the grant funds and implied that she had embezzled money. He stripped her of the coordinator duties and assigned her to teach introductory Spanish, even though he had hired her to teach upper-level Spanish courses and mentor junior and senior Spanish majors. The students rallied behind Frida and protested publicly, but after months of battle, Frida made the tough decision to resign. She is tearful as she remembers what it was like for her. "When I came through that, I was out of my mind. You keep playing it over and over. What did I do? Where did I go wrong? Well, there was nowhere. That was the good ol' boy network playing itself out. And I recognized that later. Oh, this was gender stuff! That's what I was up against. It was very crushing."

For Frida, this experience was incapacitating. She managed to find other employment within a few months, but she grappled with feelings of depression for years. Now, almost a decade later, she's still in recovery. The realization that she could be treated so unfairly because of her gender, within her beloved Black community, was devastating.

Sex in the Lunchroom?

Sexual harassment and sexual assault in the workplace can be particularly disturbing and traumatic. Too often at work, Black women are viewed as sex objects and become targets for inappropriate sexual behavior and propositions.[22] For Black women, dogged by myths that they are more promiscuous than other women, on-the-job harassment can be especially piercing. They often have to determine whether to report a White harasser and risk giving life to false stereotypes about Black women's sexuality. Or they may face the potentially wrenching decision of whether to report a Black colleague who is victimizing them, possibly damaging his career and feeding the myth that Black men are sexually aggressive.

Many women are buffeted with the message that their physical attractiveness is what's most important on the job. Denise, a 27-year-old product consultant from Rochester, New York, says, "We work in teams a lot. Instead of commenting on my job performance, male coworkers comment on how attractive I am first." Cora, a 28-year-old clerk from Mobile, Alabama, reports: "I was a cashier at an auto parts store with a staff dominated by men. I worked hard to move up to parts manager and to take on other responsibilities, but the head manager made it clear that he only wanted me to stand there and look pretty as the cashier."

A variant of the expectation to "stand there and look pretty" is the accusation that one has earned a promotion by sleeping one's way to the top. The assumption is that the woman's competence and abilities are irrelevant, that only her looks or her willingness to offer sexual favors matters. "I face prejudice from White male cops," explains Gloria, a 33-year-old police officer from central New Jersey. "I'm not seen as good enough to be on the job. They think I must have slept with someone to get my position and that I'm still sleeping with someone to keep my position."

Sometimes the emphasis on physical attractiveness slips into out-and-out sexual harassment. Vivian, a 54-year-old pension consultant from Vallejo, California, says that one of her major challenges as a Black woman is dealing with how "the men typically test the sexual envelope to see how far they can go. They start with sexual innuendo and off-color jokes." There's evidence that Vivian is not alone in her experience. The research on female professionals and managers of color, by the Center for Women Policy Studies, found that 69 percent of African American women had heard sexual and sexist jokes at work.[23] Vivian adds, "I feel most women do not report most sexually offensive talk or behavior. Most of us don't have the time or money to go through the hearings and legal maneuvers."

Faye, a 42-year-old former television news producer, had to deal with more than jokes and ugly remarks. "In an all-White newsroom," she says bluntly, "I was sexually assaulted. A cameraman mounted me from the rear when I was on the floor connecting a computer cord under my desk. He was White with an all-White 'audience.' When I started legal procedures, I had no witnesses." This incident plus the racism that Faye had experienced for years—"I always had to fight to get plum assignments, and I never got the support I needed in the newsroom"—finally drove her out of the television news business.

The message on the day that Faye was sexually harassed was that it was okay for a Black woman to be openly sexually assaulted, and for all of the witnesses, actually voyeurs, who were White, to refuse to speak up and tell the truth. Her experience graphically illustrates the convergence of racism and sexism on the job. Faye was doubly victimized—first when she was assaulted, and then when the witnesses refused to speak—and in each case sexism and racism combined to work against her.

Angela, on the other hand, a 43-year-old single woman, talks about how painful it was to be sexually harassed by men who reminded her of her brothers. When she was victimized, she was a social service worker with a Black-owned regional firm that had government contracts to provide services to the developmentally disabled. After she'd worked for about a year, the on-site chief executive was removed and the regional executives, mostly Black men, became more involved in management. Several of them would fly in every few weeks for a couple of days to work at the office. Angela says, "They would want to be entertained. They would want someone to go to dinner with them, and I never would. They really became belligerent. Then they became nasty. Like one guy just said to me, 'You want to go home at lunch and fuck?' and I said, 'Excuse me?' He responded, 'Aw, you're too good for that. Oh yeah, you're the one that went to that Ivy League school.'"

Another executive once asked her to show him around the town over the weekend. She declined. On Monday, he invited her to lunch, and she declined. Angela says, "Five minutes later, he called me into his office to ream me about something. I went from sugar to shit!"

And then there was the third perpetrator. "He came up behind me and ran his finger down my bra, and I said, 'Stop that,' but I was young at the time and I really didn't know how to handle it, and I didn't do the forceful, 'How dare you!' I did the just-play-it-off kind of thing."

Work became emotionally wrenching for Angela: "I remember getting in the car to go to work, and my eyes running full of water because I hated that job so bad, because I felt like I just ran and hid all day and made up stuff, like, 'My boyfriend's coming to pick me up. I gotta run.'"

Ultimately, Angela resigned because of the harassment. Looking back, she wishes she'd handled it more directly. "At the time, I didn't

want to offend them or be rude," she remembers. "In some ways, it prolonged what they did."

Since she left the social service agency, Angela hasn't worked much
with Black men. And though she socializes with and dates Black men
exclusively, she acknowledges that she feels safer working with non-Black
men. For Angela, like Frida, who worked at the historically Black college,
being victimized by Black men made what was a traumatic situation even
worse. Those whom she'd felt she could trust had betrayed her.

Coming Full Circle: Making a Way While Being Yourself

At its best, work can be financially, emotionally, and spiritually
rewarding. It can be a place where women find, nurture, and utilize the
best of themselves and give back generously. At its worst, it can be a
place where Black women feel disconnected from their inner being,
where they must hide out in order to survive, and where they are
pushed to sacrifice their very selves—to shift too far—to be successful.
The challenge for Black women in the workplace is to make a way for
themselves without losing themselves. Black women do this in a number of different and creative ways. Some fight back and make their way
up the organizational ladder, some become entrepreneurs and carve
out their own work spaces, and some move on to work environments
where they can exist on their own terms.

Bernice decided to fight back. Formerly an officer in the military,
Bernice was sexually harassed by Timothy, a Black male superior officer, who let her know that if she wanted to survive, she would have to
have sex with him. Bernice was appalled and filed a grievance with the
appropriate office. When Timothy retaliated by falsely classifying her
as AWOL (absent without leave), a higher officer intervened and
offered Bernice the opportunity to be relocated to a different division.
But Bernice refused. She proclaims that Timothy had "messed with the
wrong African American woman" and she wasn't going anywhere. She
confronted Timothy directly, told him to leave her and all other
women alone, and informed him, in so many choice words, that God
did not approve of his behavior. She continued to cross paths with

Timothy regularly and to have to interact with him periodically, but she had freed herself from his grip. Eventually, he dropped the allegation that she had gone AWOL.

Eleanor, 49, also fought back. When she was a program administrator for a nonprofit agency, she took a leave because she was pregnant. The morning she returned, Eleanor says, "The executive director informed me of matters I failed to do prior to my leave, and so, as a result, I was given the opportunity to resign or be fired. I told her, 'I'm not resigning.' So I was fired."

Eleanor was initially shocked and distraught, but she adds, "After my paralysis of mobility and thought left my being, I contacted a lawyer who talked, negotiated, and threatened to expose the discrimination." By then Eleanor had figured out what was going on. "All of this happened so that my then assistant, a Caucasian woman, could have my job." After much legal wrangling and maneuvering, Eleanor was given her job back plus back pay. She walked back in and did her work proudly and competently. In fact she was so capable, that a couple of years later she was promoted to executive director.

While not faced with such outright discrimination, Liz had her own frustrations on the job, and she decided to leave for a setting where she felt she would be more fulfilled. After 20 years of practicing law, and having to wait much longer than many of her White and male colleagues to be made partner, Liz, 47, walked away from a prominent firm to become a political science professor and coordinator of the prelaw program at a small college in upstate New York. She can now speak, dress, and wear her hair in the way that feels comfortable, because she has found her true professional niche, as well as a far more relaxed, accepting environment. Getting older and acquiring an ever-deepening faith in God has also made her less inclined to contort herself to fit into different environments. For perhaps the first time in her adult life, by refusing to shift anymore, she is able to feel whole in the workplace.

"An isolated part of me was there [at the law firm] and I think that's why I felt so uncomfortable because I didn't see anywhere where I could be whole. And I'd had people tell me, 'Well, you know that's not why you work anyway. You get a job, you go to work, you make money. And it's not about being emotionally fulfilled.' And I'm like, 'Well, that's you.' Whatever time I have on this earth, I'm trying to pull this all together so that it makes sense for me. If you can put up your game face and then you're someone else, that's fine. But see, I'm getting to the point where I just want to be how God made me and that's enough."

The burden of shifting is, we believe, leading a growing number of Black women to start their own businesses. With an estimated 17 percent increase from 1997 to 2002,[24] Black women are becoming increasingly prominent as entrepreneurs. In 2002, it was projected that there would be 365,110 privately held firms with majority female ownership owned by African American women.[25] Among all Black-owned businesses, 35 percent are owned by women,[26] a higher percentage of female ownership than in any other ethnic group.[27]

Lynda, a 40-year-old former banker who now works at a nonprofit foundation in Denver, is preparing to open her own day-care and after-school center for the children of single mothers. It has long been her dream, and after taking a giant step from corporate America to non-profit work—and discovering that she was still occasionally subjected to unfair decisions that she was powerless to change—she is finally ready to take charge of her own business. She began polishing off her business plan a few months ago when she discovered that a White male co-director with less education and corporate experience was earning $15,000 a year more than her.

"I realized I had to place a value on what I was worth," she says. "I think it extracts a price from your soul to stay in a place where you know you're not necessarily being valued."

The only daughter of a homemaker and janitor, neither of whom finished high school, Lynda had been her parents' pride and joy, earning a bachelor's degree at Vassar, and her MBA at Wharton. When she went to the foundation, it was the first time she could remember looking in her father's face and not seeing pride in his eyes.

"When I made the decision to leave corporate America, that was the first time I had a strong sense that I wasn't living up to what people expected of me," she says, "both in terms of my parents, in terms of me making them proud, and in terms of my friends who had gone to graduate school. And just other people in the corporate mix who couldn't believe that I'd walk away from that. Being me was going to require I free myself from other people's expectations." For Lynda, opening her own community-based center is the next step in this process.

Of course, not everyone can fight back. Not everyone can walk away. Not every Black woman can shift in a direction that is ultimately liberating. Many Black women are left with very few options. They're stuck with managing their feelings and coping every day with bigotry. They're forced, for economic reasons, to return to work day after day regardless of how disaffected and alienated they feel—regardless of how anxious, angry, and depressed they may have become. They're trapped. For these women, the real solution is for the American workplace to change.

For more than a decade now, many businesses and corporations have been wrestling with what it takes to become an effective multicultural workplace—where employees of diverse genders, ethnicities, religions, and sexual orientations flourish individually and as a collective. To achieve this aim, transformation needs to happen at multiple levels, from the individual employees and supervisors who become aware of their biases and prejudices, and their own contributions to an intolerant environment, to the top tiers of the corporate hierarchy where policies, procedures, and the organizational culture are set.[28] Unfortunately, there's no quick fix. But an essential first step is the commitment of business and industry leaders to work toward the creation of an inclusive environment.

The demographics of the American landscape are rapidly changing, and we are hurtling toward the mid-twenty-first century when there will be no majority ethnic group, only many minority groups. While the experiences of Lynda, Faye, and Ginny compel us to create a welcoming and embracing workplace, the experiences of men and women workers of all ethnicities as well as the shape and vigor of the American economy are ultimately at stake.

"MIRROR, MIRROR ON THE WALL"

Black Women and Beauty

It's taken me 41 years to get to accepting the package that I'm in—to be okay with my skin tone, my weight, my hair, with just me. For a long time I walked in a lot of shame; I walked in a lot of low self-esteem. I now realize that beauty is inside out. What do you care about? What are you passionate about? To me that's what beauty is.

JUANITA, 41, OAKLAND, CA

Lavelle, 49, rises early in the morning. She plucks the rollers from her thick auburn hair, lathers cream on her nut brown skin, and unzips the splattered makeup bag on the bathroom shelf. She lines her eyelids in Black, paints her cheeks amber rose and glosses her lips Mac Diva Red. Now she is ready to face the world.

It's Saturday morning. She's only going to the grocery store and then back home again. But her beauty ritual, even on the weekend, never rests. When asked why she is so vigilant, she says at first that it is simply because she is a woman and wants to be beautiful. Then she thinks about how "beautiful" is defined, why it is so particularly important for her, a 6-foot-tall, heavy-set, brown-skinned Black woman, never to leave home without "putting on her face."

"It's weird," Lavelle, a bank manager in Maryland, says upon further reflection. "I think part of it is because I know that Black women are not high on anybody's list . . . that Black women are seen as unattractive."

Black girls are literally not the fairest of them all. Rather their hues range from eggshell to midnight. They often fill out their blue jeans with ample rumps and wide hips, sport thick, kinky locks, broad noses, and full lips. Many are the very opposite of the rail thin, blonde actresses and models who peer out from movie screens and magazine covers. In a society where the standard of beauty remains European, where beauty still too often defines a woman's worth, many Black women struggle to feel attractive and thus secure and valued. The pressure to look like someone other than themselves, to look more European and less African, is enormous. And many Black women are pushed to obsession over their hair, their skin tone, and, increasingly, their body size and shape. This is what we call the "lily complex," the belief that the only way to be beautiful is to look as close to "White" as possible.

The Lily Complex

Altering, disguising, and covering up your physical self in order to assimilate, to be accepted as attractive is one of the most common behavioral manifestations of shifting. It can also be one of the most insidious. As Black women deal with the constant pressure to meet a beauty standard that is inauthentic and often unattainable, the lily complex can set in. In changing her physical appearance to meet the mainstream ideal, her sense of self may start to disintegrate as she rejects and even grows to disdain her natural, physical self. By reshaping her outward appearance, or feeling that she should, she alters her psyche as well. She internalizes the mainstream message that says Black is not beautiful, believing that she can only be lovely by impersonating someone else.

Black women are not the only women who must reckon with Eurocentric beauty standards. Some Asian women pay for cosmetic surgery
that rounds their eyes. Latina women who appear on television and in
feature films are often fair-skinned, their hair straightened. Even White
women are compelled to become ever thinner, ever blonder.

But because of the unique position held by Black women in this society, they have had more to overcome as they try to disprove the distorted
myths and stereotypes that portray them as less attractive, less feminine,
and less refined. The message that has resonated throughout American
culture is that they are the least desirable of all women. And while the
media images of Black women are becoming more diverse, biases against
Black women based upon their physical appearance persist. Whether hailing a cab from the corner of a New York City street, interviewing for a secretarial job at an insurance company, or trying out for a part in a motion
picture, many of the women in our research project tell us that they are
prejudged, dismissed, or mistreated simply because they have a dark complexion, are overweight, or wear their hair in a natural style. Internalized
oppression within the Black community—the end result when Blacks buy
into the negative perspectives of the dominant society—often reinforces
these biases.[1] So African American women across the country feel pressure
to alter their appearance as best they can, and many are wracked with feelings of inferiority. As Coretta, a 32-year-old social services worker from
Chicago, puts it, one of the major challenges she faces as a Black woman
is "to maintain a positive perspective on my beauty and my body shape."

But the relationship between outward expressions of beauty and
self-appreciation is complex. Not every woman who decides to
straighten her hair or change the color of her eyes by wearing contacts
believes that beauty is synonymous with whiteness. Trying on a new
look, even one often associated with Europeans, does not automatically imply self-hatred. It is possible to dye your brown tresses platinum
and still love your Blackness. For many women, such changes may simply be another means of self-expression. And for others, shifting their
appearance is just one of many conscious compromises they make to
ensure that their White coworkers and peers feel comfortable with
them and don't make presumptions about their attitude or politics

based on the way they dress, the way they style their hair, or other superficialities. These women are aware that others may find Eurocentric characteristics more appealing and that being seen as attractive can help them integrate certain circles and access certain opportunities. So they conform in order to survive, to get along, to achieve.

It is important as a woman sits at the beauty parlor getting her hair chemically relaxed, as she compulsively heads to the gym, as she etches her lips with a pencil to make them appear thinner, that she ask herself the question "why?" She needs to make sure that her outward shifting is not rupturing her inner sense of self, that she does not begin to believe that the artificial hair she gets woven in at a hair salon is better than her own. For many women who suffer from the lily complex, changing their appearance is a subconscious effort to live up to beauty standards set by others. They do not realize that they have begun to believe in them, that the blue contact lenses are not a way to enhance but an attempt to disguise their deep brown eyes; that the long golden weave is not a fun new look, or an office compromise, but a means to camouflage their shorter, naturally kinky hair. The lily complex makes Black women try to whittle their bodies down to an unhealthy size or don brassy hair shades that clash with bronze and ebony skin. It compels them to hide their god-given behinds in ill-fitting clothes and to hope that the bleaching cream in the medicine cabinet will fade their mocha skin to honey.

The rejection of self that goes hand in hand with the lily complex does not stop when the woman turns away from the mirror. The belief that one's natural self is not good enough, not attractive enough, can lead to a loss of self-esteem. Rosa, a 30-year-old postal worker from New Jersey, says, "I think many Black women lack self-esteem. We've been made to feel inferior by the media, our parents, and even Black men to the point where many of us begin to think that we are inferior. Our behinds are too big, lips too big, hair too nappy, skin too dark, . . . on and on."

Dissatisfaction with one's own natural beauty can lead to a lack of confidence in oneself, in relationships, as well as in one's work life.[2] Hearing society's message, the Black woman may take on too many tasks, becoming an overachiever to "compensate" for her lack of

beauty and prove that she still has worth. She may settle for an unfulfilling romance, believing that she cannot do any better. She may lose
faith in her capabilities, striving for less because she does not believe
she can achieve more. And she may ultimately slip into depression,
becoming another unfortunate Sisterella. Indeed, researchers have
found that Black women who internalize mainstream beauty ideals are
more likely to be depressed than those who do not.[3]

As a group, Black women spend three to four times more on cosmetic and beauty products than White women, a huge differential
accounted for in part by the lily complex.[4] And it is significant that the
first woman in the United States to become a self-made millionaire
was Madame C. J. Walker, an African American woman who developed and sold personal and hair care products, including the hot comb,
which is used to straighten hair.[5]

Today, more than ever, Black women can see their sisters working
within corporate America, and in the worlds of fashion, and entertainment. Naomi Campbell and Tyra Banks have been joined by Tomiko, and
Alex Wek, an ebony-skinned model from Sudan, on the fashion circuit's
runways. More dark-skinned Black women with natural hairstyles appear
in television commercials. Avon, perhaps the most middle-American of
cosmetic firms, signed Venus and Serena Williams, brown-skinned tennis
stars with braids, to a multimillion-dollar deal. But ironically this
increased presence and visibility has not necessarily freed Black women to
be their natural physical selves. Instead, many feel pressured to conform in
a new way to the mainstream ideal.

Black women have traditionally had higher body self-esteem than
White women, and have historically been deemed immune to the drive
for thinness that partly fuels the eating disorders of anorexia and
bulimia, often thought of as White women's diseases.[6] However, those
who study body image and eating disorders have witnessed a troubling
trend. In a study of 3700 Black and White men and women, Delia
Smith of the University of Alabama and her colleagues found that
Black women were more invested in their physical appearance than
White women and that Black and White women had similar levels of
dissatisfaction with body weight and size.[7] The one encouraging note

for Black women was that heavy Black women were more satisfied with their weight than heavy White women. But the news is disturbing nonetheless, and it appears that a newfound emphasis on thinness and body shape may be leading an increasing number of African American women to adopt unhealthy habits to try to control their weight.

Wanda Jones, the Deputy Assistant Secretary for Women's Health in the U.S. Department of Health and Human Services, says that the number of Black women with eating disorders appears to be on the rise, and like their White peers, those afflicted tend to be high-achieving and educated. In two large-scale studies, Ruth Striegel-Moore of Wesleyan University in Connecticut and researchers working with *Essence,* the largest African American women's publication in the United States, found that many Black women have abnormal eating behaviors and attitudes.[8] These studies and several smaller ones indicate that even though the rate at which Black women receive treatment for eating disorders lags behind White women, Black women may have now become equally symptomatic.[9] More and more Black women appear to be dieting chronically, inducing vomiting, abusing laxatives, and engaging in cycles of binge eating and purging, all of which put them at risk for developing full-blown eating disorders. So, although overeating is a significant problem for many Black women, severe dieting and purging may be equally problematic (see Chapter 5).

Like depression and other mental disorders, eating disorders are complex and are caused by multiple factors, including the woman's history of family relationships and her feelings and beliefs about herself. However, there's substantial evidence that the cult of thinness in western industrialized societies is a major contributing factor.[10]

While the lily complex is stoked by the larger society, it is often reinforced within the Black community where the standards of beauty can be just as rigid and intense. The length of a woman's hair, its texture, and especially her skin color too often determine whether she is seen as attractive. And this color-based pecking order has greatly divided African Americans.[11] Twenty-four percent of our survey respondents have experienced prejudice or discrimination from other Blacks based on skin color.

Mark Hill of Pennsylvania State University talks about the long history of "colorism," bias based on skin color, in the dominant society.[12] He indicates that colorism is a particular problem for Black women because of the historical association throughout Europe and the United States of fair skin with both beauty and femininity. White skin has long been connected with "feminine virtues" like purity and piety. Hill thus highlights the problem of "gendered colorism," that skin color is particularly salient in how people judge the attractiveness of women, in contrast to men. This even applies to how Black women judge themselves. In a national study of Black Americans, where a representative sample of 2,107 Black men and women from age 18 to over 65 were interviewed, Maxine Thompson of North Carolina State University and Verna Keith of Arizona State University found that skin color was related to the self-esteem of Black women—that is, women who were darker had lower self-esteem.[13] Interestingly, for Black men there was no relationship between skin color and feelings of self-worth.

In a review of studies of Black women and perceptions of beauty, Christine Iijima Hall, a professor at Arizona State University West, concludes that the majority of African Americans feel that lighter skin means better social, educational, and occupational opportunities.[14] There is, in fact, evidence that lighter-skinned Blacks lead better lives than their darker-skinned kin. Using data from the National Survey of Black Americans, Verna Keith of Arizona State University and Cedric Herring of the University of Illinois at Chicago found that Black women who were lighter in skin color were more likely than darker Black women to be better educated, to have a higher status occupation, and to have a larger family income.[15] These differences were true regardless of their parents' educational level, occupation, and socioeconomic status. This same pattern did not hold for Black men. Using the same data set, Margaret Hunter of Loyola Marymount University found that on average lighter African American women are married to more educated men than their darker sisters.[16] Hunter talks about light skin color as "social capital" for women of color, allowing them to attract a more desirable man.

Within the Black community there is also a flip side to the lily complex. While the broader society and many African Americans herald a Eurocentric standard of beauty, some Black women feel pressured to reflect an Afrocentric aesthetic. It is an aspect of what we call the yo-yo paradox, the pressure that African American women feel to shift back and forth in order to meet the conflicting expectations of others. Many feel guilty or question their own Blackness if they don't wear natural hairstyles or if they are "too light."

These mixed messages leave many Black women feeling demoralized, torn between the desire to be defiant and independent, and the very human need to be accepted. Psychologists know that the experience of "mirroring" is essential for the healthy development of a child. When children are mirrored, they see themselves positively through others' eyes; they feel affirmed by others' responses to them. Children who don't have a mirroring caregiver often struggle throughout their lives to feel secure and valuable. And there is a similar challenge when one's identity is not affirmed, when one's ethnicity and gender are not mirrored, and when one's appearance is denigrated. Oftentimes for Black girls and women, the mirroring comes from parents, friends and extended family. But it's not uncommon for the negative and stereotypical messages of the larger society to get through and to be co-opted by members of the Black community, or for the Black community to impose its own alternative but equally rigid standards.

In a society that has become increasingly multiracial, African American women are at the vanguard of the trend to redefine American beauty, challenging and inspiring us to accept our myriad physical variations. In certain segments of the Black community, one can go to a cocktail party or a college reunion and straight-haired weaves and kinky dreadlocks coexist easily side-by-side, drawing neither scorn nor presumptions. Black women have come a long way, and in their trek have paved the way for other women, whatever their skin color, weight, or age to broaden and redefine American beauty ideals.

But their breakthroughs are hard won. Their stories remind us of the dangers of America's obsession with female attractiveness, its rigid standards of beauty.[17] And they reveal to us an alternate path to self-acceptance and celebration.

Reining in the Body

Collete, 23, has copper-colored skin and a mane of thick brown hair. Since she was a little girl, her family raved how she was the most beautiful of her sisters, the most attractive girl in her Ann Arbor neighborhood. She projects confidence to the world. But she dreads going to the store, poring through racks in search of business suits and blue jeans in a size 14. Even after losing 35 pounds to get down to her current weight, she says that she still feels like "a huge hippo." She thinks about her weight virtually every moment of the day.

When she fastens her seatbelt, she peeks uneasily at the driver to see if he is looking to see whether there is any slack left. "I'm always pulling on my clothes, making sure that they're falling right," she continues. She has joined weight control programs but then been too ashamed to get on the scale at the weekly weigh-ins.

Before she goes back east for an internship with a federal agency, she has a "to-do list" to complete. She must sublet her apartment, throw herself a going-away party—oh, and one more thing. "I'm going to have to lose the weight," she says. "I don't think I judge people according to looks, but I know everybody else does, so I feel like now that's one thing I need to conform to."

Collete's comments shed light on a striking change in body image that has diminished the Black female psyche. Big legs and ample behinds have always been celebrated in African American culture. It was high praise for a Black woman to be called "healthy" or "thick." Roy Eldridge, a jazz singer, crooned "I Want a Big Fat Mama," in the 1940s. The legendary blues singer Howlin' Wolf growled that when his baby walked, she shook like Jell-O and commanded that she "shake it for me." While definitions have changed over the years, when Kumea, one of the authors, was growing up in Washington, D.C., in the 1960s, it was flattering to be called "phat," an acronym for "pretty hips and thighs." Rap artists from Sir Mix-A-Lot to De La Soul have paid homage to voluptuous Black women in rhyme. And at many a party, the thinner girls may line the walls while their heavier sisters crowd the dance floor. Such celebration is no doubt one of the reasons that Black women traditionally have had more positive feelings about their body shape than other groups of women, even as 66 percent of adult African American women are defined as overweight, and even though obesity has contributed to their high rates of diabetes and heart disease.[18]

Yet many heavy Black women who have been able to accept and love themselves regardless of their girth, still often pay a price because the larger society deems them unacceptable.

When we met with Patricia at her home, she was dressed in a burgundy cashmere sweater and matching woolen pants. An accountant in her late forties, she talks of the frustration of trying to catch a cab one afternoon when she was returning to her downtown Manhattan office. After two empty taxis sped by, the third one, driven by a Black man, stopped. She managed to get out a "thank you," but she was fuming. His response was, " 'You know why they didn't stop? First of all, it's 4:30 and they probably thought you were going uptown to Harlem and they're worried they won't get a fare back from there. Number two, you're overweight, and number three, you're Black.' I was stunned."

Patricia has been overweight since junior high, and as a young adult she had come to love herself in spite of her size. She was proud of her appearance and dressed accordingly. But sometimes the indignities she had to suffer because of her weight could overwhelm her.

She grew up with her parents and siblings in a Black neighborhood in a small town in North Carolina. Patricia was surrounded by a warm, loving family, including aunts, uncles, and cousins who were in and out of her home on a daily basis. In this affirming extended family of men and women of varying sizes and dimensions, Patricia internalized the message that being large is okay. But the Black community's traditional buffer against the mainstream pressure to be slim appears to be breaking down.

Researchers are finding that while Black women may not want to be quite as slender as the White ideal, a growing number want to be smaller than they are, causing them to chronically diet or abuse laxatives and diuretics to control their weight. Ndidi Moses, a graduate student at Pennsylvania State University, who wrote a master's thesis on the body images presented in music videos, believes it is the increased presence of Black women in the media that is fueling this trend.[19] On television, in film, in commercials and magazine advertisements, African American women who are portrayed as successful and attractive are nearly always thin, Moses says, while their heavier counterparts continue to project the stereotypical personas of a Sapphire or Mammy—loud and desexualized. She adds that even in some rap music videos purporting to celebrate voluptuous women, the dancers tend to be slim.

Moses believes that it is her generation, those ranging in age from 18 to 30, who are struggling most with whether to shift and conform to this thin ideal. "You fight with those images every day, with what you're told you should be [by the media] and what you've been told you should be by your family," says Moses, 24. "I think my generation is the transition generation, saying they don't want to be thin, but spending their time dieting. They'll explain that they simply want to get 'toned up,' 'in shape,' or to have a smaller waist," she says. "They can't say, 'I want to be thin' because that's not culturally acceptable."

Ruth Striegel-Moore of Wesleyan University says that the growing desire to be thin may be a cost of access.[20] As Black women are given more opportunities to participate in the mainstream culture, they are also subjected to the same pressures. Conversely, some experts suspect that Black women living and working in less diverse environments are less impacted by the idea that thinner is more beautiful.

Mona, 27, illustrates that conflict. Working in an all-White office in Atlanta, where many of the women are obsessed with their weight, she focuses more on her own. She knows that she doesn't have a serious weight problem. After being very thin for most of her life, she began to gain weight after college, adding 30 pounds to her medium-sized, 5-foot, 7-inch frame. Now Mona wears a size 10. But while she looks well-proportioned and healthy to us, she says that she now pauses in the mirror when she dresses in the morning and again when she takes her clothes off at night. She has become self-conscious. While she once enjoyed finally having a fuller figure, she now puts her body down.

"I'm considerably bigger than I'm used to but I didn't really think about it until I started working where I am now, where I'm the only Black and everybody else is a toothpick," says Mona, a mortgage broker. One coworker works out every day, and another constantly frets about her weight even though she is probably no bigger than a size 4. "She told me that since she was 10 years old she's been on diets. And I could not believe it. . . . I'm a cow compared to them. I could definitely tone and I probably could stand to lose 10 or 20 pounds, but I don't want to be as thin as I was." While Mona is concerned about her weight, it has not become an obsession. However, a growing number of Black women are beginning to lose control.

Unfortunately, the belief that Black women are not susceptible to eating disorders may lead many who are suffering to ignore their illness or to fail to get psychological and medical care. Another study by Striegel-Moore and colleagues, published in 2001, concluded that women of color who have eating disorders usually do not receive treatment and are underdiagnosed.[21] The same cultural stigma that prevents many Black women from receiving help for depression may also keep them from getting treatment for an eating disorder.

The Kinkiness of Kinks

The quest to be thin is a relatively new manifestation of shifting for Black women. But for generations they have struggled to maintain self-worth in a society that has failed to see the beauty in African hair, which is often kinky and short.

For many Black women, hair, more than anything else, is a symbol of how they must shift to be accepted. Hair makes a powerful statement—how it is worn is often taken as an indicator of the woman's specific identity, stance, or station in life. Thus, for Black women, decisions about whether to cut their hair, straighten it, braid it, or knot it are choices heavy with import because they know that the beholder will decide upon a meaning of his or her own. Dreadlocks are a sign of self-confidence and spiritual consciousness—or is the wearer a "radical"? A shorn head is a stroke of boldness, beauty and rebellion—or is it one of insanity? Straightened hair—short and neat or long and styled is classy and sophisticated—or is it a betrayal?

When Blacks began to toss away their chemical relaxers and hot combs in the 1960s and wear their hair naturally, it was a signal that they had discovered their own beauty and were rejecting the indoctrination that said anything uniquely Black was bad. Afros—huge puffs of hair sprung free from scalps that for years had been singed by pressing combs and lathered with lye—symbolized Black power and autonomy. Even some of the ebony afro picks used to comb them had a clenched fist etched into the handle. Rastafarians flung their ropelike dreadlocks in the faces of those who were more conservative. Black women who usually braided their hair at night and tucked it under a scarf began to wear their cornrows in the sunshine. But many Whites were put off, and many older Blacks, raised to hide their uniqueness as best they could, were appalled.

Thirty-five years later, some Whites and Blacks still see showing off one's hair in its natural state as an act of defiance—or as simply unattractive. Though many Black women today are wearing their hair naturally, beauty shops continue to do brisk business with African Americans coming in to get their hair straightened or lengthened with artificial hair, many of them coping, perhaps subconsciously with the lily complex. In New York City, one woman talks admiringly of certain hairdressers who have "growing hands," the ability to get their clients' hair to grow several inches longer. And in recent years, some Black women who wear braids or dreadlocks have had to battle with employers who felt their hairstyles were inappropriate for the workplace, even having to sue for the simple right to wear their hair the way they please.[22] While there seems to be a growing acceptance of natural hairstyles in corporate environments, many Black women continue to feel that they must shift their hairdos to fit into a professional setting and to avoid being unduly scrutinized. And many Black women learn this message very early on.

As a child growing up in a Black neighborhood outside Los Angeles, Gwen wore braces, thick glasses, and orthopedic shoes. She was short and squat in build and was nicknamed "tight end" by her cousins. But in spite of all these indignities, what bothered Gwen the most was her very thick, difficult-to-comb, disappointingly short hair.

"I never thought of myself as attractive," she says. "I felt *all* White people were beautiful. I had a big thing with hair—long hair. If you had long hair, you were instantly glorious, glamorous, beautiful. And so if you had anything other than long hair, you were not." Gwen says that when her mother cared for her hair, it always felt "like a production, a project, an imposition, inconvenient," yet it was something that *had* to be done to make Gwen presentable. Seeing Gwen now, a 52-year-old attorney who exudes elegance, it was hard for us to envision the "ugly" child whom she abhorred. Her short straightened hair was layered, framing a strikingly beautiful face. Gwen talks about how she gradually made amends with her hair, although one of her solutions is to keep a standing appointment with her hairdresser at the crack of dawn every Saturday morning. Armed with one of the best stylists in the city, she feels comfortable facing her clients and the rest of society.

Like Gwen, nearly every Black woman has memories of weekends spent in a hot kitchen, a pressing comb heating on the stove. Marti, 29, is one of the many who sat in a chair on Saturday mornings, the smell of Ultra Sheen pomade and burnt hair wafting through the house. She liked the way her hair looked when it was straight, barrettes dangling from fine pigtails. But she hated what it took to achieve it. "I just wished I could comb it and just go because it was horrible having my hair pressed."

But in high school, Marti made a discovery. She began to wear her hair in braids, and she loved the freedom that they gave her. Rather than deal with chemicals or curling irons, her hair was now wash-and-wear. She could hop out of bed in the morning, spritz her braids with oil, and be ready to go. Her hair grew thick and strong when not subjected to a weekly bout with the pressing comb. She could swim and run her track meets with abandon, not worried that her straightened hair would "go back" to its natural state, because it was already as it should be—natural and plaited.

But now, Marti rarely wears the style that she feels most comfortable with. "I used to wear braids all the time, but when I graduated from school, it was a conscious decision to take them out," says Marti, a sales representative for a pharmaceutical company in Chicago. After she's been on a job for a while, become familiar to her peers, and proved her competence and ability to fit in, Marti occasionally switches back to a braided hairstyle. But she never goes into an interview or a new job experience without first straightening her hair.

"I don't want to be prejudged. And I think a lot of times it's real easy for them to do that because they don't understand how our hair works, and that it's just a hairstyle. I think it's just different to them. And I don't know what their experience has been with Black women with braids. I don't know what they think but I don't want that to be the reason that I don't get the job."

Some women take more risks than Marti and Gwen. We spoke with two women who wear dreadlocks in conservative work environments. Yet they also go to great lengths to hide or disguise their hair. Mavis, 39, an administrator of a nonprofit community agency in Ohio whose responsibilities include networking with potential donors, has developed the habit of securing an advance roster of who will be attending a business meeting or a work-related social function. What she does with her dreadlocks depends on the politics of the crowd. "When I'm meeting with conservative people whose support is critical, I pull back my locks as a way of neutralizing attention to them."

On the days she's on-duty, Rolanda, 34, who works for a law enforcement agency in the San Francisco area, carefully wraps and secures her waist-length dreads, crown-like around her head. "I'm sure that if I hadn't done that, they would have found any way they could to fire me. I think it would have been too Black for them, so people never see my hair down."

These women have had to learn to shift to manage society's limited tolerance of Black hair. They've had to shift to ensure that they aren't immediately dismissed based on their hairdos, and that they're given a chance to demonstrate their competence and skills. They've had to shift so that their hair doesn't blind their employers to their talents.

While both Rolanda and Mavis face bias when they head to work but are quite comfortable at home, Alana and Miriam, best friends in Atlanta, tell stories that illustrate the yo-yo paradox, the pressure to shift between two vastly different identities, or sets of expectations.

Alana, 25, recalls how just two years ago, she was told by an administrator at a Black-owned employment agency that she would need to take out her braids before she was sent on interviews. Alana obliged, getting her hair straightened, and during her career as a school counselor, she never returned to her braided style. For the past year she has coiffed her brown locks in a sleek bob.

But when she and Miriam ventured out one night to a poetry slam at a smoky café downtown, straightened hair no longer seemed like such a good idea. The flickering candles cast shadows on the walls, making Nubian knots and dreadlocked crowns look 3 feet high. Poets took to the stage, their hair knitted in cornrows, scalps swathed in scarves, rapping about poverty, hypocrisy—and self-love. The whole place seemed to pulsate, the crowd reveling in its negritude. And Alana with her bob and Miriam with her relaxed shoulder-length hair felt out of step. They felt conspicuous, like they didn't quite fit. Miriam dreaded that someone would stand up, grab the mike, and recite a poem lambasting whitewashed, lye-fried sisters. It never happened. No one criticized them to their faces or from the stage. And the women managed to have a decent time. But they spent much of the evening feeling self-conscious, uncomfortable in themselves, maybe even a little guilty. They worried that some might look at them as sellouts, that some would assume that they had bought lock, stock, and barrel into the lily complex. They worried all night simply because they had chosen to straighten their hair.

The Color of Beauty

The message that White beauty is the standard to aspire to has clearly come from the broader society. But centuries of discrimination and the perpetuation of distortions and stereotypes have led many African Americans to internalize these negative messages, to reject their physical selves, to not recognize their own beauty and to be as critical of each other as the mainstream.

Colorism is perhaps the most potent manifestation of the lily complex. Many of the women we interviewed shared painful experiences of being snubbed or scorned simply because of their skin tone. Colorism is so pervasive and toxic that it affects the self-esteem of Black women all along the color spectrum. Talisa, a 22-year-old from southern California, says that she is often considered too dark to be pretty or told, "You're cute for a dark-skinned girl." Fifty-four-year-old Shirley speaks through tears about how for years she was made to feel guilty by darker-complexioned Blacks because she had light skin. And a 49-year-old probation officer from Kentucky named Nora talks about how her medium brown in-between color has always been an issue for her. "Sometimes I think that I'm just smack in the middle. I'm not really, really light. I'm not dark, dark, dark. I'm just smack in that dang middle, and sometimes it seems like an ugly spot to be in." For so many women, skin color is a source of shame.

Shelly, a 26-year-old college student in New York, talks about her grandmother, who was "color-struck," showing favoritism to her light-skinned grandchildren. The lighter-complexioned children got taken to Red Lobster for dinner, to a Michael Jackson concert, to Disneyland. Shelly, on the other hand, her skin the color of coffee dappled with just a hint of cream, "was only good enough to clean house." She internalized the notion that dark is ugly, dreamed of looking like Vanessa L. Williams, and for several years shunned dark men.

Tall and stocky, with very dark skin, Briana, 24, grew up in Oklahoma believing that she was "ugly and overweight and had unattractive hair." Since early adolescence, she has tried to minimize attention to her skin color by losing weight, and she even had a special prayer. "I can remember laying in bed at night and thinking, 'Oh, if I'm not going to be light, God, please help me get skinny, and then nobody's going to worry about the color of my skin.'" She found she could shed 10 to 20 pounds rather easily but invariably after a few months, she regained every one of them.

When Briana got engaged to Reginald three years ago, she was concerned about how she would be received by her fiancé's fair-skinned family. Only moments before the wedding ceremony, as Briana stood trembling with anticipation and emotion, she met Reginald's grandmother for the first time—a blue-eyed, long-haired, White-looking matriarch. There was no question that Briana wasn't accepted. The grandmother walked up to her and said, "Well, I'll be damned if he marries this Black bitch. Her skin is too dark. We're trying to make beautiful White babies, and there's no way that she can give me no White baby. Get her out of my face."

This was hardly an auspicious beginning. Briana walked down the aisle on the verge of tears, deeply wounded by the words she'd just heard. But she recited the marriage vows anyway, and a year later, she gave birth to a very light-skinned baby boy. They named him Reginald Jr. "I took my baby to her, before this woman who told me I would never be a part of her family, just to see her face. And she took my baby, and she kissed him, and she loved him. And she had the nerve to tell me, 'Thank you, looks like we might have hope with this one.'"

While Briana deeply resented the grandmother's extreme colorism, she found herself feeling badly about her deep brown complexion and eager to win the elderly woman's approval through a fair-skinned baby. "I wanted her to know that I had to be a beautiful person 'cause I created something beautiful. I was dark-skinned and it didn't matter. I had a beautiful baby."

Barely 18 years old and recently graduated from high school, Marisa fought for years to be treated in a humane fashion by her peers. It seemed almost impossible for her classmates to see her as pretty or attractive. From her early days in elementary school, Black students teased her about her deep mocha-colored skin and her height. Throughout grade school, she usually towered 4 inches over the next tallest girl in the class. Children would call her "beanpole," "too-tall," "blackie," and "cockroach," "They wouldn't like to touch the same things as I would because they'd say, 'She's got dark skin; she's got the cooties.' It was a normal thing for me to get called names and be picked on."

Much of the time Marisa felt isolated and alone. She'd try to manufacture a sniffle or cough so her parents would let her stay home from school. And though she prayed that her classmates would outgrow this behavior by the teen years, the taunting continued into high school.

But then things suddenly changed. Marisa's town had an annual Founder's Day celebration, and one high school senior was crowned "Miss

Springfield." Though not labeled a beauty contest, Miss Springfield was always very attractive and personable, an excellent student and an active volunteer. On a lark, Marisa decided to apply. She endured three rounds of tryouts, along with close to a hundred of her peers, and to her surprise, she was one of five finalists, which was considered quite an honor. After her photo and name appeared in the local paper, Marisa could feel the difference in how she was viewed by her classmates. The teasing and taunting ceased. Marisa's view is that because she was seen as beautiful enough to be a finalist, dark skin, tall frame and all, she was no longer a pariah. Being validated by the larger, predominantly White community made her more acceptable within her own. She felt redeemed for all the years of abuse that she had tolerated, and most importantly, she began to see herself as a pretty young woman.

It is sad and striking that women as young as Marisa, Briana, and Shelly are still wrestling with blatant color discrimination from other Blacks. The 1960s rallying cry "Black is beautiful" is now almost 40 years old, but the message has not been fully grasped, internalized, and passed on. For many Black women, the notion that there's something wrong with their color burrows inside. Many are left with a sense of shame, a lack of confidence, and feelings of inadequacy. For some women this means diminishing themselves and accepting situations that are truly intolerable.

Cynthia, 35, first met Lucas, a chiropractor, at the grocery store. She was standing on her tippy-toes, trying to reach the paper towels when he walked up and grabbed them for her. He was tall, his dimples framed a gleaming smile, and his deep brown skin matched her own.

Their relationship was always ambiguous. He took her phone number and called immediately, and in the coming months, they grew intimate. But he hesitated to commit to her. They were lovers and friends, but never, for some reason, girlfriend and boyfriend. During those times, when the friendship overtook the romance, Lucas would see other women. And Cynthia noticed that all of his other dates had light skin.

"He would always refer to them as pretty or beautiful. He *never* referred to me that way," she says, her voice etched in pain. "He would have magazines and he would never ever find a dark-skinned woman, even on the magazine cover, that he would refer to as pretty. I really internalized that."

Cynthia would come home from a night out with Lucas, an evening in which he gazed longingly at a light-skinned waitress or a tan model in a magazine, and soak her pillow with tears. "Oh yeah, I cried a lot. I loved him. I really loved him." She put on makeup and straightened her kinky mane, but she knew there was only so much a dark-brown woman with nappy hair could do. "I can't change my skin color," she says. "I can't change my hair texture. No. I could not change myself. It was very painful. I'm telling you, my heart was very hurt. But I couldn't change it."

Throughout her life, there had been moments when she wished she could have. She and her darker-skinned cousin Tressa saw the color distinctions within their own family from the time they were young. Each of them had lighter-skinned siblings, Darryl and Kiara, who were irresponsible, did poorly in school, and were bratty and rude. Yet their grandparents, aunts, and uncles adored them. "We were always doing well in school. We got high marks," she said of herself and Tressa. "But we never seemed to be able to get the praise that our siblings got because they were supposedly good-looking, because they were high yellow. They always made us feel inferior. They always had 'good hair.' We had 'bad hair.' They always looked good; we always looked bad. There was always this comparison, and yet I felt like we're working hard, we're doing all these things and we're getting no credit. And they don't do anything except show up and they're special."

Cynthia began to expect rejection from other Blacks. "I always thought I would be inferior because of my skin color. . . . Even to this day it's something I still carry."

A successful interior decorator, Cynthia says that she has come to appreciate her own beauty. "At this point in my life I wouldn't change anything. If you had asked me 20 years ago, I would definitely have said I would have been lighter-skinned. I would have long hair, have 'good hair.' Today I would change nothing. I'm happy with the way I look. I've become confident in myself. When I walk into a room now, I know I can take the room."

Yet it was clear in our conversation that Cynthia's confidence in her appearance, her sense of self, was still wavering. The thought still crosses her mind when a light-skinned woman enters the room, that the other woman will be the center of attention. And she endured her painful relationship with Lucas for more than three years. Her affection for him, and a lack of self-esteem, compelled her to stay involved with a man who did not respect or appreciate her enough to tell her just once that she was beautiful. "I really thought that he would love me so much that it would become a nonissue," she says of her dark skin. "It never did. I guess it was a fantasy."

Cynthia, Marisa, Briana, and Shelly illustrate colorism's typical pattern, with dark skin being seen as bad, ugly, and evil, and light skin as good, pure, and beautiful. But sometimes it operates in the reverse. Sometimes women are victimized for being too light.

Clarice, a 51-year-old nurse in southern California, who with her vanilla-colored skin and dark, wavy hair has often been mistaken for Hispanic, fights tears as she talks about the verbal abuse in her own home while growing up. Her siblings, who were darker than she, would call her "high yellow" or say, "Get your dirty, yellow butt over here." Visiting cousins asked, "How can you be so light?" and teased that she must have a different father than her brothers and sisters.

"It caused me such hang-ups that I used to scrub my arms until they turned red, trying to get rid of the dirty yellow," explains Clarice. "I used to stay out in the sun trying to get dark. I've been sunburned a few times."

Clarice's experience represents yet another troubling phenomenon. Sometimes, Black people, both men and women, who have bought into the lily complex, who have internalized the notion that dark skin, kinky hair, and African features are ugly, turn on other Blacks who are less African in appearance. It's what psychologists call "reaction formation," an unconscious defense mechanism by which the person transforms a threatening or unacceptable belief—"Dark-skinned people like me are ugly"—into its opposite—"Unlike me, light-skinned people are ugly." To accomplish this maneuver, the defense mechanism of splitting is also utilized. Splitting involves seeing one part as all good and the other part as all bad. In other words,

"Both light and dark can't be beautiful. One must be good and one must be bad."

So the coffee-colored person who has been bombarded with negative imagery about Blackness finds a way to handle the uncomfortable thought that she's fundamentally not okay. Reaction formation and splitting allow her to foist the problem onto someone else in a desperate attempt to hold onto her own fragile sense of self. This is sophisticated and dangerous cognitive and emotional shifting that occurs outside the person's conscious awareness.

The more common type of colorism, bias against Blacks who have dark complexions, is easier to come by. It doesn't require as many subconscious machinations. To dislike those of dark skin, one need only listen to society's messages and mimic them. Perpetrators of color bias often unknowingly identify with mainstream society, with its values and beliefs. These people have internalized the aggressor. They've gained a sense of inner power by taking on the views of the seemingly indomitable enemy. Their sense of self, and by extension, their sense of community, has shifted thoroughly.

Skin-color bias is not only perpetuated by Blacks upon Blacks. Non-Blacks can be colorist as well. They too make distinctions about good and bad, smart and stupid, pretty and ugly, based on skin color gradations. Many women are well aware that being Black in ethnicity and dark in color can compound a woman's difficulties in the majority culture.

Some Black women who have light complexions are uncomfortable with the distinction made by Whites between themselves and their darker sisters. Dawn, a 55-year-old high school librarian from Minnesota, says, "I think my light skin made me more acceptable to White people, and they really embrace me. When I had my first child, I prayed for a brown baby so that he or she wouldn't have to deal with that uncertain position."

Pamela, a 44-year-old high school graduate and the single mother of 27-year-old twin daughters and a 15-year-old son, suffers at the other end of the color spectrum. Tall, wiry, and energetic, she has a face whose lines bear witness to the trials she's endured. After getting pregnant during her senior year of high school, and with no family support, Pamela landed on welfare and has languished there most of her life. In her struggles to get work, she has become keenly aware of how her almost blue-black complexion impacts her prospects. She talks about how routinely she feels dismissed when she walks into companies and applies for a position:

> I've been building myself to have enough background and training to get a job. I've got good clerical skills, but when I go for a job, they don't want dark Black women. I've been to lots of job fairs, tried to apply to the city. But I just got so tired over a five-year period. I was just hitting that pavement, getting out there, dressing up nice, going to interviews. They know what they want. And for some, all the people there were light-skinned or of another race. Nobody wanted to open the door for me!

Pamela sums up race and color relations this way. "There's a deep rift, like a scar, an open wound, like a gash, a deep, deep rooted hate against dark-skinned Blacks, and I don't know why it is, but it's there. It's still there, and it's just as strong as it ever has been."

Black Women in Hollywood

The media, the chronicler and mirror of American life, is also the creator of images. If billboards and television shows connect thinness with beauty and wealth, the association takes hold in the national psyche. If movies tend to depict less desirable women as darker-skinned or fuller-figured, those are the images that the public internalizes and believes. Brenda, a 22-year-old executive assistant in northern California, says that she struggles to keep her self-esteem afloat in the face of such portrayals. "The media image of what beauty is takes a toll on my self-image. I have been raised to love my body with all of its curves, yet always being bombarded with women no larger than a size 6 sometimes makes me feel fat and ugly, when I know I'm not. Black women are naturally thick and healthy, and I have to make a conscious effort to remember that and love who I am."

Black women like Brenda are constantly struck with messages that they are not beautiful. Andrea moved to New York almost a decade ago to develop a career as a Broadway set designer. She came to talk to us with her hair straightened and with an added weave that flowed partway down her back. "I used to wear a short afro and I loved it," she says. "But here on Broadway, it's such a male-oriented business, and I know men like hair, so that's why my hair is long now. Anything I do at this point is for my business."

Andrea is even considering getting aqua-colored contact lenses because she knows that they will add to how attractive she is deemed in this beauty-conscious environment. Despite all of this shifting, Andrea fundamentally feels good about being Black. Yet she senses she's got to change herself to play the game.

Tanya, an actress living in Los Angeles, makes it clear how blatant the message that Black women are not considered attractive can be. Tanya speaks of how she and many other darker-skinned actresses shift emotionally after each rejection, struggling to feel beautiful when they are told in casting call after casting call that they are not. They numb their sadness and anxiety and ignore their insecurities to get back up the next morning and try again. Tanya's stories, told from inside America's dream factory, make it easier to understand why so many Black women suffer from the lily complex; why they feel they are no one's fantasy, and why they feel inadequate as they watch the embodiment of society's rigid beauty standards flicker across the screen.

Petite and striking, with dark brown eyes and rich cocoa skin, Tanya, 41, was not prepared for what occurred at a casting call in Los Angeles one afternoon in the late 1980s.

She hadn't been in California long when an agent called and said that she wanted Tanya to try out for a part in a television movie. "So I went over to the casting place. And they had me stand there. You had to read in front of a camera. And then they put the bag up next to me. A brown bag. And they put the brown bag up next to me and they said 'Okay, thank you.' I never did read." That evening her girlfriend asked her how the audition went, and after Tanya described what happened, her friend exclaimed, "'Girl they gave you the paper bag test!' She said that down South, elitist Black colleges used to make you stand next to a paper bag, and if you were darker than the paper bag you could be rejected."

The role ultimately went to a very fair-skinned Black actress with straight hair. "I guess they weren't going to waste my time," Tanya says of those in charge of the casting call. "But that was very hurtful. I was really sad after she told me that. And then just other experiences where I would want to audition for the leading lady and they would say, 'Oh you're too dark.' I heard that so many times it's not even funny."

In the "breakdowns," descriptions of how a casting director envisions a certain character, Tanya says that they often specify skin shade for roles featuring Black women. "That shouldn't be," she says. "They don't realize what they're saying and doing. Instead of saying 'African American woman, 20 to 30,' it will say 'African American woman, very fair, 20 to 30—fair skin, light skin, lighter complexion.'"

Tanya remembers a television show in which the White casting director said that she specifically had Tanya in mind for the part of an upscale professional. A very light-skinned friend of Tanya's had tried out for the role. But when Tanya asked her friend's agent and then another to send her in to audition, they refused. She came to understand that in their minds, upscale, professional, and dark-complexioned did not go together.

Tanya feels the images of Black women have gotten a bit more diverse, and she continues to persevere. She vigilantly tries to stamp out the lily complex when she sees it in others. She has walked out on auditions where casting directors have tried to make her play a lesser role than what she was seeking. And she is trying to create opportunities for herself and other Black actors by writing scripts and pitching her own projects. She has shifted into a proactive stance, reshaping her career in order to counter the bigotry she has experienced as a darker-complexioned Black actress.

But sometimes she succumbs to how others would define her, if only for a moment. "I even got the outfit for when I go to play the prisoner's wife," she says. "I know just what I'm going to put on. Some old jeans, a gray turtleneck that's loose. And a hat."

Shattering the Mirror

And yet, while some are trapped inside America's mirror, many others shatter it and craft their own. Ernestine, a 53-year-old loan coordinator from Louisiana, says, "One of my great joys is my full lips on a red lipstick day!" Dinah, a 30-year-old police officer from Connecticut, says, "I love my big rear end. I love the way I walk, talk, breathe air. I love the fact that Black women come in all shapes and sizes. We don't all look the same." And Syrah, a 30-year-old logistics manager from Georgia, says, "I love my complexion; I think I'm a beautiful brown. I love my 'stereotypical' Black woman figure. I'm a size 16, and even though I want to lose weight, I only want to get back down to a 12 or 14. To go any lower would eliminate my Black woman's glory on the top and bottom."

A number of women say that they have managed to sidestep the lily complex, learning to believe in their own natural beauty and to change in their appearance only to please themselves.

Rhonda, a 61-year-old teacher in upstate New York, speaks of her journey to wholeness. "In my early years I straightened and later permed my hair so that it would not be kinky. I used words like 'bad' as opposed to 'good' hair, learned to apply makeup to decrease the fullness of my lips and the size of my nose. I was constantly dieting in an effort to decrease the size of my hips. It took my husband's unconditional love for me as a person to make me appreciate me for me."

Paulette, 51, grew up in Birmingham, Alabama, in a family of dark-skinned people who were proud that their blood had not mixed with Whites, unlike most African Americans. She remembers that her mother and father always made her and her sister feel like the most beautiful children in the world, and Paulette didn't doubt it. Except on Saturday morning, when she had to endure the sizzling hot comb like all the other little girls in their tight-knit community. Despite her family's pride, the message seeped through that there was something bad about kinky hair.

Then one day, she picked up a Black community newspaper and noticed a photograph of a woman who wore her hair in a short afro. "She was beautiful to me," Paulette remembers. "When I saw that Black woman . . . that really made an imprint on my brain. I remember that so well. And I remember just staring. And I guess as I was looking, I was looking evidently for the ugliness. . . . I turned that way, and I turned that way, and I looked at her, and I was looking for the ugly. Because this is supposed to be ugly, you know, nappy hair. All Black kids know that."

The memory of that photograph stayed with her, even as Paulette wore fine plaits in her elementary school play, a pressed and curled flip to her high school football games, and a beehive to the senior prom. Then, nearly 30 years ago, Paulette cut off her long hair and stopped straightening it. At times she even shaved her head. There was no dramatic impetus. It was just a look that she wanted to try. And while she knew that some people would react negatively, she was even more surprised by another reaction; over the years, so many Black women have tapped her on the shoulder and told her how much she inspired them. They thanked her for having the courage to be herself.

Paulette explains that on some level, shearing her hair and wearing it natural was a statement, though not a political one. It was a personal affirmation, an expression of her unique style. "I figured hell, if anybody else wanted to, they would do it. That's how I rationalized it. I mean you do it or you don't. You are who you are. You're no less of a person either way. But this is what I'm gonna do. And don't mess with me about it. You don't like it, keep it to yourself."

For Paulette an external transformation followed many years after an internal change, whereas for Reva, now 46, it was the opposite. Reva, a brownie-hued woman, who has wrestled with extra pounds since childhood, grew up in a small town in upstate New York and was the first kid in her area to wear an afro. She decided on the new style one Friday afternoon in junior high when she'd had it with being put down as "Black" and "fat" by her classmates. Always the rebel, she decided, "Okay, I'll show you. The Blacker I am, the better."

She washed out the press and curl and begged her mother to trim her near-shoulder-length hair into an Angela Davis–style afro. Afterward as she gazed into the bathroom mirror, she realized that she was beginning to own her Blackness, yet she continued to see herself, as she always had, as ugly. "I accepted being Black a whole lot sooner than I accepted not being ugly," she says. So while first her hair and later her dashikis seemed to telecast that she felt good about her African beauty, inside she remained the ugly little girl whose skin color and weight were a source of ridicule.

Reva attributes the early Afrocentric exterior to "knowing first of all that I'm *never* going to be blonde-haired and blue-eyed. No matter what I do, it's not going to work. Once I realized that, I had no other choice but to embrace myself totally." But she admits that the process took decades of work. Now as a middle-aged adult, and with the help of a support group for Black women, she's gotten there. She finally accepts herself, loves herself, and feels attractive. The short twists that she's now wearing along with her mud-cloth garments match up with how she's feeling on the inside.

As Reva and many others demonstrate, the lily complex is powerful and hurtful, but it can be surmounted. It is hard to compel the broader society to appreciate the physical bouquet that is Black beauty if African Americans do not do so themselves. The creativity with which Black women style their hair, the fact that their skin shades are a rainbow, and that their features mirror all the peoples of the world are just some of the characteristics that make them admirable and unique. Black beauty, in all its forms, is worth celebrating, at home and in the mainstream.

Traditionally, the African American community has done a remarkable job in blocking out the message that thinness should be achieved at virtually any cost, allowing generations of Black women to appreciate their unique body shapes and to feel beautiful no matter how much the broader society might have disagreed. That buffer must be reinforced. Trying to whittle yourself into a size that is unnatural and using self-destructive methods in order to do it dishonors your body, the physical manifestation of yourself. In extreme cases, it can be fatal.[23] It is important that Black women recognize that they are not immune to eating disorders, and that they truthfully share their fears and obsessions with each other. For those who appear to be dieting too often or acquiring other unhealthy eating or purging habits, Black women should point each other in the direction of professional treatment. Reinforcing the idea that health is most important, whatever size you happen to be, can help slow what appears to be a dangerous trend.

The fixation on weight is just one aspect of the media-fueled overemphasis on external beauty.[24] The rigid, sexist code that says that women must be physically attractive needs to be confronted roundly. Men suffer much less than women from the demands to be a certain color, have a particular hairstyle, and adhere to a specific size and weight. All of us need to work together to challenge the destructive biases about looks and beauty.

Black women can feel more whole not just by carving out spaces where they can speak and act in the ways that feel most natural, but also by embracing every facet of their unique beauty. Similarly other Americans can do much more to assist Black women in their quest for self-acceptance, celebrating the physical diversity of Black women, and thus, ultimately the physical diversity among themselves. As we burst common myths about Black women and encourage people to transcend America's rigid racial codes, beauty will come to be seen more broadly and African American women as well as women and men of all ethnicities and hues will feel more confident about being dark or light, skinny or corpulent, long-haired or nappy-headed.

The wisdom of Justine, a 25-year-old child-care provider from Brooklyn, stays with us, "Beautiful is how you feel and how you look. You have to love who you are—that's the way you were made, beautiful and surely special. If I can't love who I am and what I look like, how can I love or be loved?"

8

FORGING A
DELICATE BALANCE

Romance and Relationships
Between Black Women and Men

*I want to be appreciated for what I do and what I am,
and I don't want to have to suppress. I always find myself
kind of downplaying my independence and my role and
my accomplishments, so they [Black men] don't think
that I'm better than them.*

PATRICIA, 42, WASHINGTON, D.C.

We meet Naomi when she is on the upswing, when she is beginning to put
the pieces back together, reshaping her marriage with her husband Harold.
A 39-year-old associate dean of students at a liberal arts college in New
England, Naomi is a dedicated professional who gives her all to her job. At
work, she is a caretaker, helping to handle the myriad difficult situations
of a few thousand young adult students. But she is also an assertive, no-
nonsense leader, respected for her directness and forthrightness. Though
she works incredibly hard, requiring staff to call her whenever there is a
crisis, even if it interrupts her days off, she is also able to set limits.

Yet at home, in the past, her skills in self-expression and assertion would dissipate. She had convinced herself that her task was to support her husband emotionally and financially no matter what. And when she stumbled upon feelings of resentment, she engaged them for a moment then stuffed them away—until the day came when she no longer could.

She and Harold married 15 years ago, in a huge wedding at her childhood church. He was a very bright, well-educated Black man who had been working for years on his first novel, and who, off and on, taught African American literature as an adjunct professor at various universities in the area. Teaching in that limited way meant that Harold had time for his writing, which was his passion, but it also meant that his contribution to the family income was nominal.

Both Naomi and Harold were politically conscious. They once took a day off work to drive to New York City and participate in the mass protests over the police shooting of African immigrant Amadou Diallo. And Naomi had always been proud that Harold was active in local Black community affairs, serving on various boards and in a number of organizations. In the mornings, as Naomi rushed off to work, Harold would often look up from the newspaper and begin ranting about the latest brother who was being targeted politically. And at the end of many a day, Harold would come home complaining about how poorly he was being treated at the school where he was currently teaching. Naomi was always sympathetic. When Harold announced that because of a racist dean, he had refused to accept an adjunct contract for the following year, Naomi was worried about the financial impact on the family. Still, she rarely spoke up.

They had two boys—5-year-old Trevor and 2-year-old Brandon—and though Naomi spent most of her week on campus, 35 miles away, while Harold worked at home, Harold rarely participated in managing the household and child care. Since Trevor's birth, Naomi had instead developed a sophisticated network of formal and informal child-care providers and chauffeurs who helped out when she worked late and on weekends. When she had to travel out of town for professional meetings, she usually took the children with her and arranged for child care at the hotel where she stayed.

After a particularly challenging spring term, when there was a flurry of suicide attempts on campus and Trevor was hospitalized for two days with severe asthma, Naomi reluctantly decided to see a therapist. At that moment, she had reached a breaking point. She was physically and emotionally exhausted and depressed, and she realized this had been building over the past two years. She loved Harold dearly and deeply admired his talent and flair for writing as well as his commitment to and advocacy in the local Black community, but she could no longer identify what she was getting from the relationship. He was a good friend, but he wasn't much of a partner. They were financially strapped, and he could barely pay the utility bills. Though he loved the children, he was content to play with them an hour or so a day during breaks from his writing. Yet Harold always found time to have lunch or dinner with friends or fellow politicos.

Through her therapy, Naomi began to acknowledge that there were problems in the marriage. She came to realize that their friendship was based on her listening to and being a sounding board for Harold, whereas he seemed uninterested in her life at the college and the challenges that she navigated daily.

Naomi also came to realize that she had colluded with Harold's disengagement. Concerned about his struggles as a Black man and an activist and the uphill battle to establish himself as a novelist, she had done whatever she could to soften his experience of oppression. But she'd shifted so much in order to cushion Harold that she'd endangered her own health. Naomi had become another Sisterella—a depressed Black woman, silencing her self and shifting into hyperperformance largely to protect and support Harold, whom she saw as a besieged Black man. But carrying both her load and his meant emotional collapse.

Black women are often forced to shift in intimate relationships with Black men, sublimating their own needs, strengths, and desires. Our research reveals that many Black women feel pressured to calibrate their directness and assertiveness, and minimize their accomplishments and success, to make the men in their lives comfortable with and confident in their manhood. It is a supreme irony that Black women, mythologized and relied upon for their strength, so often have to submerge their savvy and fortitude to make their partners feel at ease—an aspect of the yo-yo paradox, the pressure to conform to conflicting expectations and demands. On the other hand, some worry that if they show their vulnerabilities, some men may take advantage of them or deem them weak and unstable. Black women pursuing Black men romantically often face a host of troubling questions: *Can I be myself and have a relationship? Do I need to suppress my strengths, pull back, hide my success in order to keep him? Must I be a superwoman to hold onto my partner? Does staying in this relationship put my health and well-being at risk?*

All intimate relationships are challenging, and many of the areas of conflict that Black men and women experience mirror those found in any relationship, regardless of the couple's ethnicity. There are struggles over space, power, money, sex—over how much of the outside world's pressures should be brought home each day and how much needs to be shut out. But the variable of race adds significant extra layers to these oft-fought battles. For both Black men and women, having to shift to deal with constant bigotry in the larger society can intensify the need for home to be a refuge where you can truly be yourself. Thus, it is all the more frustrating and wearying when home life is not idyllic and calm, when there are additional demands to change one's self to accommodate someone else. And, in part, because of these pressures, home life for African American women increasingly means life without a partner.

Our nation is in the midst of a precipitous decline in the rate of marriage among African Americans, and racial oppression and the lack of economic opportunity, particularly for Black males, are major culprits.[1] According to the U.S. Census Bureau, in 2000, 38 percent of Black women ages 18 and older had never married.[2] In contrast 18 percent of White women and 25 percent of Hispanic women in the same age group had never married. Moreover, the divorce rate for Black women is higher than that for women of other ethnic groups.[3]

Unfortunately, Black women are dealing with a stacked deck. Because of the high rates of homicide, suicide, and imprisonment among African American men,[4] the ratio of Black adult heterosexual women to men is skewed, and much more dramatically than in the general population. Black women outnumber Black men roughly 19 to 17,[5] and they live seven years longer on average.[6] Moreover, more Black women than Black men are in the labor force,[7] and there's evidence that unemployment and underemployment affect Black men's willingness to marry and stay wed.[8]

Of course being single is a viable way of life as well, a sliver of the relationship spectrum that also encompasses the choice to marry, to divorce and marry again, or to be part of a same-sex relationship. But for Black women, especially Black women with children, being single too often means a lifetime of poverty. Thirty-five percent of Black female-led families are living below the poverty level.[9] And while many Black women embrace singlehood and the freedom and opportunities that it provides, others bemoan the fact that they are not able to form a lasting partnership, and that they're left to raise children without the benefit of a father in the home.

Nineteen percent of the women we surveyed, and 39 percent of those who were single and had never been married, volunteered that the major difficulty for them as Black women had to do with relationships with Black men, including garnering respect, developing a healthy relationship, finding a good man who's not intimidated, and getting support from their children's father. Among our survey respondents, difficulties in relationships with Black men ranked second only to difficulties in the job market or workplace.

The research literature shows that African Americans who are married experience higher levels of personal happiness and general life satisfaction than Blacks who have never married or who are separated or divorced.[10] Yet Black married women experience more life stress than their male counterparts,[11] and, notably, Black women are less satisfied with their marriages than White women.[12] Middle-class Black women who are married also experience more depression than White middle-class married women.[13] These findings tell us that while marriage generally contributes to emotional well-being, this is more true for men than for women, and more likely for Whites than for African Americans.

Ironically, although marriage rates and degrees of marital satisfaction are lower among African Americans than in the general population, Blacks have been particularly successful in forging egalitarian relationships. Black married couples are more likely to be open and fluid with regard to the responsibilities and tasks that men and women assume,[14] perhaps because the history of slavery and oppression has made it harder to cling to a strict set of narrowly defined behaviors or codes based on gender. To some extent both Black men *and* women have had to nurture children, cook, clean, and work outside the home.

But gender bias still creeps into Black couples' relationships. And the White community's centuries-old fear and subsequent devaluation of Black manhood has contributed to the problem. Since being a man is often defined as being in charge and being in control, and since Black men are so often denied this opportunity, they sometimes turn to relationships to realize this aim. And Black women at times collude with this solution, shifting out of the way at home so that their partner can feel empowered. Yet our research shows that Black women sometimes shift so much that they endure emotional or physical abuse. The silencing of the self, as we discussed in an earlier chapter, can lead to depression. And submissiveness can put Black women at risk for contracting deadly sexually transmitted diseases, like AIDS. A diminution of the self, a lack of self-assertion—in other words, too much shifting—can kill.

Functioning for Two: Buffeting the Impact of Racism

While Black women clearly suffer the blows of racism, society's irrational fears about Black people and its physical violence against them are manifestations of bigotry that more often fall on Black men.[15] Ironically many of the descendents of Whites who enslaved and brutalized Blacks are fearful of Black male violence. Some of the children of White men, who sexually assaulted and raped Black women during slavery and for a century after, have created the myth of the Black male sexual predator whose target is White women. When Black men come home at the end of a day, whether they've been hanging out on the corner, looking for employment, working in a menial job, or functioning as a professional, they often bring with them the residue of these myths that pervade our culture. They often need someone who can absorb and deflect the stings of racism. And at times the wife or girlfriend becomes that person. She may become the recipient of anger that he could not express outside the home, the target of rage that he had to contain to function in his workaday life. At other times she is expected to understand the weight of his burden, to adapt accordingly, perhaps by tolerating his joblessness, his emotional unavailability, or his absence from the home as he commiserates with friends over a bottle. Black women sometimes find themselves suppressing parts of their selves in order to keep the peace or overfunctioning in order to pick up the slack. Ashanti, a 25-year-old student and office manager from Los Angeles, sums up the problem succinctly: "I'm overly sensitive to their plight but don't feel that they're sensitive to mine."

The tendency of Black women to overfunction, to step in, handle responsibilities and keep going even when their partners have retreated and withdrawn, converges with the myth of Black women as unshakable. Because of societal assumptions and cultural expectations within the Black community, many feel that they have no choice but to play that role, but many say that they would rather not have to. Pauline, a 27-year-old single, paralegal from Greensboro, North Carolina, says that her major difficulty as a Black woman is "carrying the weight of the world on my shoulders and not feeling as though I can depend on men to help me out."

Rachel, a 35-year-old attorney in Washington, D.C., has both overfunctioned and suppressed her own needs in relationships, giving much and asking little. A petite, attractive woman, with shoulder-length braids and pale gray eyes, Rachel has almost always dated highly educated professionals—doctors, professors, politicians, attorneys. Though she is often just as accomplished, Rachel so admires what some of her boyfriends have been able to achieve despite racism that she often finds herself saying and doing little when they treat her insensitively or with disrespect. In too many of her relationships, she has written out her boyfriends' bills, planned their vacations, even cleaned their apartments.

She has listened to their complaints about work and brushed aside the pain she felt when they refused to listen to hers.

One boyfriend, a physician named William, was particularly inattentive. While she went out of her way to cater to his needs—running errands for him on her lunch breaks, staying up late listening to his work woes when she needed rest to deal with her own stressful job—he would often let her down. He was thoughtless, telling Rachel he was going to social functions thrown by his ex-wife and refusing to take her. And he was selfish, growing impatient when Rachel occasionally tried to talk about her own professional frustrations. So it was disappointing, but not a surprise, when three years ago, he completely forgot her birthday.

They spent the evening together, watching *Butch Cassidy and the Sundance Kid* on television, as though it was a night like any other. When finally she reminded him that she was now 32, he gave her a kiss, wished her happy birthday, and promised he'd go "all out" the next year. Rachel, struggling to hold back tears, went to the bathroom to collect herself. But by the next day, when she told incredulous friends what had happened, she chalked up William's forgetfulness to the stress he was under at work. A month later, when William turned 43, she baked him a cake, bought him a pair of monogrammed cuff links, and took him to Georgia Brown's, his favorite restaurant, for dinner.

"I was in that relationship at least a year longer than I should have been," Rachel says of her time with William. "But you know, some of my not confronting him [was based on] giving him all kinds of leeway because he was this good, smart man. 'He's intelligent, he worked really hard, he's oppressed in a White man's world,' that kind of thing."

And Rachel has realized that her acceptance of such shoddy treatment is also fueled by the endless discussions among her Black female friends about the shortage of marriageable Black men, and her own ensuing fears that if she demands too much, she will spend her lifetime alone.

"I think that's part of it. It's out there. 'You're so lucky to have a good man.' And the message that there are no good Black men, that you're lucky if the man does anything at all. . . . I think in my previous relationships, I probably went by their agenda more than mine. I didn't sit and think, 'Am I happy? What would make me happy?' It was more 'How do I keep him or how do I make him happy?'"

Crystal, the 26-year-old mother of a 4-month-old daughter, is unmarried and younger than Naomi and Rachel, but she has found herself falling into a similar pattern with men. Crystal earned her bachelor's and master's degrees and is currently working as a program officer at a community foundation in southern California. But while she has thrived educationally and professionally, she has recently given up hope of a continued relationship with her daughter's father or even of his being responsible and involved in the child's care. Crystal has become aware of her own tendency to overfunction for boyfriends who seem chronically beleaguered and in need, and to demand little of them in return. "Always what happens is the person becomes dependent on me in terms of financial support, emotional support. You're taking care of that person as if they're your child and not a significant other. And that brings stress into the relationship because you're taking care of them and not yourself." Now that Crystal has her own child, it is more difficult to tolerate a romantic relationship where much of the time she feels cast in the role of mother.

Fully Emancipated?

Black women often get mixed messages about how they should behave in their relationships with men. On the one hand, many feel pressed to excel educationally and careerwise, raise children single-handedly, and overfunction for their male partners, but there are often countervailing pressures to submit and yield to Black men and to make sure that they never eclipse a boyfriend or spouse. It is a stark manifestation of the yo-yo paradox. They are compelled to take charge yet also pressured to be docile to defeat stereotypes that they are less ladylike than other women, to bolster the egos of Black men, and to adhere to society's general codes about the roles of women versus men.

Not all Black women succumb to this push and pull. In our survey, we asked women if they ever felt they needed to downplay their abilities or strengths with Black men, and a number of respondents said,

"Never!" or even "Hell, no!" Camille, a 35-year-old divorced administrator of a community-based organization in Mobile, Alabama, admits
that she feels the pressure. "I recognize the expectation that some men
may have for me to 'dumb down.'" But she quickly adds, "I never have
and I never will!" Thelma, a 59-year-old divorced realtor from Maryland, says that she doesn't diminish her talents, but notes, "I guess
that's why I've had three failed marriages." Other women, like Shana,
an 18-year-old single college student from Miami, don't feel pushed to
play down their gifts. "I don't have to downplay anything," Shana says.
"The Black men I deal with are strong and confident about where they
are in life right now. They bring experiences into my life that will help
me to become a better and stronger Black woman."

But 40 percent of the respondents said that in relationships with
Black men, they have at times hidden their talents under a bushel. For
example, Jasmine, a 30-year-old single administrative assistant from
Pasadena, California, says, "I don't completely and freely express myself
for fear that I may intimidate them. I rarely challenge them for fear that
I may end up isolating myself." Bernadette, a 37-year-old single manager
in the Department of Labor in Washington, D.C., writes, "In relationships I am forced to be much more submissive and appear less capable to
keep the peace." Penny, a 39-year-old married department store supervisor from Culver City, California, says that she's constantly diminishing her talents. "Being married, I do this daily. When I don't, I'm often
told that I think too highly of myself or that I know it all."

Gina, at 26, is already frustrated with the pressure from Black male
partners to fit into rigid gender roles. The mother of two toddlers who
are barely a year apart in age, Gina has been on welfare but currently
works for an insurance company handling claims. She lives with her
children and their father, Greg, but she has recently come to realize
that the relationship with Greg has no future. Currently living in
Cleveland, Gina is considering leaving the area to start a new life near
her relatives in Tallahassee, Florida.

"Some of our Black brothers feel that our role is to cook and clean
and walk behind our men," she says. "A lot of us are outspoken. I don't
bite my tongue, and Greg feels sometimes that I should. I'm not going to

bite my tongue just for you to be comfortable. I'm not going to let you say what you have to say and then not say what I have to say in return."

Toni, even younger than Gina at age 21, has found herself criticized in relationships for her independence. "A good example is my ex-boyfriend," she says. "He thought I was too strong, too aggressive, and too independent, and that made me unfeminine, because I don't wait for men to do things for me. If I want flowers, I go and buy myself flowers. If I want to give myself a nice dinner, I take myself out to dinner. If I want to see a movie, I go see a movie, and I think he was a little threatened by that. It was very frustrating because I wanted him to understand that I'm used to doing things for myself out of necessity. I'm a very big advocate of being a whole person and being okay by yourself, but I wanted our relationship to work."

Joyce is just now getting back into the dating scene and trying to figure out how to present herself to men in a way that's attractive and appealing. She doesn't particularly like what she's learning. A 37-year-old bank manager in New York City, she's never been married, but she was in an on again, off again relationship for 12 years until she finally realized a couple of years ago that it was going nowhere. On the dating scene, she's been getting the not-so-subtle message that she must tone herself down to spark the interest of someone new. "I feel like I can't talk as much or I shouldn't talk as much. I never used to think that I was attractive enough. Now I feel more attractive, but I'm too intellectual or I'm too experienced. I have too much life. There's no demureness about me, nothing about me that will make the primal 'I want to take care of you' thing in men come out."

Like Joyce, Nzinga too is wrestling with what is appealing to Black men. The difference is that Nzinga, a 39-year-old woman from Cambridge, Massachusetts, is already married. But her husband Sam moved out a few months ago after becoming romantically involved with a White woman, and she believes that he chose his new girlfriend because she was more docile than Nzinga. "I know what Black men want from us," she says. "I think they want the White woman—someone who's mealy-mouthed, who's not opinionated. I think they want that type of woman, and we're not. The thing that really upset me is here I am, more educated than this little woman, and here I am work-ing, two kids, pretty much supporting him, supporting myself, support-ing the kids, and you go and run to this White girl? And for what?"

For Renee, it was her maturity and increasing independence that destroyed her marriage. Now 40 and living in Bowling Green, Ken-tucky, she was married at 19 to a man who was nine years older. She chronicles the ending:

> When I hit 30 and started saying, "No, I don't want to do that, I want to do this," then we started having problems. If I acqui-esced, the world was a wonderful place. I started getting to the point where I would disagree with him—it could be something simple like he said, "Let's have string beans," and I said, "No, let's have brussels sprouts." It got to the point where he started feeling like, "You don't love me. You don't listen to anything I have to say." In my mind, it was his weakness and insecurity. When I'd come home with things that I was feeling really good about at work, it didn't make him feel good. There was no support for anything I was trying to do. As long as he laid down the law and controlled the situation, everything was fine. I gave up a lot of who I was.

Renee adds, "It was painful to give myself up." While her husband was comfortable with her working outside the home, sharing financial responsibility for the family, he felt that she should be silent and submis-sive as soon as she crossed the threshold into their living room. During the latter years of her marriage, Renee saw a therapist to help her with feelings of depression and to provide a sounding board as she wrestled with the difficult decision of whether to file for divorce. When she finally decided to leave her husband, she was relieved. Renee ran into an acquaintance who said, "You look great! What's going on in your life? You've lost weight. You look fit. There's a glow about you!" "I hadn't really told anybody what was going on," says Renee. "From that point for-ward, I said I'm not going to give up who I am for anybody."

But for many women it is a struggle to be both self-reliant and to make their partners feel indispensable. "I don't know or understand how to keep my independence but yet allow him to feel needed," says Anisa, a 26-year-old married civil engineer from Phoenix. Nicole, a 46-year-old divorced banker from Austin, Texas, sums up her major hardship as a Black woman: "balancing being independent and self-sufficient yet sensitive to not emasculate the Black man." Harriet, a 44-year-old married woman from Somerset, New Jersey, who works in marketing, says her major difficulty is "packaging the strength and vision within without overshadowing my partner."

Ironically, while many Black women feel pressured in relationships to be less independent and self-reliant, being more needy and dependent can at times leave them feeling at risk. It can be a no-win situation, both for those who are used to taking control at work and in other areas of their lives, as well as for those who have exposed their vulnerabilities in the past only to be taken advantage of. Saudia, a 45-year-old divorced mother in Dallas, longs to have a partner, in part to share the burden of round-the-clock parenting, maintaining the house, and all the ups and downs of life. She'd like to be able to let her guard down, to not have to be so strong all the time, but she also fears being seen as dependent. "I want to be able to be comfortable in my vulnerability. I've been exploited for my vulnerability in relationships with Black men. It's been seen as weakness rather than as softness or kindness."

Ultimately, says Aja, a 29-year-old single health-care consultant from New Haven, Connecticut, honesty in relationships is paramount. She shares her philosophy with us: "Men, especially in relationships, should always know the real me. If we aren't comfortable with each other, we shouldn't be together. I don't believe that downplaying my abilities will make the 'right' man find me more interesting." Listening to Aja, suddenly it seems quite simple.

The Underside of Success: When Competition Strains the Relationship

If independence and strength are sometimes seen as a problem, being successful can cause even more turmoil. Numerous women feel direct and indirect pressure to downplay or hide their career successes from their boyfriends or husbands. For some, the same promotion or pay raise that was cause for jubilation at work creates tension and strain at home. Of course, it's one thing to not be satisfied with one's life, to yearn for something different. It's another thing to feel like you can't fully appreciate your achievements because of others' criticism or resentment. The message too many Black women hear from some Black men is that if they were less ambitious and less accomplished, they'd be more desirable. Such commentary casts a shadow over their lives. It makes some feel guilty about their successes, and steals a portion of their joy.

Nanette, a 29-year-old social worker from Bloomfield, Connecticut, writes that her achievements are making it harder to find a relationship. "The more I acquire as a Black woman—successful job, education, house—the harder it is to find a self-confident Black man." Neva, a 38-year-old data entry supervisor in High Point, North Carolina, says that a former boyfriend constantly complained that she was trying to show him up. "I was in a relationship for 11½ years and had more income coming in than my live-in boyfriend. I've always moved up because I need to stay challenged, and I was always being accused of trying to make him look stupid." And Elizabeth, a 54-year-old small business owner who lives just outside Boston, declares that she has had to contend with her husband's jealousy. "My very spouse became unhappy that I always succeeded or got ahead of him. He complained when I made greater income."

Shirelle, a 49-year-old divorced mother and scientist who works in a pharmaceutical laboratory in Rochester, New York, is not looking for financial help from a man. Instead, she yearns for a companion with whom she can share interests and communicate openly. "It would take the right person to know that equality is not based on matching funds," she quips. Shirelle, who lives in a modest townhouse close to the center of the city, sometimes finds that she's denigrated by men for being middle-class and ambitious: "I think they're insecure with themselves intellectually and they don't know how much they have to offer, so it's almost acted out on you, as 'Oh, you think you're a White girl.

You want to live in the White world.' Why? Because you want to have a house, you want to have a car, you want to send your kids to college? It's mind-boggling. It's such a cop out. It's not fair."

Unlike Shirelle, Ethel, age 68, has never been married. She is retired from 40 years of teaching, and we met with her one afternoon in her bungalow on the South Side of Chicago. Ethel grew up in a small town in Alabama, begged her parents to send her to Tuskegee for college, and arrived there by bus, all alone, with less than $5 in her pocket. She found a job as a live-in nanny to cover her room and board, and she picked up part-time jobs on campus to pay for tuition, books, and other expenses. Academically, she'd been poorly prepared, but she persevered, taking an extra year and a half to earn her bachelor's degree. She migrated north where some of her mother's relatives lived, began teaching kindergarten, did graduate studies, and developed a satisfying career as a high school history teacher. Looking back from the vantage point of six decades, Ethel confides that she feels successful in everything she's taken on, except for romantic relationships with men. After years of soul-searching and agonizing, she realizes that those very successes and her many goals impeded her love life.

> I have always, always, always had a problem with Black men. I used to think it was something wrong with me, but now I know it's because I was ambitious at a very early age, and I had goals. I don't think I was that smart. I just have mother wit. I must accomplish something every year in my life. Men always had problems with me. I was bossy, I wanted too much. I wanted a home, and I wanted to travel—that kind of thing. I might want some diamond earrings. I might buy myself a mink coat, and I might want a chandelier. It was always, "You want too much." I felt that I could never be happy married. Every time I heard that I wanted too much, I knew this wasn't the person for me, no matter how I felt about him. I'd been thinking all these years that I would meet the right man and I just never did, and for years, I just thought it was my fault. I don't anymore because I'm basically satisfied with my life. And I

always managed to get things for myself, when I was able. I wasn't expecting them to get these things for me.

Ethel has come to terms with remaining single while holding fast to her desires and ambitions, but Beverly has just begun to squarely face these issues. We talked with her one afternoon in her midtown Manhattan office, complete with a panoramic view of the Hudson River. Beverly, who is single and 43, began work after college as a copy editor, gradually worked her way up the publishing house ladder, and serves now as an editor and earns a six-figure salary.

Beverly reveals how painful it is to date Black men who are uncomfortable with her career success and her income. "I don't have to tell them how much I make, but they just kind of know, and they make a lot of cracks about it, and that's when I realize that they're not comfortable. I was dating this guy, and whenever we would go out, he would say to the waiter or the salesperson, 'She's rich, oh, she's rich!' I was so embarrassed. I would go through the floor. I'd tell him, 'Don't say that,' and he was like, 'You know I was kidding.'"

She laughs about it now, but at the time, it was far from funny. What's not amusing, Beverly adds, is how difficult it is to feel really good about her own accomplishments.

I do in my heart believe that it would be nice for African American men to be head of the household, and I do have strong feelings about that traditional picture, so therefore, since I don't live it, I find myself often being somewhat embarrassed about driving a BMW and buying a condo that costs more than $300,000, and therefore, I can't feel as good about things as I'd like to. I can't enjoy it totally, because in my heart, I want the traditional husband who is doing better than me. I want to show that the African American family structure is intact, but by my own success, I feel that sometimes I represent the opposite—that the African American family structure is not intact. Is being an independent, successful woman really success?

The message that Beverly, Ethel, and Shirelle hear from too many Black men is that if they were less accomplished, they'd be more appealing. Such a message, and the self-flagellation that it can cause, is particularly dangerous for the Black community, which desperately needs more, not fewer, leaders who will make a difference in the quality of life for all.

Not Pretty Enough: Finding Love Under the Specter of the Lily Complex

Black women may be asked to downplay their intellect and diminish their success, but they're often expected to play up their beauty. Too often Black women have to shift to manage Black men's expectations, desires, and demands about how they should look. It is a chore that women of all ethnicities take on, but living in the shadow of the lily complex—the belief that the way to be beautiful is to look "White"—makes Black women feel even greater pressure. Some women alter, amend, and augment themselves to try to fit the mainstream mold, while others, convinced that it is no use, give up altogether and are wracked with feelings of inadequacy and low self-esteem.

Marilyn has been traumatized by Black men's beauty ideals. A 43-year-old jazz singer, who has recorded and toured with some of the greats in the industry, Marilyn is 5 feet, 9 inches, with deep brown skin and a trim figure. She came to the interview dressed youthfully in Black form-fitting slacks and a fuchsia rib-knit top. When asked about her romantic relationships, she became edgy and it was clear that she didn't care to share the details of her experiences. "That's a very touchy subject for me," she begins. "I've not found any Black men that I feel were loving enough. Either I felt like I wasn't attractive enough for them or wasn't light enough, especially professional Black men, that they wanted a lighter-skinned woman. So I've just never found love, and I have tried."

Cheryl, a 35-year-old sales clerk who has been separated from her husband for the past two years, believes that many Black men are choosing White women because they simply find them more beautiful.

She says, "We have a war going on with the White women taking the good Black men. And the sisters, the Black women, are just as good as the White woman. But the Black men who're making millions—the doctors, the lawyers, the athletes—are going after the White woman. And I think that's the reason why we change our appearance." Cheryl, who wears her hair straightened with an added weave, says that Black women try to look more European, wearing colored contact lenses, for example, in order to be more appealing to Black men: "We're hoping a Black man will say, 'Hey, she's just as pretty as this White woman right here.' We're trying to get their attention."

For Claudia, wearing colored contact lenses is not likely to make a difference. For her, skin color is the issue. Claudia is the color of ebony, and she often stands out as the darkest person in a group. She grew up in a suburb of San Francisco, went off to college at Northwestern University, and then secured a job in urban planning in Chicago, settling there. Her Black college roommate and close friend Shannon grew up on the south side of the Windy City and became Claudia's entry point to the town's social life. But somehow, no matter how many sorority functions and house parties Shannon took her to, no matter how many Black professional networking lunches she attended, Claudia never seemed to really connect or be accepted, and she was almost never asked out. As we talk with her, we realize that she certainly has the personality to attract people; she's witty, vivacious, and warm. But she confides that eligible men chat with her in an obligatory but distracted fashion before rapidly moving on.

Finally, one evening when she and Shannon were sipping merlot in Claudia's apartment, Shannon pulled her coat. Hemming and hawing, Shannon, whose complexion resembles light caramel, said, "I think it's your skin color." From that point on, Claudia began to look more closely at who talked to whom, for how long, and how cliques were formed. As she began to take stock of the dynamics, she realized that, "You could be a dark somebody, but you couldn't really be a dark nobody. If you were already somebody, then being dark was okay, but if you were nobody like me, then being dark was a liability." Claudia still clung to the hope that once people got to know her, they'd look beyond her skin color. Now at age 36, 14 years after her move to Chicago, she admits that she doesn't feel this has happened. It feels like the message is, "You're a nice person, but you're just way too dark." Claudia says that though it helps to understand what's going on and to realize that she's not the one with a problem, it still hurts.

In contrast to Claudia, Veronique, a 25-year-old registered nurse in Tuscaloosa, Alabama, worries that Black men seek her out because of her pinkish-white skin color and long, naturally straight hair. She's keenly aware of the prevailing messages that light skin and flowing hair make you beautiful, and she hates it when Black men want to date her simply because of her appearance. When asked how she knows that guys are riveted to her color and hair rather than to her person, she says, "they often just tell you right out." Veronique sees these appearance fetishes as a way of dividing Black women, and though she could potentially benefit from these biases, they've never felt advantageous. Like her darker sisters, she struggles with whether her true beauty is being seen.

A central motif in Iris's life has been concern about whether she's deemed attractive or even physically acceptable to Black men. Iris, 21, is almost 6 feet tall and rail-thin. With her baby face, she looks like a tall junior high school student, yet she speaks with a maturity and thoughtfulness beyond her years. A full-time college senior in Virginia, she remembers an experience that deeply scarred her when she was 11 years old:

> When I was in D.C., I was actually traumatized, because I've always been small. I don't put on weight. It's just not going to happen. I've always felt inadequate to Black men, because I tend to view Black men as wanting bigger women, wanting more voluptuous women, wanting curvier women. I remember when I was in sixth grade, I was slow to develop—not slow, I did it in my own time, but the girls that I was friends with were much bigger than I was. I was the only one who didn't wear a bra, and I'll never forget, one day I was eating lunch, and these guys in my class were sitting behind me, and they were talking

about all of the girls in my class, and about who had the biggest breasts and who had the biggest butt, and they got to me, and I don't know if they realized I was sitting there, but they may not have even cared, because they were guys and they were being obnoxious. And they were talking about, wow, she doesn't have breasts, and she doesn't have this, and saying things like, "You couldn't do anything with her." And hearing them talk about me, that was horrible. That was where it started, me feeling really bad, and that sort of started me avoiding Black guys.

The following year Iris's family moved to a largely White suburb in Montgomery County, Maryland, so Iris was able, without a lot of effort, to steer clear of Black boys. She adds, "After we moved, I developed this attraction to White males, I think, because I was trying to be White. And I felt uncomfortable with Black guys, because I felt inadequate with them. And even though I've dealt with some of this, it's still hard to get rid of those feelings of inadequacy."

Of course, many Black men adore and luxuriate in the beauty of Black women, in all of its sizes and shapes and colors. And for many Black women, being seen as beautiful by Black men is an important antidote to the larger society's racist messages. Jean, a 52-year-old married woman, whose hair is very short and natural, who's a little thick around the middle, who never shaves her legs, and who hardly owns a pair of heels, talks about how wonderful it is to be told by her husband of 28 years that she is absolutely gorgeous: "Sometimes I think that I should grow out my hair and do something more feminine with it, and sometimes I wonder, 'Am I the only Black woman who still doesn't shave her legs?' And I would like to lose a few pounds for me, but you know, Randy really loves me and he thinks I'm just beautiful."

The Dangers of Submission—Abuse and Violence

Shifting can be deadly. Some Black women, because of the pressures to defer to and accommodate men, stay in abusive relationships, putting themselves at risk for emotional and physical injury or even death. Other women put their lives at risk when their difficulty asserting themselves with men means that they say yes to sex when they really mean no or when they don't insist on the use of safer-sex practices. Some of these women get pregnant when they're not ready, and are left to raise a child alone. Other women contract sexually transmitted diseases, including HIV, the virus that causes AIDS. Submission, which is often touted as a virtue in women, is actually a vice when it means that women are not able to take care of, protect, and defend themselves. Submission to an abusive or uncaring partner can be among the most dangerous of shifts.

Intimate partner violence is a serious problem in the United States. Far too many women and men are threatened or physically attacked by a current or former boyfriend, girlfriend, or spouse, and sometimes death is the result. Women are far more likely to be victims of partner violence than men, and Black women are more often victims than White, Asian, or Hispanic women.[16]

Maxine, a 40-year-old woman living in Denver, worked for years as a radiology technician and has recently returned to school to finish her bachelor's degree and become credentialed as a teacher. Maxine always assumed that she would marry by her early twenties and have a couple of children by the time she was 30. It has not worked out that way, and Maxine explains why. "I was told I was unattractive because I was fat, and that I wouldn't be wanted because I was fat, so whenever I would get some male attention, I'd be so grateful, until I would almost do anything, like 'do whatever to please your man,' and I would end up being hurt.

"I got into a relationship with an abuser, Frank," she says. "He would throw temper tantrums for no apparent reason and yell and rage at me. I was saying stuff like a lot of women, 'Well, he hasn't hit me.' It took my cousin, who's a social worker, to tell me that he was abusing me. I couldn't believe her and I couldn't let him go because we were supposed to get married, and this may be my only shot. My mother, bless her heart, coming from the old school, was telling me to do whatever it takes to get along with him. And I believed everything I'd been taught, like when you get a man, you make him happy."

Maxine shifted dramatically to try to make the relationship work. She tolerated her fiancé's abusiveness. She even denied that it was abuse. Fortunately, Maxine was able to extricate herself before it was too late.

In a review of studies of Black spouse abuse, Odell Uzzell and Wilma Peebles-Wilkins of North Carolina State University conclude that oftentimes Black abused wives blame themselves if the violence occurred when their spouses were unemployed or were drinking.[17] So Black women who have been victimized often bear a double burden—abuse and self-blame. We see this pattern clearly with Regina.

We met with Regina, a 32-year-old married woman, in her home in Decatur, Georgia, where she lives with her 10-year-old son, Marcus. A tall, slender, and commanding woman, Regina was eager to talk about the recent difficulties she'd endured and to share her analysis of Black male-female relationships. Regina's husband Phillip had been incarcerated for four years for burglary and assault with a deadly weapon, and he was soon to be released. He had been a cocaine user who had spiraled out of control. A few months prior to his incarceration, he had moved in with another woman, and Regina had gotten a restraining order to keep him away from the house because he had begun to steal her belongings in order to sell them for drugs. One day he arrived at the house, apparently wanting to reconcile with Regina. When Regina refused to open the door, he broke in. Regina was able to get Marcus out of the house and instruct him to go to a neighbor's and call 911 before Phillip barricaded her in the house. He threatened to kill her, and then cut her under her ear. The police arrived, and 10 tense minutes later—an interlude that seemed to stretch on forever—Phillip released Regina and was carted off to jail.

While it was horrifying that Regina had been held hostage, threatened, and assaulted, what is most surprising is that she doesn't consider herself a victim of abuse. She's excused Phillip for his actions, and she even blames herself. This is particularly notable given that Regina sees herself as a woman who isn't easily trampled by others. She attended college for two years and works as one of several managers in a large food service company that subcontracts with cafeterias throughout the area. She is the only Black person in management there, and has spent lots of energy fighting to be seen by her peers as competent and equal. At work, Regina speaks up, advocates for herself, and challenges coworkers who are dismissive of her. But at home, it's quite different. She explains: "When Phillip met me, I was very independent, doing pretty well on my own, able to take care of myself. I think that makes them feel inferior. You know the old saying, 'The man is supposed to be the king of the house.' And I believe that we do become too dominant with our men. We do need to let our men have some of that because the world takes it away from them. And with Phillip, even now, I don't fault myself, but I will take part of it, because I didn't let him be a man."

Regina wishes she had related to Phillip differently. "If I had to do things over again and knowing what I know now, Phillip would love it, because I would treat him like a king. And I think that would make him, his outlook on things, a lot better, and maybe he wouldn't have turned to drugs to make him feel so manly." It was hard to miss the inch-long scar on Regina's neck, and as we gazed at it, we worried about how she was setting herself up for further abuse once Phillip is released from prison. Regina's sentiments were disturbing and frightening.

More Dangers Ahead—HIV and AIDS

In recent years, the reality of what can occur when a woman shifts too much to accommodate a romantic partner has become devastatingly clear. Black women have the highest rates of HIV (human immunodeficiency virus) and AIDS (acquired immunodeficiency syndrome) of any group of women in the United States. Of the roughly 40,000 new HIV infections each year in the United States, 30 percent occur among women, and 64 percent of those newly infected women are African American.[18] For Black American women between the ages of 25 and 34, AIDS is now the number one killer, according to the Centers for Disease Control and Prevention.[19] The rise in the prevalence of AIDS is primarily due to an increasing number of Black women contracting the virus from sexual relations with HIV-positive men.[20]

Other than abstinence, the consistent and correct use of condoms is known to be the best defense against contracting HIV sexually, and a number of researchers have explored the factors that impact women's use and nonuse of condoms. Gail Wyatt and her colleagues at UCLA deduce from their research that because of the perception of mate unavailability, African American women may not challenge Black cultural norms that encourage unprotected sex.[21] In a study of 128 Black women in San Francisco, Gina M. Wingood and Ralph J. DiClemente of the University of Alabama at Birmingham found that women's assertiveness in asking men to use condoms was a key factor in whether condoms were used.[22] And in a study of 423 Black women in a southern city, Janet S. St. Lawrence of Jackson State University and the Centers for Disease Control and Prevention and her colleagues found that consistent condom users were more likely than inconsistent or nonusers to communicate about AIDS with their partners.[23] In a review of a number of studies of HIV risk among African American and other women, Hortensia Amaro and Anita Raj of Boston University conclude that girls and women who feel that they have less control and less power in influencing relationship decision making are less able to initiate and sustain safer sex behaviors in their relationships.[24] Amaro and Raj invoke the notion of silencing as one way of understanding the gender-based power dynamics that prevent women from insisting on the use of condoms. Thus, while information about safer-sex practices has been available for two decades, the high HIV infection rate of Black women may reflect their relative powerlessness in relationships with men.

People often do not acknowledge to themselves, much less admit to others, aspects of their sexual lives and sexual behavior of which they are ashamed. But Inez, a 28-year-old manager of mental health services in Queens, New York, is at least able to own up to the self-denying behavior she's engaged in over the years. She writes, "In the past I have felt unattractive and therefore engaged in risky sexual

behaviors and in behaviors depictive of low self-esteem in relationships with men."

Lauren, on the other hand, had always been careful. A former
radio disc jockey, Lauren, 42, grew up in Hartford, Connecticut, the
only daughter of a mother who never seemed to know her own worth.
Lauren and her older brother, Ray, endured two stepfathers and count-
less boyfriends who often physically abused them and their mother,
and Lauren vowed that when she became a woman, her life would be
different. "I wanted to marry one of the Jacksons," she says laughing at
her little-girl fantasies. When she got older, and her marital picture
evolved, she wanted "a nice family, like the Huxtables on television."

She left home at 17, enrolling in a community college in a neigh-
boring state and renting an apartment with an older cousin. Eventually, Lauren got an internship at a local smooth jazz radio station, and
before long, her smoky voice became her calling card, landing her a
spot as a disc jockey and sometime talk show host. On the air, life was
good. But away from the station, she had, sadly, fallen into her
mother's pattern.

There was Joey, gorgeous with his ebony eyes and toffee skin, who
charmed the world but belittled her behind closed doors. There was
Jeremy, who insisted that they live together, promising that they would
eventually marry, only to cheat on her constantly and move out a year
and a half after he had moved in. And then there was Paul.

He wasn't particularly handsome, Lauren says, but he had a presence. He was 6 feet 2 inches, and broad-shouldered, and he filled the
room with his rich baritone. He had his own car-detailing business
that afforded him a beautiful four-bedroom home in the suburbs, and
he made a point of giving after-school jobs to teenage boys from some
of the poorest neighborhoods. He took charge, she remembers. "He
seemed like he could take care of me."

Lauren wanted to take it slow. They dated a couple months, going
out to romantic dinners, checking out Will Downing and Ladysmith
Black Mambazo in concert, before they finally made love. By that
time, she was head over heels. She would do anything for this man.
She wanted to be his wife.

So when the sweetness stopped, she was too in love to just walk away. "He would not want to talk and just be mean and evil," she remembers. One minute he loved her, and in the next she could do nothing right. In between the bouts of emotional abuse, Paul would often disappear, taking off for days at a time. He wouldn't even leave Lauren a number where he could be reached. She'd find out Paul was gone when she called his office and was told by his business partner that he was traveling "on business." When Paul returned, and Lauren asked about his trip, he'd tell her to "stop sweating me," and leave her questions hanging in the air.

In hindsight, Lauren says, it was clear that Paul was cheating on her. But, at the time, "I did not pick up on that," she says, "because I was so busy trying to find somebody to love me, instead of trying to love myself. You know, we always try to look for love in all the wrong places, instead of within ourselves. That's the right place."

Lauren had had an HIV test not long before she met Paul, but she never insisted that he take one as well. She didn't want him to feel that she didn't trust him. And after the first two times they made love, when Paul began complaining that the condoms irritated him, they stopped using them. Lauren ignored her misgivings, telling herself that Paul was health-conscious, smart. She didn't have to worry about catching a venereal disease from him—or anything else.

They were together a year, though Paul's kindness toward her had ended months before. Lauren says that she had wanted desperately for things to get better, to not have yet another failed relationship to con- template.

She says that she will never forget the last time that she and Paul slept together. They hadn't seen each other for a couple weeks. Paul had asked her to come over, and when she got there, he told Lauren what she already knew—that it was no longer working. She cried. They sipped wine. And she went to bed with him, a last-ditch effort to try and hold onto the relationship.

But Lauren also remembers the message her instincts tried to send that night. Paul just didn't look well. It was faint, subtle, but there was something about his eyes. "And I did not listen to that, to that little thing inside of me," she says quietly. "And I remember so well me saying to myself, 'He does not look right. Something's wrong. He does not look right.' But I looked past that, and I think that probably was the time that I became infected."

After that evening, she and Paul never spoke again. Eleven months later, Lauren tested positive for HIV. "I found out I was positive in 1996," Lauren says, matter-of-factly. "The first thing I thought was, 'The Lord wouldn't let this happen to me.'" She stayed in denial for the next four years, continuing to work in radio, and only telling her closest relatives and a few friends that she had been infected. But when she became very ill in 2000 and was hospitalized for more than five weeks, she had an epiphany. She told herself, "Either you're going to get better, you're going to get out of here and you're going to let the world know that God is good, or you're going to sit back and you're gonna cry over it, and talk about the things that I didn't do that I coulda did. . . . I prayed, I cried, I fell out, I did all the things that I needed to do, [so] when I came out the hospital I was going to go out and I was going to shout out to the entire world that I have the virus. And who don't like it, I don't care."

She tried to reach out to Paul, leaving him messages that were never returned. And Lauren went on to become an AIDS activist, a powerful speaker who comforts those who are infected and uses her story as a cautionary tale for those who are not, particularly African American youths. "It's just interesting that me contracting the virus would bring me to my real calling," she says, a look of serenity on her face. "And my real calling is to go out and to minister to people and to show them that, hey, this is how it is for me too, but I'm looking beyond that and I'm moving on and I'm on to bigger and better things."

Adoring Our Men, Cherishing Ourselves

For Black women, relationships with Black men carry the potential for danger, sadness, pain, grief, excitement, passion, joy, and, of course, deep and abiding love. While many women in our study shared their struggles to feel powerful and confident and loved in their relationships with men, many others proclaim that they are already in strong, healthy relationships buoyed by mutual respect and affection. Georgia, a 47-year-old woman from Carson, California, who's been married 26 years, has recently left the corporate world to start her own organizational consultation business. She talks passionately about how loving and supportive her husband Bobby has been, particularly as she has transitioned from the security of a well-paying day job with great benefits to the uncertainty and instability of self-employment. Years ago Georgia and Bobby dedicated themselves to keeping their marriage healthy and vibrant. She says, "Now, I love my brothers more than anybody out here. I love Black men! They're rich and wonderful. I sleep with one every night. I bore one. How could I not love them?"

Georgia's passion and love for Black men also extends to herself. "Do I accept negative behavior because they're male and they may have pain? No! I do not. Is it okay for my husband to treat me any way he may choose at any particular moment he's in pain? No! It is not. Is it okay for my son to speak any way he chooses? Will I coddle him because of his pain? No! I will not. Will I comfort him? Will I love him? Will I embrace him? Yes. Will I do that for my husband? Will I hold him and see the tears he cannot shed? Yes. But is anything acceptable? No. Pain is not a license for you to lash out and beat someone else."

As we all know, successful relationships, like Georgia and Bobby's, require work. Couples sometimes get stuck in dysfunctional patterns of relating, but just as people can change and grow, so can relationships; they can be renegotiated and reshaped. When couples are able to acknowledge their differences and their varying needs and desires, when they are able to listen attentively and communicate honestly with each other, they can build a partnership of respect and cooperation.

Compromise is a fundamental part of this process. Some accommodation, ideally by both parties, must take place in order for relationships to survive after the initial honeymoon phase. As we learn more about the other person and realize that he is a separate, clay-footed individual, and that he's not the flawless, idealized being we'd fantasized about, we must adjust and adapt to that reality or end the relationship. As we learn more about ourselves, we realize that we too are not perfect, that we have failings and frailties, and that the wonder of love is that it sees us as better than we are. When couples share their vulnerabilities and fears and come to understand each other more deeply and intimately, they almost always find greater empathy for themselves and their partner, and they often discover a profound and unalterable love.

For Black couples, mired in a nation where racism and sexism are rife, it's especially important to find a way to allow each partner to process and sort through what happens "outside" while simultaneously creating a barrier that provides protection on the "inside"—that preserves a sacred space that only the couple inhabits, a space where love can be nourished. The external myths, stereotypes, and distorted perceptions, the slights, the snubs, and the insults should, as much as possible, be kept at bay. In the best of circumstances, the coupling becomes a bulwark against the larger world—allowing the individuals to lead lives that are somewhat shielded from the assaults. And this bulwark can protect children too, providing a shelter in which they can grow and flourish, as well as modeling for them egalitarian relationships where Black women and men converge as true partners.

Yet couples shouldn't have to do it all on their own. Extended families, churches, and Black organizations can and do work to undergird and strengthen couples' relationships. But clearly more reinforcements are needed. A laudable example is Couples, a group established in 1991 in Los Angeles, with the sole purpose of supporting and strengthening Black married couples. Members of the club meet monthly, engage in social and cultural activities together, and participate in an annual weekend retreat designed to help each couple learn more about their relationship dynamics, improve their relationship skills, and become more intimate.

For some couples, marital counseling is a valuable tool, often helping the partners to learn the communication and problem-solving skills that most of us were never explicitly taught but that we all desperately need to function effectively in a relationship.

For Black women the challenge is to find that delicate balance that allows them to connect and commit without being silenced and victimized, the balance that permits them to engage without losing themselves, to retain their individuality in the midst of partnership, and thus to genuinely and fully love and be loved. To achieve this, both partners must be able to speak for themselves, to share their hearts and souls, and to stand on their own feet. Georgia seems to have found that balance.

Yet partnership is not the only route to fulfillment. Black women are well placed to show that there are many paths to love, happiness, and self-actualization. They show by example that there are numerous healthy family structures. Married with children is only one. And while some Black women long to be in a relationship with a man, others celebrate their singleness and the opportunity to share themselves more fully with a broader circle. Cora, a 60-year-old, never-married community college instructor in Houston, has not given birth to any children, yet she tells story after story of her mentoring relationships and friendships with Black women students at the college. Cora repeatedly goes above and beyond the call of duty—to find housing for a student who is evicted, to advocate for more substantial financial assistance for a student who would otherwise have to drop out, to be available by phone at midnight when a student is going through an emotional crisis.

Still other single Black women find contentment and joy through the opportunity to learn to more fully accept and love themselves. June, a 43-year-old single mother from Akron, Ohio, shares her growing realization with us: "I've got to love myself before I can love anybody else anyway. And that's why, when I'm not in a relationship, when I'm by myself, I'm just great."

9

THE ABCs OF SHIFTING

Mothering Black Children

I feel very strong in family values. And it's not that I want my children to live like they're White, but to live as themselves and be able to achieve—don't let being Black hinder your achieving. Because look at all the statistics: How many of our young Black boys will succeed in life? How many of our young Black girls will succeed compared to the White race? To Hispanics? To Asians? In raising my children, I just feel that we're not trying to be White, we're just trying to be equal.

SYLVIA, 37, CAMDEN, ARKANSAS

Serette, 43, a purchasing specialist for the municipal government, lives in Boston, where she's raising four children. And when she is tending the flowers in her front yard, talking about life with her neighbors, she is only too proud to boast about Thalia, her oldest daughter, who went off to a Black college in Virginia two years ago.

Thalia made the dean's list her first semester, interned at a local radio station this past summer, and pledged Alpha Kappa Alpha during her sophomore year. A communications major, she hopes to work in television when she graduates.

But when she sits back and reflects, Serette remembers how hard the trek was to get Thalia where she is. She had always been a good student and a sweet-natured, obedient daughter. But when she went to high school, Thalia seemed to become an entirely different person. Her freshman year she brought home C's in math and history, subjects in which she had always excelled. She adopted a Southern lilt and dropped slang into conversations at the dinner table, even when her elderly grandmother was present. Sophomore year, she and her best friend, Carla, went and got their belly buttons pierced—and Serette was so terrified about the cleanliness of the shop that she visited it herself and had Thalia tested for hepatitis and HIV. Serette lay awake for several nights, waiting for Thalia to receive her results, which were negative.

Serette also worried constantly about whether Thalia would have a weak moment and become sexually active long before she was ready. In their heart-to-hearts, Thalia always denied that she was having sex with Dwayne, her high school boyfriend. But Dwayne was a year older than Thalia and seemed a little too suave for his own good. He was a popular track star, and Serette could just imagine him sweet-talking Thalia in a darkened movie theater, proclaiming his love and letting Thalia know that if she didn't, many other girls would.

Divorced for 12 years, Serette for the most part fretted alone. Sometimes she and her mostly non-Black coworkers would discuss the universal trials of raising a teenager. But Serette had layers of worries that they could never understand: the youthful transgressions of their children that might be dismissed by a teacher, a potential employer, or a police officer, because they were Asian or White, might irreparably damage her children's futures because they were Black.

She muses about those more difficult times when her daughter was headed down the wrong path:

> She was bombarded with drinking, smoking, and the pressure for sex. . . . All of that is a humongous battle, I think more so for our kids than it is for White middle-class America, who can move away from situations and shelter their kids a little

more, who can put their kids in private school. They can close their doors and hide things like alcohol abuse. They don't have to take it to the clinic for treatment, where everybody knows. They can get the special help. They can get the tutor. Whereas our stuff is in the open, and as such, our business is public, which means it's on display, which means people point at us and say, "See I told you."

For Black mothers, the primary caretakers and socializers of Black children, the extra yet essential tasks needed to raise Black boys and girls add to their already considerable burden. They have the same worries as their White counterparts, but then they have so many more. Our research shows that Black mothers spend significant energy shifting emotionally and psychologically, constantly anticipating and coping with the assaults that their children encounter. They buffer, filter, deflect, defend, bolster, fortify, and embrace—even as they wrestle with their own sadness, fear, and anger about what their children must endure as Black people in this society.

Black mothers must constantly decide whether the challenges and disappointments their children face are race-specific. They must figure out whether Johnny really was disruptive in class or was targeted because he is an energetic little Black boy; whether Tanya received a poor mark in seventh grade English class because she wrote a mediocre final essay or simply because the teacher is White and viewed her through racist eyes. Black mothers struggle too to protect their girls from sexualized images and messages, as well as from outright sexual abuse and exploitation, even as they try to convince them that they are attractive whether or not they reflect the mainstream ideal.

And in the midst of teaching their children the multiplication tables and drumming in warnings never to talk to strangers, Black mothers must also offer their children primers on shifting. They must teach their children that knowing when to be rambunctious and when to be quiet and obedient can mean the difference between placement in a gifted program or being shunted into a special education class and down a dead-end road; that shifting can save their lives if they encounter a trigger-happy policeman—or a violent youth. African American mothers have the daunting task of making their children aware of the discrimination they may one day face, yet convincing them not to give up on life before it truly starts, to recognize society's double standards and negative messages, yet not be filled with hatred of others or themselves.

While dispensing these lessons, many Black mothers may have to answer questions that they have yet to personally resolve—when to roll over, when to fight back, how to respond, how to shift. And how do you hold onto a positive feeling about yourself through it all? How do you build an internal strength that's impervious to the myriad external assaults?

In the United States there are more than 5 million Black mothers with children under 18 in the home. While 41 percent of these mothers are married, the other 59 percent are single parents,[1] and single mothers are raising more than half of the Black children in the United States.[2] It is a particularly tough job because about half of the children in Black female-led families struggle in poverty.[3] Yet more Black mothers (78 percent) than White (72 percent) or Latina (62 percent) mothers with children under 18 are in the labor force,[4] and thus juggling outside work with the responsibilities of parenting.

The truth is that the majority of Black mothers have managed, in spite of the realities of single parenthood, poverty, prejudice, and limited opportunities, to beat the odds and raise healthy and productive young men and women. However, oft-told myths continue to obstruct the many positive attributes and accomplishments of Black mothers today. In the first half of the last century, Black women were stereotyped as Mammys—caustic and unkempt, caring more about White children than about their own. That image was supplanted in the national psyche by the archetypal welfare queen, an irresponsible, unmarried teenager who loved her government handouts more than her sons and daughters, or worse, the crack monster, who at the height of the drug plague in the 1980s was portrayed as a woman who would use her last dollar for a vial of cocaine and let her own baby go hungry. Since the 1960s, in the social sciences as well as in the mass media, Black mothers have often been maligned as the root cause of problems in the Black family and the Black community.[5] They have been denigrated as castrating matriarchs who make families dysfunctional and who are largely responsible for the social ills that some Black children and youth face—delinquency, gang membership, and teenage pregnancy.

Stung by such portrayals, the women we surveyed and interviewed, 58 percent of whom are mothers, speak of the real-life truths that contradict the hurtful myths. They speak of the strength, wisdom, and love of their mothers, their grandmothers, their sisters, and themselves. But they speak, too, of profound fears and anxieties. They speak of shifting.

Home Schooling—Race 101: Racially Socializing Black Children

While the task of all parents is to educate and socialize their sons and daughters, Black parents must also teach their children about the meaning and dynamics of race. Across color lines, mothers are the primary socializers of children, and Black mothers have the additional task of being the primary *racial* socializers, of developing child-rearing approaches and strategies to prepare their children to live in a racially charged America. Racial socialization means raising a child to like herself, to have positive feelings about and connections with the Black community, and to be competent and successful in the broader society while carefully navigating bigotry and discrimination.[6]

Reporting on the National Survey of Black Americans, Michael Thornton of the University of Wisconsin at Madison and his colleagues noted that two-thirds of Black parents convey racial socialization messages—messages about what it means to be Black.[7] Thornton's analysis, as well as other studies on racial socialization, indicate that mothers are more likely than fathers to rise to the occasion by teaching their children how to handle the daily assaults of racism.[8]

"I feel like I have to teach them some of the same lessons I learned about America and White America and dealing with it, without making them racist," says Faith, a 36-year-old mother in Ohio, who with her husband is raising a son and daughter. "And that's very, very challenging and I'm not even sure that I know how to do it. My son is 7 and I think about what is he going to get, where is he going to live, and when is he going to hear that N word. And so we have that burden. And then we have to teach them all the cultural things. What's going to happen if you slip and say something in front of a White person. 'This is what you say in front of them, this is what you don't say.' All of that stuff on top of the ABC's and 1, 2, 3's."

Black mothers struggle to achieve the right balance between educating their children about race and racism so that the child feels good about herself and is realistic in her approach to the world, and overwhelming the child, such that she gives up altogether. They must decide how long to wrap her in a cocoon, be it by enrolling her in an Afrocentric learning academy, or simply staying silent on the subject of bigotry, and when they must expose the child to life's inequities. And they constantly wonder: *How much is enough? How much is too much? What can a 6-year-old handle? What must a 12-year-old be aware of? Am I exposing my child to enough Black history and culture? Will my child be able to interact comfortably with people of other cultures and races? Will my child be "Black" enough? Will my child become too "White"?* The question of how long to shelter and when to teach haunts many.

Toni, a married mother of two living in the suburbs of Washington, D.C., was unsure when to tell Kyle and Avery about the hostility they might one day face. She says that it was lessons about the past that compelled her to tell them the realities of the present:

> I didn't initiate it with them. Their school did with Black History Month, with Martin Luther King. So in the last couple of years . . . they brought the questions to me. "Mama did you know White people didn't used to do this?" or "Some White people did this." And so I went over the stories with them. We got books at the library, we do our Black history projects and I just try to stress to them that what they're learning about is history and there were even some good people then. And still

there are some people that don't like Black people. And they are like "Why? God doesn't like that." So they're trying to figure it out within themselves and I just stay with the truth and try not to overburden them as well.

Some mothers are forced to talk to their children about discrimination after they experience such cruelty firsthand. Ruth, a 42-year-old mother on public assistance, living in southern California's San Fernando Valley, anguishes over the emotional brutality heaped on her 9-year-old son, Robert, by classmates:

Even though he's at a mixed school, kids pick on him. It's very subtle. Certain things kids do to let him know "You're not quite as good as we are," to let him know "We're running the show, just do what we say." For me that's a hurtful thing because I see my kid suffering and hurt by this racial stereotyping. . . . He feels bad about it sometimes. He asks me, "Mama, why am I Black? Why am I made this way? Why don't people like me?" It fills me with so much bitterness because of what I've been through and what my grandparents went through. We still haven't come to realize human equality. There still is that division of race. And I can't fight it alone. All I can do is just get a grip on myself and just keep pushing my kids around it. And just keep letting them know that they're somebody and they come from a rich heritage.

While she encourages him to ignore the slights and believe in himself, she fears her words are no match for the anger that must be growing inside him.

I don't have a lot of the things that my kids see other kids have, and it's hurtful for them. . . . My kids see the struggles that I go through as a single mom, and they see when people discriminate against me too, like how people treat me standing in the line in the store. They see how people treat me on the bus.

They see how cab drivers treat me. They just see how individual people treat me going down the street. It makes me feel bad
that my boy has to see me going through this in this day and
era, as a young boy. And this is instilling hate; this is instilling
hiding it in his heart so when he grows up, he's going to have
some bitterness in him. Now this is going to come out later, and
they're going to want to know, "What's wrong with you?" And
they don't understand that they instilled this in my boy.

Delores and her husband Joe, who live in an ethnically mixed area
in Denver, are trying hard to prevent the sorts of problems that Ruth's
young son is already contending with. They were delighted to find a
Black private elementary school for Renita, for kindergarten. They
wanted to make sure that their daughter was in a nurturing school
environment and in a place that fostered her identity as a Black girl.
For a couple of years, the school seemed perfect. It had high academic
standards and a strong curriculum, with an emphasis on African heritage, history, and culture. Renita excelled academically and seemed to
thrive emotionally.

But as Renita entered third grade, the social dynamics of the classroom began to change. The girls in the class became more cliquish.
Some girls who were new to the class further fueled this trend, and
Renita, who is chubby, suddenly became the brunt of teasing and social
ostracism. Delores and her husband started getting reports that Renita
was getting into physical fights at school. They were shocked because
Renita had never been aggressive or violent. But in spite of numerous
visits to the school, discussions with the teacher and principal, and
talks with Renita, the fighting and the calls from the school escalated.
Renita also seemed increasingly isolated and withdrawn, even when
away from the classroom. Finally, after much agonizing and soul
searching, Delores and Joe made the decision, in the middle of the academic year, to move Renita to another school—a private, predominantly White institution.

They felt that they were compromising their principles in making
the decision. They believed strongly that an Afrocentric environment

was healthiest for Renita, but they knew it didn't make sense to keep her where she was if it was no longer working. At the new school, Renita began to be her old self, to make friends, and to interact comfortably with her peers. Delores and Joe are relieved but still worried about the long-term impact of this change. They worry that Renita will lose out by not being in a more Afrocentric school environment, that she will not get the extra reinforcement that she needs to succeed, and that she will encounter discrimination before she is mature enough to handle it. But they do not have many options. There is no other Black-run elementary school in the area.

Tiptoeing Through the Streets: Tutorials in Shifting

The racial situations that Black mothers must prepare their children to handle range from inequities in the classroom and cruel words on the playground to scenarios far more brutal. Many mothers worry about whether their children will be assaulted by peers, arrested unfairly, or beaten by the police. Some worry about whether their children will make it home at the end of each day.

For these reasons, and many others, the lessons in shifting often have to begin early. Helen, 48, and her husband, Ray, raised their only child, now a young adult, in a predominantly White town outside of Chicago. Helen says that the tutorials in shifting began when Derek was a toddler.

Raising a Black boy in a White environment is about giving him small details of survival, such as, early on, at age 4, this little child had to learn to go in a store, buy something, and get a bag. I'd tell him, "You must always ask for a bag, any time you buy a little this or a little that. You ask for the bag and you ask for the receipt." I deliberately took him into settings in which he had to look and not touch, and learn not to put his hands in his pockets. Details and details. . . . I would tell him, "if you visit one of your [White] friends and the friend isn't home and the mama's there, do not go into the house. Wait for the child on the porch." I would never have given that kind of advice if his friends were Black. . . . Trick or treat, I used to hate it, because I always felt that he was the most vulnerable. . . . Teaching him that he couldn't play the same way as White boys because the White teachers would see it differently.

For Helen, raising Derek involved constant and ongoing monitoring, educating, and interceding. She adds, "Being in a predominantly White setting, I felt that I had to be on it. Everything was intentional. Every aspect was intentional parenting."

This need to be hypervigilant in teaching Black children how to protect themselves also stands out with Ruth, who is raising her children as a single parent and living in very different circumstances than Helen. Though she is pleased to have found an apartment in an area that she feels is "less gang-plagued" than others, she still wrestles with anxiety and feelings of powerlessness as she anticipates the dangers her children face in their neighborhood and beyond. "I'm so worried about my boy," she remarks. "He's already been attacked by the gangs in the neighborhood. By bigger boys—one boy was 12 and one was 9 and my son was just 6 or 7 at the time. . . . The kids in the neighborhood have tried to push my girls into gangs also. I try to watch my 16-year-old all the time. Other girls are rough with her; they push her around. . . . Darker [complexioned] boys and girls, they get the bulk of the hatred from people."

While aggressive kids and youth gangs are frightening for Ruth, the police loom as her biggest concern, particularly when she thinks of Robert.

I've already taught him, when he's stopped by the police, what to do. I've taught him, "Don't talk back, quiet down." I've got this little card that I show him, "What to Do When Arrested." "Keep quiet, put your hands up." Even at 9 years old, I'm teaching him how to conduct himself around the law. Give full cooperation. . . . I have to keep a hedge of protection around him because the police are after him every chance they

get; they're after the Black boys. They think he's in a gang, but
he's not. That's why I keep him well-groomed. I don't let him
go out and play too often by himself because of the drive-bys.
But there are certain things I have to instill in my son—his
pride, his roots, and the danger of being a dark-skinned boy.
There's dangers that come with your race, your color. All your
life you're going to face this. A lot of times you're not going to
be able to always explain. They're just going to look at your
color and say, "You're it, you did it." . . . I worry about my boy
every day.

Serette, who had so many fears for her daughter when she was in
high school, is now worried about her 19-year-old son. "My son concerns me because he's lately picked up with some White kids whose
daddies can bail them out if they get in trouble. My son will go to jail.
I have no doubt about that. I've told him if the three of you get caught
in the car smoking marijuana, they'll be out before the night's over.
You're going to prison."

Her son has never been arrested, but that doesn't lessen the anxiety. She feels that his view of the world must evolve to reflect the reality of being an African American man. "He's naïve and he doesn't see
the racism in the world. He doesn't see the full institutional picture."

While the concerns about police brutality are mostly about the
victimization of Black boys, many mothers are aware of the dangers
that their girls face as well, and thus early on train them, too, in how to
deal with those in authority. Lynell, who has 3-year-old twin girls, says
that she did not tolerate the "terrible twos." Already her daughters
know to pick up after themselves, not to play at the dinner table, and
not to make any excuses when their mother says it is time for bed. Her
strict love, she says, is necessary.

"As Black people we don't have the luxury of questioning authority, especially armed authority," Lynell says while her girls take a nap in
the next room. "We'll always come up short. And when that authority
is packing a gun, you're going to come up dead. As long as they're
racial profiling when you're driving a car, when you're flying in an air-

plane, your kids can't jump up in a cop's face and say anything. They can't be in the wrong place at the wrong time. . . . So it's my responsibility as a parent to protect my children's well-being by making sure that they have the proper respect for authority. Well, right now, that authority is me."

Feeling Good from the Inside Out: The Special Challenges of Raising Black Girls

While, the racism and brutality of cops conjures up concerns about life and death, for girls there are also other dangers that are often more subtle, yet perhaps more internal and chronic. One can preach to even a hardheaded son about *behaving* a certain way and expect him to eventually get it. But how do you get a girl to feel better about herself—not necessarily to behave in a different way but to *be* different? The challenge with Black girls is to help them develop a secure sense of self that counters the prevailing stereotypes and messages that convey that they're unattractive, unworthy, and insignificant. Several scholars use the term "armoring" as a way of capturing the particular socialization process that Black girls must undergo in order to defy both racism and sexism.[9] Armoring gives Black girls the fortitude to venture out in the larger world while simultaneously protecting them from the bias and discrimination they will find there. Yet there are no blueprints, no pat answers to how this can be achieved.

Like any parent, Black mothers want to spare their children from the pain that they have suffered. So even if their own sense of self has wavered at times in response to society's myths and messages, they hope that their daughters will be able to avoid such self-doubt. Many mothers know that it is critical to inculcate positive self-esteem and confidence in their daughters. Still, this is easier said than done. It can be difficult to instill in one's daughter a sense of inner and outer beauty when the world is ignoring or actively maligning her.

Often mothers of Black girls find themselves battling the lily complex, the notion that the only way to be beautiful is to look "White." Sharon, the divorced mother of a 10-year-old girl, recounts that when her daughter Keisha was 6 years old, she had a White boyfriend at school. When a family friend asked Keisha about him, the little girl's reply was "None of the brown boys pay attention to me." Keisha has a complexion the color of bittersweet chocolate, and Sharon was deeply pained by how early in life her daughter had learned about the color distinctions that too often arise among African Americans. Sharon suddenly became acutely aware of how hard she'd need to work to counter the negative messages, to keep her child from internalizing the lily complex.

Toni's daughter Avery had barely turned 4 when she began to question why she was the color of nutmeg, and her brother and mother, much lighter.

> She's very pretty but she was concerned about her skin color for a minute there, and I couldn't figure out where it came from. It bothered me that it bothered her. I'm light-skinned and my son is light-skinned. She's brown and my husband is very dark. She thought Kyle and I were White for a while, so we had to undo that, clarify that we weren't, we were Black too. Then she started saying "I'm brown and brown is pretty too." You know, I could tell she was kind of self-conscious about it for some reason, all of a sudden, . . . like a light just went off that we were a little bit different. And so we just went around stressing that we're all the same, just lighter or darker. And everybody's beautiful.

Toni will likely have to be careful to affirm Avery's beauty, since the little girl is constantly being reminded that she looks "different" from her brother and is also receiving the message that to some, brown skin is not so beautiful. When praising Avery's looks, some African Americans have implied that she is pretty *despite* being darker-complexioned. "[Black] people used to refer to my daughter, and still do, as 'a pretty little Black girl.' And it's like, 'Hmmm. What is that about?'"

Maisha, whose hair is in dreadlocks, talks about how she constantly works to keep others' biases from contaminating her daughter's sense of her own beauty.

Until she was about 14, Kamilah's hair was rarely straightened. When she was young, it was in braids or cornrows without any extensions, and when she got older, it was in twists. The amazing thing was that I kept getting completely unsolicited offers from fellow church members to press her hair. One day, after service, a friend handed me a pressing comb, which I still don't know how to use. Later when Kamilah chose to have her hair cut at age 13, people reacted with shock and disbelief: "You cut your hair? Why?" This was the nineties, but it wasn't much different than the reactions I got in the late sixties when I went from my pressed hair to an afro. I feel like I've had to work hard to keep other Black folks' biases in check and to protect Kamilah from their comments and feelings.

Carille, a mother of three young girls, is keenly aware of how the differences in her daughters' skin colors and facial features have led to teasing from peers and rivalry among them. She finds herself constantly reassuring her oldest girl, who has dark brown skin rather like Carille's, that she is beautiful, and that, in fact, "from the darkness comes the light." Carille must also console her lighter-skinned, sandy-haired middle daughter, who physically looks very little like Carille and is teased by friends that, "She can't be your mother." And then there's the youngest who can't stand her very full, well-defined lips that look just like her mom's. If this weren't enough to keep Carille busy, she recently overheard her middle child criticizing her darker sister's complexion.

Carille is constantly shifting to respond to and manage her daughters' distress over the negative messages they've received and internalized. The tasks of educating, protecting, reassuring, and of course, loving and nurturing can be all-consuming, especially if, like Carille, you're a single parent struggling to pay the rent and get food on the table.

The possibility of sexual victimization invokes fear in many mothers as well, particularly in a society whose popular culture continues to perpetuate the myth that Black women are sexually promiscuous. Ruth, who was so concerned about the police brutalizing her son Robert, talks about her dread that her 16-year-old daughter will be sexually assaulted or raped. "For girls, the boys in the community are more of a danger than the law," she says. And Sharon, the divorced mother of a 10-year-old girl, doesn't hesitate in naming "sexploitation" as her single biggest challenge in raising her daughter Keisha. Recently she took Keisha to see the Black British singer Sade perform, "because Black women in music videos take their clothes off. I wanted her to know it's not about shaking your appendages and being sexual to be an artist, to be a performer. It's about our heart and soul. I find ways to get my point home."

Many mothers can't shake the worry that their daughters will get pregnant as teens and that their lives will forever be thrown off course. Janet, a 34-year-old mother of three, who has never been married, has two teenage boys, one of whom is in juvenile detention and one who was recently arrested and is in an adult jail. In spite of this and the sadness and pain that she experiences around the decisions her sons have made, she asserts with confidence that rearing a girl is tougher than rearing boys. "Because girls can have babies. Boys can't," she says simply.

More than anything else, Janet is struggling with what to do to keep her 14-year-old daughter Pam, who is now menstruating and beginning to show an interest in boys, from having sex prematurely. Her fear is that her own pattern of much-too-early pregnancy and single parenthood will be repeated. She desperately wants to help her daughter to break the cycle but she's unsure of how to have an impact.

While Janet frets over her daughter's future, some mothers in similar financial straits are too preoccupied with basic day-to-day survival to worry about something so intangible. Carol, now in her thirties, who was first pregnant at age 16 and who is raising three children without a father, says that there is no room to think about "the special challenges of raising a Black girl or boy. I am just trying to survive—to keep a roof over their heads, and to keep them fed and clothed and off the street."

Over the Transom and Back Again: Bridging Two Worlds

Hazel, the mother of two teenage daughters, speaks passionately about how she struggles to teach her children to code-switch, to shift between speaking Black English in their neighborhood and Standard

English when dealing with the White world—as she puts it, "to be 'bilingual.'"

> I'm constantly fighting the battle with my children in terms of, I call it, their bilingual education. In other words, when you can go straight up 'hood, shake our heads, and use Ebonics, and when you don't, and learning the difference between the two. I've tried to teach them there's a time and a place for everything. When you're with your girlfriends, it's "Awww, gir-r-rl!" but you don't want to walk into a job interview carrying those habits. You want to be able to shut that off at least for the time being and make sure you're perfectly and clearly understood. . . . You need to be able to talk to the mayor and you need to be able to talk to the homeless person and anyone in between.

Right now, it's in the classroom where Hazel's children must be most vigilant about speaking Standard English. Like many African American mothers, Hazel has high academic expectations and career aspirations for her children. A number of studies indicate that regardless of the family's economic situation, Black parents, and Black mothers in particular, are at least as likely as, and often more likely than, White mothers to expect their children to achieve good grades, attend college, and graduate from college.[10] Many Black mothers see educational achievement and success as the only defense against racism and sexism.

But many mothers are also concerned that if their daughters and sons venture over the transom, mastering the skills that enable them to assimilate into and succeed within the White world, they may have difficulty fitting in or feeling comfortable back in the Black community. For these mothers, a carefully crafted "bilingual education" strategy is crucial—one that helps the child to live in two worlds, to know when and how to shift in order to manage the bigotry they encounter, yet to always be able to find his or her own voice, to always be able to find their way back home.

While Hazel carries the fear that her children may not master the art of verbal shifting in time, Lucy, who lives outside Atlanta, is afraid that her 14-year-old daughter has no understanding of the need for linguistic dexterity. Her daughter Christina has spent most of her schooling in a gifted program in a predominantly White school where none of her classmates is Black. Lucy confides that though Christina has become skilled at shifting to fit in at her school, she's unable to put it in reverse when she comes back home:

> She definitely is not what, in our house, we call "a 'hood girl."
> She doesn't understand a lot of slang. She doesn't understand
> Black people's attitudes or what she perceives as Black people's
> attitudes about not wanting to be smart. She doesn't buy into
> that. But by the same token, because she doesn't follow a lot of
> Black people, it makes it hard for her. Even as I watch her
> interact with other girls of her same race, they perceive her as
> being different because she speaks different, because she speaks
> very well and always uses words that most people even my age
> don't necessarily use in normal conversation.

Lucy is concerned that Christina's experiences might weaken her in other ways as well. Lucy makes a point, for instance, of communicating to all three of her children that they've got to be "a little smarter" than their White peers, a lesson that Lucy learned from her mother.

> I tell my children it's not enough to know it, you have to *really*
> know it for the people to recognize that you do know it. And I
> say this to prepare them, because I don't think by the time
> they enter the job market that we are going to have this color-
> blind society, this utopia where it's based upon nothing else
> and people don't see your color. . . . They're going to have to
> be a little bit sharper and a little bit more tenacious.

But Lucy is troubled that Christina in particular doesn't grasp the message and can't read racial and gender dynamics. Lucy feels good about the formal education that Christina has been afforded at the schools she's attended, but she worries about the informal one. She's fearful that Christina is vulnerable to significant disappointment in the future.

> I try to tell her that even though all these [White] kids you go to school with are your friends, they might move into a world that you're not going to be a part of. I try to prepare her for that because I'm afraid that because of her social setting now—which I don't really discourage because I think there is gonna come a time when some of those kids she's going to school with are going to do some really, really good things, and she might need those contacts, so I never discourage that—but by the same token, we had a discussion last week about dating. I'm trying to prepare her, that as her friends go out and date she might not be included in that little clique because she's Black.

Lucy is not always sure about the best way to guide and shape her daughter's life.

> I think it's time to find that balance between maintaining a sense of Blackness and at the same time teaching them that they are part of this larger society. And the two don't necessarily go together, because when you teach Blackness, that implies some separateness, and you still have to come back into this larger society. And I think that's probably been one of the biggest challenges for me.

Even though Lucy is not sure what the strategy should be to get there, she's very clear on her two aims: that Christina get the best education possible, and that she stay connected to and give back to the Black community.

> My thing is that your job is to go to school and get an education. I don't care what Sue or John or Mustafah think. I don't

care what they are doing. You are here to go to school, but by the same token, having her recognize that Black people are her family in a sense. You share a heritage. And part of your responsibility in being one of the talented tenth is you have to look out for the other 90 percent.

Joyce poured herself into ensuring that her daughter Ramona mastered concepts and skills that never appeared on the syllabus at school. A 55-year-old critical care nurse who lives just outside Buffalo, New York, she talks wistfully about what it took to raise Ramona, 24, who is now a college graduate and a program director at a YWCA. "God knows it's a challenge to raise Black girls," she says. "They kind of have to live in two worlds. They have to live in a Black world to know who they are, but they have to live in a White world in order to survive. The thing I used to say to Ramona was, 'You're going to Casewell Academy [a private, predominantly White school], and you must never be a follower. You must be a leader. You're going to Casewell to learn how to pass the White man's test, to get the White man's job, and make the White man's money, not to marry a White boy.'"

It was very important to Joyce that Ramona always embrace her Blackness and that she not feel superior to Black people who were less fortunate.

I just tried to be realistic with her about who she is and what she is and what her mission is in life. Her father and I would put her on the bus and ride her downtown, and [we'd] see prostitutes, and we'd say, "Look, these are your sisters; they're out here because they have to feed their children." We didn't think that she was better than anybody else because she was in a private school, and we wanted her to know that any Black woman you see is your sister.

Like Joyce, Kumea, one of the authors, has been struggling for more than a decade to carefully craft the right "mix" of experiences for her daughter. "Okay, we've decided to put her in a school that is mostly

White, so how are we going to balance that? The neighborhood is ethnically mixed, but our block is mostly White, with no Black kids. How
do we compensate? Thank goodness, we're active in a Black church—
the youth group and youth choir are especially good for her. But she
doesn't know a lot of Black kids who are college-bound. What group
can we get her involved in to fix that?" It's felt like a constant juggling
act to make sure that her daughter is both grounded in her Blackness
and able to move beyond the boundaries of the Black community—
skillful in getting over the transom and back again.

Beating the Odds: Raising and Inspiring Self-Confident Black Children

Despite the obstacles, many Black women have been successful in teaching their children how to confront and transcend racism and sexism.
Olivia, who lives in San Francisco, talks about how she counseled her
daughter Alexis on how to respond to a racist incident in the classroom.

"I remember one instance when she was in the sixth grade and
they had to do some kind of report, and this White kid innocently
came in with blackface," says Olivia, a corporate management coach.
"And Alexis's favorite teacher didn't realize the impact of that. Alexis
was disappointed, came home and told me about it. We talked a lot
about what you do in this kind of situation, and finally, I asked her,
'What are *you* going to do?' She said, 'I'm going to talk to the teacher,'
and we rehearsed what she'd say, and I went with her. And at 11 years
old, she's confronting the teacher but using 'I' statements instead of
accusing. Alexis said to the teacher, 'I feel that when this happened I
was offended. I was disappointed that you didn't say something about
it.' Well, when this little child finished talking to the teacher, I was so
impressed. Then Alexis said, 'I'm going to talk to Samuel [her class-
mate] and tell him, because he doesn't know.' And she did it. . . .
That's the work of parenting."

Olivia's encouragement and education of her daughter, along with
her decision to let her take the lead in handling a problem, empowered
Alexis to stand up for herself. She acknowledges that her professional

experience in human relations training gives her the skills to effectively coach her daughter. But while Olivia has a PhD, most Black mothers have to develop similar skills without a university's teachings.

For her part, Katrina, a married social worker in her early forties, has been a very devoted and involved mother, continually wrestling with how to create the optimal space in which her only son can be himself, explore, and grow. As a child, entering a high school in Seattle, where she was one of a handful of Blacks, Katrina had suddenly felt ignored and unseen, and in one fell swoop, her confidence and assertiveness vanished. Her aim was to make sure that this didn't happen to her son Matthew.

> Understanding racism, I was very watchful of his experiences, how he could learn about himself, and to make sure he would not be invisible and to make sure that none of his world would ever be invisible to him. I was very concerned about him connecting and finding himself and being prepared for those moments when he could possibly fade away, since that happens to everyone, but more to Black males. [I asked myself] "How do we help him broaden his world in a way that's healthy and helpful for an 8-year-old child?"

"As people of color, we don't get to see the world the way we want it," Katrina stresses.

> We don't get to hear our own voices out there. We have to hear our own voices internally. So my job then shifted when he was about age 6 from just teaching to protecting him and helping him be whoever he was. And nobody, bigger, Whiter, Blacker, was going to shift him out of his own. He can learn but you're not going to make him do this or that. So that became the real job of protecting him, and during that time he got more and more strength, and he became his own fighter.

Katrina stayed constantly attuned to the messages Matthew was receiving and to what was going on in his inner world. Matthew attended a predominantly Black school in his early years, and then went to a predominantly White high school. He seemed to be doing well there, but one day, he came home and told his mother, "I'm not smart. The White kids are smart." She promptly took him out and put him back in a predominantly Black school, where he received more encouragement, and he came home and said, "Oh, I guess I am pretty bright." And so he went on and excelled.

At age 13 he went through an intense rites of passage program where many of the kids were more Afrocentric than he, wearing for example, dashikis and other African clothing. She told him, "I want you to know that no one can define for you Blackness and you're entitled as a person of African descent to claim your Africanness in any situation. No one owns that. So you can walk in and stand in the power of your African identity and learn and feel at home anywhere, in any community." Katrina wanted to make sure that Matthew didn't get the message that there's only one way to be Black, or that a select few have a monopoly on Blackness, or that some aren't "Black enough." She wanted him to know that there is not one way to be—whether it's defined by Whites or by Blacks—that Matthew could be himself.

Matthew is launched now, having graduated from college several years ago. And it's clear that Katrina's dedication to shaping a world for him in which he could grow, and providing him the skills to make sense of and challenge that world when necessary, have been vital to his success. As a high schooler thrust into a racist environment, she had to develop her skills at shifting, and she continued to hone those skills as a mother—listening, sensing, intuiting, responding, speaking, encouraging, facilitating, initiating, advocating, fighting, sometimes fleeing, and managing her feelings all the while. The aim of her shifting was to minimize Matthew's, to keep him from having to "shift out of his own."

Otherkin: The Role of Extended Family in Raising Black Children

Katrina, like many Black mothers, has been able to rely on extended family and friends, particularly other women, to help with the tasks and decisions of childrearing. One of the great strengths of Black families has long been the extended family network, which provides extra hands, added wisdom, as well as auxiliary shoulders to lean and cry on.[11] Thus, rather than being left to the mother or even both parents, the tough task of socializing Black children around race is shared by relatives. In a study of racial socialization, Vetta Sanders Thompson of the University of Missouri at St. Louis found that messages from other adult family members about how to cope with racism were more numerous and often had a greater impact than such messages from parents.[12]

"It takes a village to raise a child" is an African saying that Black communities understood and embraced long before Hillary Clinton popularized the notion.[13] Patricia Hill Collins at the University of Cincinnati talks about the central importance of "othermothers," who often share the burden of raising the child and function as coparents.[14] Othermothers are sometimes the mother's blood sister, mother, aunt, or cousin. At other times they're close family friends who function like blood relatives.

In some cases, othermothers are an absolute necessity. Barbara, a 45-year-old clerk from Cleveland, talks about how she was reared by a team of othermothers. "I didn't have my mom around when I was growing up. My grandmother was there, but my mother was out there, back and forth. She was a party girl and an alcoholic." In the past few years, "my grandmother has died," Barbara says, "but I still have six people in my life who are really, really close to me and whom I call mom. All of them are a mother to me in some kind of way."

As a single parent, Barbara is now raising an 8-year-old daughter, and she has recreated a network of mothers *and* fathers who love and nurture her child and who provide her with support and advice.

Usually othermothering is an informal arrangement, but sometimes it's more structured. Black women have founded organizations, like Jack & Jill of America, which have the central task of providing cultural, social, and educational opportunities for the healthy development of Black children and youth. In addition, sororities often provide othermothering. The National Sorority of Phi Delta Kappa, a Black educators' group, sponsors Xinos and Kudos, a program to promote the positive development of high school youth. Numerous churches and community-based organizations support rites of passage programs and other projects that extend the parenting function. The aim of many of these programs is to teach Black children how to be successful in mainstream society while retaining their identity and connection to the Black community. These programs help youth to learn effective shifting. And they bolster Black children as they embark on their journey into the larger world.

In the best of circumstances, mothers, fathers, othermothers, and otherfathers use their collective experiences, know-how, and wit to teach the community's children how, when, and where to shift in order to grow up to be sane and successful members of the society. And they affirm each other, helping to sort out the anxieties, fears, and conflicting feelings so many Black parents wrestle with as they try to steer their children through society's racial and gender hurdles. "God has been at the center of this," Katrina says of her experience in raising her son Matthew. "And we're going to figure out how to do it—all of us, my husband, my mother, and my sons' many other mothers, and many other fathers, and many siblings."

"CAN I GET A WITNESS?"

Black Women and the Church

I have been very upset with my church, that women are downplayed, and there are certain things that only men can chair or do, although 99 percent of the time, women in the background are making it possible. . . . though they're invisible.

MILDRED, 63, SILVER SPRING, MARYLAND

Houses of worship have long been havens for African American women, places where they felt they could lay down the burden of shifting, briefly forget about the myths of color, and be accepted for who they are. They could leave the lily complex on the church steps, and with their flamboyant hats and going-to-church clothes feel regal, beautiful, and embraced by a distinctly African American world. For Black women, developing spiritual practices and getting involved at church have provided significant resources for coping with the challenges of being Black and female—for managing the myths, negative stereotypes, and discrimination of the outside world. For many African American women, the church has been crucial for their very survival.

But while our research shows that many women find their involvement with religious organizations to be nurturing and sustaining, it also reveals that too often Black women are asked to give up personal power in exchange for the spiritual sustenance and sense of community that they seek. They are asked to be quiet and deferential and to yield leadership to men. They are asked to deny parts of themselves—their ability to lead, to be analytical and critical, to do more than just settle into the pews and follow the flow of a service. The religious message itself is sometimes a disempowering one, relegating women to second-class citizenship. They're coerced to shift, to act "ladylike," to be submissive. They feel subtly, or not so subtly, put down by the church experience despite all of its spiritual offerings.

Research indicates that African American women are perhaps the most spiritually devout group in the United States. Based on a review of five national studies, Robert Joseph Taylor of the University of Michigan and his colleagues concluded that Black people have stronger religious feelings than Whites, and Black women are more religious than Black men.[1] The National Survey of Black Americans revealed that more than 71 percent of Black women attend religious services at least a few times a month and more than 68 percent of Black women are members of a church or congregation.[2] In another study utilizing data from the National Survey of Black Americans, Clifford Broman of Michigan State University found that prayer was the second most common strategy used by Black men and women to cope with a stressful episode in their lives.[3] Black women were especially likely to use prayer as a strategy to manage the stress of health, emotional, or interpersonal problems. For many Black women, spiritual beliefs are at the core of their inner being, and participating in a religious organization is a central and lifelong commitment.

The religions of Black women span the gamut. They are Muslims, Jews, Buddhists, and adherents of many other faiths, but the overwhelming majority is Christian. In the National Survey of Black Americans, 88 percent of the respondents identified as Christian, and this was also reflected in our own survey.[4-5] The majority (approximately 80 percent) of Black Christian women are adherents of seven historically Black denominations, the first of which developed in the late eighteenth century in response to the racist beliefs and practices of White denominations.[6]

These Black Christian denominations, often collectively called "the Black church," have been a centerpiece of Black life since the slave era.[7] They have historically met a multitude of needs within the Black community, serving not just as a spiritual and religious resource but also as a refuge from the racism of the larger society, a locus for social and political leadership, a community of like-minded souls, and an extended family. For the past two centuries, the Black church has been by far the most significant Black institution in the lives of African Americans.

In this chapter we will talk about the solace that religion provides African American women. But we will also reveal the surprising extent to which society's codes creep into the pulpit. Many Black women believe that cultivating a spiritual community is a positive, necessary way for them to deal with the racism and sexism they encounter in day-to-day life. But some also tell us that too many leaders within these communities of spirit have not yet learned to fully respect Black women.

The Highs and Lows of Religious Involvement

When we asked, "What helps you to get through difficult times?" fully 75 percent of the women whom we surveyed volunteered "faith," "prayer," "God," "my church," or similar responses stressing the centrality of religion and spirituality in their lives. For many, the Sunday service is an opportunity to refuel emotionally and spiritually and to arm themselves for another week of ups and downs with family members, supervisors, colleagues, and even strangers on the street. For many, making it through each day requires constant prayer and the companionship of God.

Cherie, a 55-year-old project manager from Seattle, is sustained by "my trust, faith, and relationship with God; reading the Bible and applying the scriptures to my walk and talk daily." She adds that her faith tells her that though she's sometimes knocked down, when she gets up, she'll rise even higher. Lavonda, a 37-year-old teacher from Pomona, California, writes, "I don't face any major difficulties because of my relationship with Christ and who He says I am and what I can do." Nia, a 30-year-old sales account manager from Atlanta, remarks that what helps her is "knowing that God is on my side and has my back." And Irene, a 30-year-old staff sergeant in the U.S. Army, has a simple formula for making it through the day: "Prayer, much prayer."

Some women point to the particular significance of their church involvement. Renee, a 24-year-old sales clerk from Greensboro, North Carolina, says, "I feel that being raised in the church gives me inner strength and peace to make it through difficult times." Bobbi, a retired physician from Los Angeles, talks about "the comfort, joy, history, and hope afforded by my affiliation with the African Methodist Episcopal (AME) Church."

Research confirms what these women already know—religiosity and religious participation is health-enhancing. A number of studies indicate that Black women who are more religious or who attend religious services regularly are less likely to be depressed and more likely to experience personal happiness and satisfaction with their lives.[8] Having deeply felt spiritual beliefs and being active in religious organizations are valuable coping methods that allow Black women to minimize the impact of stressors. When Black women are struggling to fend off racial or gender assaults, spirituality and church involvement serve as important shifting strategies. Consequently, it is particularly ironic that the church can also compound the difficulties of Black women.

The Christian church has struggled for centuries with the role of women, and while substantial change has occurred in some aspects of church life—for example, in many, though not all Black denominations, women can now be ordained as ministers—women are still far from being equally represented in church leadership. In a study published in 1990, the late C. Eric Lincoln, the Duke University professor who was the preeminent scholar on Black religion and theology, and Lawrence H. Mamiya of Vassar College, estimated that only 5 percent of clergy in the seven principal Black denominations were women.[9] In 2000, Reverend Vashti McKenzie, the author of a book aptly titled *Not Without a*

Struggle, was elected a bishop in the AME Church, the first ever African American woman bishop in one of the major Black denominations.[10] Yet, ironically, Black women typically account for more than two-thirds, and sometimes as much as four-fifths, of the congregation.[11]

Eve—a Lesser Adam? The Struggle for Equality

Black women are often referred to as the backbone of the church, cooking for the socials, selling tickets to raise money for a new piano, organizing the summer vacation Bible school, feeding and clothing the needy.[12] Yet these same women often have difficulty asserting leadership outside of traditional female-designated arenas, and they often hear little from the pulpit about the creativity, independence, and strength of women. Thus, even in these Black-run centers of spirituality, we see the yo-yo paradox at work. Black women are expected to be strong and capable in one realm, while remaining passive and deferential in another.

In 1991 and 1992, Marian Whitson of East Tennessee State University conducted focus groups with 100 Black women church members, including some clergy, on their perceptions of sexism and gender issues in the Christian Methodist Episcopal Church.[13] She found that the majority of her participants were concerned about limited female leadership, sexual harassment and other forms of sexism, and about the church's failure to speak out on these issues. These women were troubled by the pervasive gender silence within their houses of worship.

Many of our research participants have similar concerns. Monisha, a 26-year-old college student and single mother in Tulsa, Oklahoma, bemoans the fact that at her former church, "They believe that the woman is a child. She can't say or do anything without the husband." Monisha had aspired to be on the deacon board of her church but was unable to because of her gender. "Women can only be missionaries or part of the nurse's guild," she says.

Several other women pointedly describe themselves as "second-class citizens" in the church. Natalie, a 45-year-old security officer in West Haven, Connecticut, grew up in a military family and lived in six states in the South, the mid-Atlantic region, and the West by the time she was 18. The family connected with a Black church wherever they were posted, and Natalie talked of how painful the "second-class citizenship" was for her. "The message was biased against women. We were expected to be a certain way, do certain things, and not really have a brain, not really have the ability to speak out the way you want to. If the pastor didn't say it, you couldn't do it." What made this particularly damaging for Natalie was that the message at church was echoed at home. Her father was emotionally abusive and repeatedly told her that her destiny in life was "to do nothing but clean White folks' floors and have babies."

Even when women are able to hold positions that have been traditionally male, their competence is sometimes questioned. When Betty, a 46-year-old teacher from Oak Park, Illinois, served as treasurer at her predominantly Black church, she recalls that "a couple of board members assumed that my husband was the 'real' treasurer behind the scenes."

Gaye, a 38-year-old print shop owner in the suburbs of Washington, D.C., experienced a gender-based double standard at church. When she was 16 and became pregnant, she remembers how painful it was to be told she could no longer teach her Sunday school class. On the one hand, she understood why the pastor didn't want her standing in front of a class of 4- to 6-year-olds, but she was well aware that had she been an unmarried teenage father, she would have been able to continue and no one would have said a word. Feeling hurt and abandoned, Gaye stopped attending church for several years, losing touch with the place that had been her emotional anchor. Without it, she felt adrift, more vulnerable to life's setbacks. But it was difficult for her to go back.

Terri, 29, became so disillusioned with the bias she experienced that she recently left her home church as well. A life-long member of the Church of God in Christ, Terri began attending services at a large sanctuary outside Atlanta two years ago and quickly became active, leading workshops on entrepreneurship, organizing weekend retreats, and eventually becoming a youth minister along with a male congregant named Ron.

As the owner of her own small gift shop, Terri was adept at communicating with people, coming up with innovative ideas, and taking charge. But as youth minister, she seldom got to exercise those skills. All the authority went to Ron.

> We were both the same age. But they were always investing in him spiritually, backing him, and giving him the kind of support that he needed, but I was getting nothing. What I was getting is "Your skirt is too short. You need to come to [class] so we can teach you how to be a minister's wife." And I was like, "Who told you I wanted to be a minister's wife?" But that's what they did and I felt that they were always wanting me to be more subservient and he could be the hero. I'm supposed to sit up and type all his stuff for him, and I'm supposed to always be, "What do you need, Pastor Ronnie? I'm here for you." And I don't think that's right. I just don't think that my job is to get him water. Forget that.

Finally, four months ago, Terri resigned her position, and three Sundays later, instead of getting dressed to go to church, she stayed in bed, watched *Meet the Press*, and later met a friend for brunch. Since then, she has never returned to that particular church. "I felt the prejudices and discrimination were slowing my progress and weakening my strength as a leader in the body of Christ," she says. No longer content to downplay her talents, she is currently visiting other sanctuaries with friends, hoping to find a place of worship where she can make more of a contribution.

Sometimes the rigid gender roles prescribed from the pulpit are simply unworkable. Pauline, a 42-year-old divorced telecommunications company administrator in Oakland, recently visited a Black Protestant church. During the service, she says, "One of the preachers talked about how the man should take care of the woman, and the woman should stay home and take care of the man, and when the kids come, the woman should take care of the man and the kids, and I kind of looked around the room, and thought, 75 percent of these brothers in here are unemployed, now how's she going to do that? This sort of message is not healthy."

For the women with whom we spoke, it was not always evident whether these messages that seemed to justify a lesser status for women emanated from a particular interpretation of Christian theology or simply from gender biases rife in the broader society. Some women make it clear that the sexist messages they hear at church are explicitly proclaimed as biblical, although there is substantial controversy within Christianity about the correct interpretation of the Bible with regard to gender issues. Feminist Christianity and womanist theology—two strands of Christian scholarship that have developed in the past three decades—critique the traditional subordinate position of women and instead affirm women and their vital place alongside men in the history, beliefs, practices, and leadership of the Christian faith.[14]

Renita Weems, an African American minister and theologian at Vanderbilt Divinity School, defines the "womanist" perspective in biblical studies as the viewpoint of a Black feminist—a woman who is committed to both men and women, a woman who is committed to whole people. Her book *Just a Sister Away* is representative of the scholarship of Black womanist theologians. In the foreword, Weems says that her aim is "to probe beneath the surface of biblical texts to discover a place for everyone in the Kingdom."[15] Sadly, what many Black women are hearing from the pulpit has not been influenced by such womanist theology. Instead, they are being led in a very traditional, patriarchal Christianity.

Donna, a 41-year-old high school history teacher in Shaker Heights, Ohio, describes how devastated she was when, in the context of a Bible study class, her relatively new Black male pastor put an organizational chart on the overhead projector that put women last. The top box fittingly was "God," directly beneath "God" was "man," and directly beneath "man" was "woman." This visual aid corroborated the condescending and dismissive attitude that this twice-divorced minister seemed to have toward women. Fortunately, Donna was not the only woman who began to steam. Several women spoke up and challenged the pastor, though he refused to budge. Donna became even angrier when she noticed the self-assured smirk on the face of one of the few men in attendance.

Sabrina is a 27-year-old substance abuse counselor who grew up in a Black Baptist church in central Mississippi. She, her parents, and her siblings were all very active in the church, and Sabrina sang in the youth choir, served on the youth usher board, and attended Wednesday evening as well as Sunday morning services. But in spite of her outward attachment to the church, Sabrina remarks, "Something was missing for me. I didn't feel like I was at home there. It felt like an obligation." Sabrina had learned at an early age about the importance of nurturing her own relationship with God, and her mother had taught her the power of prayer. However, as Sabrina matured, she found that the church itself was offering less and less with regards to her spiritual growth.

An excellent student, when Sabrina was 15, she was offered a scholarship to a residential summer program at a college in Michigan. She found a church to attend nearby. "And they had a woman minister!" she exclaims, her excitement still palpable more than a decade later. "And I thought, oh, okay, this is different. And she was talking about God could be a woman, and I'm like, whoaaa! This is totally different. And I had to ask myself, why is this so jarring to me? I'm female."

When Sabrina returned home, she remembers her minister railing against seminaries that were teaching that God could be a woman: "I couldn't get behind a lot of what my minister was saying," she says. By the time Sabrina graduated from high school and left home for college, she could no longer abide the intolerance and rigidity of her childhood church. She no longer considers herself a Christian; instead her spiritual life is cultivated through involvement in a Science of the Mind congregation, which in her words, is "accepting of my whole beingness."

Like Sabrina, Judith, 51, has had difficulty quelling her discomfort with the biases at church. Judith was raised in her maternal grandmother's Baptist faith, but grew away from it in her teens. Her parents were not very religious, rarely attended service, and didn't balk when Judith and her younger brother begged to stop attending. A child of the 1960s, as Judith journeyed through her late teens and early twenties, she increasingly felt that going to church was irrelevant to Black people's struggles and needs. She felt her church was too conservative and at times outright oppressive. But even so, she would periodically

attend services with family or friends, in part as a way of exploring
whether there might be a place where she'd fit in. It didn't happen.

After college and law school, Judith moved to Atlanta and became a
public defender. A decade later, she married, became a mother, and was
drawn back to church, where she hoped to find a community and Christian values for her children and a place to develop her own spirituality.
Her husband Steve had been raised as a Black Methodist, and he and
Judith decided to join his more progressive church.

Judith grew to love the church. It was a congregation of about 150
people where she and the family came to know just about everyone.
The children found surrogate aunties, uncles, and grandparents. Judith
immediately became active in the community outreach ministry, and
later she was invited to join the trustee board. There was only one problem: the pastor was innovative and creative with respect to outreach
and children's ministries, but he was traditional when it came to gender
issues. God was a He. The role of women in the Bible and in biblical
times was rarely addressed or examined. And most disappointingly, the
pastor sermonized that God expects men to serve as the "head of the
household." For Judith, this seemed so antiquated, so patently sexist,
that she bristled whenever she heard it. And she hoped that at these
moments her preadolescent son and daughter were daydreaming or distracted, as they sometimes were during the 40-minute sermons.

Judith and Steve, who was a computer analyst, prided themselves on
raising children who were not constrained by gender roles. They cared as
much about their daughter's educational and career development as they
did about their son's. Though Judith played the lead role in arranging for
school, child care, and activities for the children, Steve was right there,
rearranging his work schedule as best he could, taxiing children, shopping, and cooking. Steve didn't feel particularly irritated, however, by the
pastor's beliefs, and his lack of irritation annoyed Judith. She talked with
other women at the church, a number of whom were professionals her
age, but they didn't seem bothered either. One friend told Judith, "Oh,
it's just the way preachers talk. He doesn't mean any harm." Another
confessed, "Well, I think it's okay for men to be head of the household.
We need to encourage them. Sometimes they feel so powerless. Maybe if

we did a better job of giving them their just due, fewer of them would abandon their families." And a third church member pushed Judith to look at the matter differently, "Well, if the Bible says that men are the head of the household, I need to accept that. I may not like it, but I need to try to understand it and support it."

After a while, Judith felt that only her nonchurch friends could understand her. One told her, "That's one of the reasons I haven't been to church for 30 years. It's such a sexist, chauvinist institution. It's worse than the work world." Judith finally got the courage to talk with the pastor one-on-one about her concerns. Pastor Taylor was a warm, intelligent man whom Judith respected and with whom she'd had a good relationship, but Judith didn't feel that he addressed her concerns directly. His response was, "I preach what God has said to us through the Bible. I know it may be hard to fully understand or make sense of, but I'm confident that it's what God wants us to hear and to strive for. I'd like you to study the scriptures and pray on it."

Dissatisfied, Judith began to visit other churches. At one very ethnically mixed New Age–inspired service, she was thrilled to hear lyrics that were gender-inclusive and to hear God spoken of as "He/She" and "Father/Mother." At a predominantly White Episcopal church, she knelt for communion and was overcome with tears when she realized that for the first time in her life, a Black woman minister—someone who looked like her—was serving her the bread and wine.

Judith continues to wrestle with where she fits best. She loves her home church—the extended family network, her opportunity to serve, the comfort and familiarity of the music and the rituals. But she can't abide what she sees as devaluing messages about women. Still, it's her family church, so how can she really leave? Her children love the friends they've made and the Sunday school activities and youth events. Steve is content, reliving his childhood church experiences. Presumably Judith is the only one with a problem. She's the only one who has to shift to try to make it all work.

Although we talked with a number of women like Donna, Sabrina, and Judith, who, sensitized to gender bias, found themselves making tough decisions about whether to leave or stay in their church home, we also met many Black women who were not concerned about gender issues in the church. It seems that the same cultural norm that compels so many Black women to be silent about gender disparities in other areas of their lives—to focus on racism only and to always stand by Black men—pervades the church as well. Some women excuse the gender inequities that they witness because they are glad the church affords Black men the kind of platform and power so often denied them in the outside world. Margeaux, a 34-year-old seminary student in New York, does not necessarily agree with such thinking, but she understands it. "There's this sense of 'this is one of the few places where they can run things, so we need to let them do this,' in the sense of affirming and preserving their manhood," she says. "I also think there is this sense that we need to be in solidarity with men and not break over the sexism issue like White feminists do; that racism is so bad, that we just need to put up with this sexism stuff and present a united front. And so I think a lot of that is part of our conditioning. I was listening to somebody else talk, and they said for a lot of Black women in church, Sunday is the one day that they get to have access to a Black man. So they like the fact that there's a Black man up there preaching, who's in leadership and running it."

But while their silence may have an explanation, one can't help but wonder whether many of these women, blind to or quiet on matters of gender, pay a steep emotional price by deferring to institutions that often constrict opportunities for Black women, limiting what they can aspire to and who they can become.

Fighting for the Pulpit: Black Women in Ministry

If many Black women sitting in the pews wrestle with the message that they are not fully equal to men, a number of women ministers seem to feel this even more acutely. Anastasia, a 55-year-old ordained minister in Colorado, says, "In the Black church, my voice has often been discounted because I am a woman." Eleanor, a 47-year-old minister in southern California, talks about the problem of "male clergy who want to limit my involvement or have me sit some place other than where the other male clergy are seated." Robina, a 42-year-old minister from the Bronx, New York, reports that her major difficulty as a Black woman is "being cast aside and pushed back by male ministers."

For some Black women ministers, the bias begins in seminary. Florence, who's now serving as an associate pastor in a Baptist church in Chicago, attended a Black seminary eight years ago when she was in her late thirties. Florence says, "I faced gender bias from the moment I walked in the door. It hit me that nothing was expected of me, nothing was being asked of me. A lot was being asked of my male counterparts. Where are you going to go with this? What church are you looking at? Those questions were not asked of females, openly or one-on-one. There was no expectation."

Sheila, a 44-year-old minister in a Black Methodist denomination, experienced gender bias during the ordination process. "Women are definitely being discriminated against in the ministry," Sheila says. "They were holding me back every chance they could for ordination." The day before the ceremony, the bishop said with resignation, "I guess I am going to ordain this big-legged woman." Sheila was aghast at the blatant, unabashed sexism. And, now after almost a decade of ministry, she continues to feel crippled by her gender. She serves as an assistant pastor at a church, working with a male pastor, and she feels sorely underutilized. "It's as if he doesn't know what to do with me," Sheila says. But though her talents are stifled, and she must hold her tongue or go to great lengths to be diplomatic in her protest, Sheila has so far chosen to stay. She loves the congregation, and she feels that her leadership role, however limited, sets an important example for both the women and men of the church.

Laura was so traumatized by the obstacles that she encountered on her way to being ordained that she dropped out of the process, abandoning her dream of becoming a pastor. A 41-year-old insurance underwriter, Laura was married with one young son when she heard the call to the ministry. The family had long been active in a Black Methodist church, and Laura immediately began to study and to be mentored by the male pastor of the church. But her marriage was beginning to fray. Her husband Howard had a tendency to drink too much, and when he

SHIFTING

did, he often became verbally abusive. Laura had done her best over the years to try to avoid him during his binges and, when he was sober, to try to persuade him to get treatment. As her son got older, she became more and more concerned about the lessons he was learning from Howard's dysfunctional and at times frightening behavior. After her call to serve, Laura felt God telling her that she needed to straighten out her personal life. She implored Howard to go into counseling with her, but he adamantly refused. And his drinking and emotional abusiveness only escalated. At her wit's end, Laura began to consider separation. She confided in her pastor, Reverend Manning. His advice to her was, "Stay and continue to pray and believe that God's going to make it all right." In addition Reverend Manning made her advancement in the ministry contingent on the marriage. "My pastor told me he couldn't move me forward in ministry if I chose to leave my husband. 'After all,' he told me, 'he didn't hit you, did he?'"

Eventually, Laura separated from and divorced Howard. She affiliated with another church of the same denomination that had a male pastor whom she had gotten to know through work on various community projects. Laura felt comfortable with and supported by her new pastor, but she came to dread the periodic reviews, which were required for all ministers in training and which were conducted by a committee of ordained, mostly male, clergy. Invariably, her status as a divorced woman became a focus of discussion. "I was grilled about being single, about having divorced. A couple of them said, 'You have to have a covering'" which she explains is, "a male in domination over you—a husband, presumably."

When Laura asked John, a divorced male minister in training, if his marital status was the focus of discussions with the same committee, he looked puzzled and said no. Frustrated and angry about the way these issues were handled, Laura eventually pulled out of the ordination process. She realized that she had to change course, to find another way to do the Lord's work. She still feels called to serve God, and she's developed a ministry to incarcerated women, but she's clear that she's unwilling to shift to the degree that was expected in order to be ordained.

For her part, Melinda, 35, is mulling over whether to abandon her beliefs for a Sunday. A newly ordained minister, she has had to think about whether she should insist upon speaking from the pulpit, where she feels she belongs, or preach from the floor in the church where she was baptized.

She has many sweet memories of Sunday mornings spent in that small Baptist sanctuary three blocks from her family's Cleveland home. She recalls the nurses of the church smelling of jasmine and baby powder, stiff in their White stockings as they walked through the aisles. She remembers how she first cowered in fear, then watched in amazement as the older women jumped up, flailed their arms, and "got happy," so caught up with the spirit that it took two of the church's brothers to hold them down and carry them to a back room.

Sitting through the long services as a child, Melinda daydreamed about what she wanted to be when she grew up—a teacher, a veterinarian, an artist—but never about being a preacher. And if she had wanted to become one, the message was subtle, yet clear, that she could not be. "I knew that on fifth Sunday you wear White and they have a woman speaker come, and she speaks from the floor because they won't let her stand in the pulpit," Melinda says. "I never really thought about how that woman felt. . . . Because at the time I had no aspiration to work in ministry, it's not as though I was cognizant of the barriers for women who did want to be in ministry." Now, however, she knows.

Although Melinda had a successful career as a graphic artist for a large advertising firm, she began thinking in her late twenties about pursuing the ministry, and three years ago, she entered the seminary. When she was ordained last year, she became an associate pastor at a large multiethnic, nondenominational church that she'd started attending several years ago. But Pastor Williamson, the minister of the church where Melinda grew up and which her parents still attend, told her that one Sunday he would like her to come back home and speak. Melinda knows, even without his saying so, that women have never been allowed to stand in the pulpit.

> I think one of the decisions I'd have to make is, would I preach from the floor. Here are the old folks who knew me growing up,

and a lot of these very same people who affirmed and encouraged me as I was going to college. Now I'm a woman minister. Are they still pleased with me if I show up as a pastor? So I think I will be forced to make some of those decisions going forward. How much ministry can I do in the Black church if they do not affirm me as a woman? Will I take the stand as the evangelist who says, "It doesn't matter that they won't let me stand in the pulpit? I'll proclaim God's word from the floor?" Or, [decide] if I can't stand in the pulpit, I ain't coming?

Melinda remains unsure whether she will shift in her principles. "I think it depends. I think if it's my parents and it's the people I know and love, I might stand on the floor for them. If it's random folk I don't know at all, it would be much easier to tell them, 'No thank you.'"

Cynthia, 34, has faced both racial and gender bias at different junctures in her ministry. She graduated from seminary seven years ago and initially served as an associate minister with a White male pastor, Reverend Fred Lambert, in a liberal, predominantly White suburban church. At the outset she felt welcomed and accepted as an equal by the pastor, and the congregation was warm and embracing. But as she matured in her role, Cynthia became aware of the pastor's paternalism and lack of sincerity. Reverend Lambert seemed to take great pride in the fact that, unlike most of his White peers, he had a Black minister on staff, and Cynthia came to feel more and more like a showpiece.

At one ministerial staff meeting, Reverend Lambert unveiled a plan of partnering with an economically challenged inner-city Black church in order to provide mentorship and assistance to the church's pastor and lay leaders. What was missing from the plan was any meaningful dialogue with the other church's leadership. Cynthia was appalled at Reverend Lambert's arrogance and racism. There was an assumption that any small Black church in an economically depressed area would want and need his help. Cynthia, who, until that point, had kept a low profile and said very little when she disagreed, finally decided that she must speak. She talked about how shortsighted the plan was. She also quietly began exploring other options for herself. She knew she wanted to move to a Black church. When her husband Adimu was offered a career-enhancing position in the city planning department in a town a thousand miles away, Cynthia encouraged him to take it. They were both ready for a change.

There she was welcomed as an associate pastor at a large Black Baptist church. The pastor, Reverend Hugh Brownlee, was mature and secure in his ministry, and he treated her collegially and supported her fully, as he did the male ministers on his team.

One Sunday morning after Cynthia had preached at the 8 A.M. service, Reverend Brownlee said to her, "You're a very gifted speaker. In a couple of years, you should think about getting your own church." Three years later, Cynthia decided to pursue it. But when she began to apply for positions, she ran headlong into gender bias. After each interview, she says, "The chair of the church committee would call and say, 'You're the best, but we've got to have a man' or 'We really like you, but the congregation won't accept a woman pastor.'" After lots of prayer, reflection, and discussions with Adimu and Reverend Brownlee, Cynthia decided to start her own church. Through this, she hopes to develop a ministry free of the racial and gender bias that has impeded her and so many of her sisters across the nation.

Freeing the Body, Mind, and Spirit

Liberation has been a central theme in the Christian theology of African American people.[16] Historically, the Black church has been a vehicle not only for spiritual freedom but for social and political freedom as well. Slave churches were sometimes subversive, flouting the law by teaching slaves to read and providing the impetus for enslaved Blacks to fight back or flee. The spirituals, a uniquely African American religious music form born of slavery, often included a cloaked message of empowerment. "Swing low, sweet chariot, comin' for to carry me home" speaks of freedom through one's eventual journey to heaven *and* via the underground railroad that could carry the slave to freedom on Earth. Black clergy, congregations, and religious organizations, as exemplified in the leadership of the Reverend Martin Luther King Jr. and the Southern Christian Leadership Conference (SCLC), were the foundation of the civil rights movement of the 1960s. Biblical stories like that in Exodus, telling of the Hebrews' dramatic escape from the Egyptians, have long been centerpieces of Sunday morning sermons.

Yet it's clear that liberation, both outside and inside the church, has not been fully realized. Within houses of worship, gender bias and sexism have often been ignored, tolerated, and even directly promoted. Though the church has been an oasis, a place that provides solace and spiritual sustenance for many Black women, it has too often been hurtful and damaging as well. Women's voices have been muffled, and at times, completely silenced. Many Black women are left with mixed feelings, seeing the church as a source of spiritual and emotional guidance and support, but also as a place where they have to fight to be seen as equal, as capable, as valuable, as whole. They end up shifting—maneuvering, conforming, adapting, and often settling, to make it work. Or they fight back. Or they walk away.

Sheila, who was insulted by a bishop the day before her ordination and who's still struggling to create a role for herself as an assistant pastor, contrasts sexism in the Black church with painful incidents of bigotry that she experienced in the workplace. Long before she was ordained, she earned her MBA and worked in information systems for two large corporations. In one case, she had to resign under duress because of the blatant gender discrimination.

Yet, she is more disappointed by the bias she has experienced in the church, a space that is expected to be a safe harbor from the inequities and hostility of the outside world. "I get angry at gender bias in both arenas—at work and at church," Sheila says. "But when we look at what the church is supposed to represent, then I really get angry, because the doctrine around love and acceptance and caring and nurturing and empowering and all that is still in tension with that old need to be in control and for men to yield to their own insecurities."

Cynthia, who recently made the decision to start her own church after being turned down as pastor by several church committees, sums up her thoughts this way: "It's not all right to be kept out because you're a woman, or kept out because you're Black. And doing it in God's name does not make it any better." She continues: "In our sacred places, it's not all right to do unkind things. You don't have to look in the Bible to see which one of the commandments that is. Try the commandment to love. [Refusing to share power with women in church], that's not loving. We need to begin to figure out this belief system that we have overlaid on this thing called Christianity."

The Black church has been critical for the survival of the Black community. It has been a lifeline. Yet to fulfill its mission of fostering spiritual and sociopolitical liberation, we strongly believe that the church must work actively and deliberately to empower *all* of its people—women and men alike. True spiritual liberation requires people to be whole—to use their gifts and abilities, to develop their leadership skills, to share all of themselves. The Black community can hardly afford unused talents and untapped potential. Yet this is exactly what gender bias promotes.

Sexism is damaging to all of us—to those who feel spurned and betrayed and whose hopes are dashed, to those who are blind to the bias, to those who collude silently with it, and to those who directly perpetuate it. It impedes women directly—stealing from them a belief in their own possibilities—and it constrains men indirectly—robbing them of the gifts of half of their kin and pressing them into limited, rigid, gender-defined roles as well.

We encourage Black men and women, lay people and clergy, to join together to address the issue of gender bias in the church. In her years as a member of Black Baptist and Methodist congregations, Kumea, one of the authors, is struck by the virtual absence of conversations about women's issues and gender inequity. The unwillingness to acknowledge and dialogue about gender bias—the gender silence—must first be conquered in order for churches to move forward. Ultimately, the Black church can play a pivotal role in challenging sexism outside the sanctuary as well—as a champion of nonsexist beliefs, policies, and practices in the larger society and world. Thankfully, some churches, pastors, and lay people are already engaged in this work.

What's clear is that the growth and vitality of the Black church depends upon Black women being fully included and supported—encouraged to use all of their God-given gifts and to spread their wings and soar.

AFTERWORD

I'm a Black woman. I'm an African American queen, and it is very important because I feel that I am a chosen one to show the way to others that can't see the way. I feel that when I was given birth, the plan was, "We need her to be a woman, and we need her to be Black, because we need her to show that nothing can stop you." I definitely feel that's what we demonstrate—power, more than any other woman that walks this Earth. I tell people that it is an honor and a privilege to be a Black woman.

CHARLOTTE, 42, NEW YORK

During the two years we spent researching and writing this book, we were struck by the power of Black women—not just the storied acts of courage that have brought fame to a few, but the everyday resilience displayed by a school teacher in Dallas, a scientist in Chicago, an unemployed mother in Denver, and so many others. As we listened to hundreds of our sisters around the country, we were also touched by their vulnerability, their all too human need to be understood and appreciated, not only as African Americans and as women, but as individuals who have much to share.

Shifting, all the ways that Black women navigate bigotry—as well as the emotional ripples that they experience because of it—is, for now, a necessity. But it doesn't have to be. By listening to the voices in these chapters, we as a society can begin to see African American women in all their dimensions. Black women can finally break free from the myths and stereotypes that have shrouded them for so long, as we recognize them for the whole, vibrant, and complicated beings that they are.

Their stories not only illuminate the common experiences all Americans share, but they help us realize that there is value in differences. Each of us can learn from someone unlike ourselves. We may find that we are enriched by the experience of speaking with a different voice or adopting a style of worship that we once discounted or were unaware of. We may learn a new, more satisfying way to cope with the travails that are an inevitable part of life.

What's needed is a mutuality of accommodation between diverse groups. The more our misperceptions and prejudices break down, the more we come to understand and celebrate differences, the less shifting Black women and other stigmatized groups will have to do. All people will have more freedom to be who they are, to accept themselves, and to contribute their unique voices and style to this nation and the world.

And for those of us who care about social equity, justice, and the well-being of others, knowing the realities of Black women's lives can make us more conscientious, more compassionate. It can push us to become leaders and activists in our own families, in our communities and beyond. It can help us to speak up when we might have otherwise kept silent. It can spur us on to bring about real change.

Most of all, we hope that the women who speak out in *Shifting* will be a source of inspiration for African American women everywhere, as they are for the two of us. However Black women shift, it is imperative that each and every one remember who she is; that she affirm her own gifts and those of her sisters; that she recognize that her opinions have value, that a stranger's beauty does not outshine her own and that she carries her own unique song. It is important, too, that she know her own threshold—when the shifting is too much—and that she always remember that no matter how far she wanders to make her way in the world, it is never too late to find the way back to her self.

The African American Women's Voices Project

This appendix includes:

- Results of the survey of Black women
- Demographic profile of the survey participants
- Demographic profile of the interviewees

Results of the Survey of Black Women

From August 2000 to April 2002, 1700 surveys were distributed and 333 Black women completed and returned them.

Kumea Shorter-Gooden and two research assistants reviewed the surveys and developed a coding manual based on the responses. Then they each independently coded a sample of 30 surveys in order to determine if they could be coded reliably. All three coders agreed 95 percent of the time. Given that this is a very acceptable level of agreement, the remaining surveys were each coded by one of the three researchers. Data were then input into SPSS 11.0 for Windows.

For more details on the research, see the description of the African American Women's Voices Project in Chapter 1.

1. In the United States, do you think there are negative stereotypes about Black women?

    NOTE: *For yes/no questions and other multiple-choice items, the percentages are rounded off, so they don't always equal 100 percent.*

Yes	97%
No	3%

2. If so, what are the stereotypes that you are aware of?

    NOTE: *Where respondents are asked to list responses, they sometimes listed none and sometimes listed more than one, so percentages don't add to 100 percent.*

Sexually promiscuous, loose, immoral, whore	31%
Hard to deal with, "ghetto," hostile, rude	27%
Uneducated, unintelligent, incompetent	24%
Domineering, demanding, emasculating, aggressive	23%
Poor, on welfare, unemployed	23%
Unwed mother, lots of babies	19%
Loud, flamboyant, boisterous	16%
Money-hungry, gold digger, shopaholic	12%
Lazy, not ambitious, doesn't want to work	11%

3. How have you been affected by these negative stereotypes?

    80% indicated they had been affected

    20% indicated that they had not been affected

4. What are the major difficulties that you face as a Black woman?

Difficulties in the job market or workplace	39%
Issues in relationships with Black men	19%
Having to prove self, underestimated, difficulty getting respect	15%
Having to fight stereotypes	14%
Having to play numerous roles, responsible for others	5%

5. Have you ever had to deal with prejudice or discrimination because you're Black?

Yes	90%
No	10%

Examples:

Workplace discrimination	41%
Discrimination in service in stores or restaurants	20%
Treated like a criminal, e.g., followed in stores, harassed by police	13%
Target or witness of racial slurs	10%

6. Have you ever had to deal with prejudice or discrimination because you're a woman?

Yes	69%
No	31%

Examples:

Workplace discrimination	34%
Discrimination in service in stores or restaurants	8%
Sexual harassment or assault	4%

7. Have you ever felt that you needed to change the way that you act in order to fit in or be accepted by White people?

Yes	58%
No	42%

Examples:

Blend in, talk about things they're interested in, can't be myself	24%
Change way of speaking, use of slang, enunciation	23%
Change hairstyle or clothing	7%
More restrained, less animated, quieter	6%
Play up education and accomplishments	5%

8. When you're around Black men, do you ever feel that you need to downplay your abilities and strengths?

Yes	40%
No	61%

9. Have you ever experienced prejudice or discrimination from other Blacks?

Yes	85%
No	15%

Examples:

Disliked or mistreated because of skin color	24%
Envied/mistreated because seen as more successful	20%
Put down for acting/sounding "White"	12%
Disliked or mistreated because of hair texture, length, or style	8%
Looked down on because of less education, income, or status	6%

Demographic Profile of the Survey Participants

Following is demographic information on the 333 Black women who completed the survey.

1. Race/Ethnicity

African American	91%
Bi/multiracial	5%
Caribbean	2%
Other	3%

2. Age

18 to 25 years	15%
26 to 33 years	25%
34 to 42 years	22%
43 to 54 years	21%
55 to 68 years	12%
69 to 88 years	5%

3. Do you have children?

Yes	60%
No	40%

4. Employment status

Employed	64%
Student	13%
Employed & Student	9%
Retired	12%
Unemployed	2%

5. What is your current job position (or your most recent position)?

Professional or technical	38%
Manager or administrator	21%
Sales	5%
Clerical	25%
Service worker	9%
Other	3%

6. Most of my work experiences have been in:

Settings with very few Blacks	41%
Settings which are very racially mixed	33%
Settings which are mostly Black	18%
Other	8%

7. Education

Some high school	1%
High school graduate	7%
Technical school	2%
Some college	28%
Bachelor's degree	18%
Graduate work or graduate degree	44%

8. Marital status

Single, never married	40%
Married	32%
Separated	2%
Divorced	18%
Widowed	5%
Living with partner	2%

9. Sexual orientation

Heterosexual	94%
Lesbian	4%
Other	3%

10. Current household income (per year)

Up to $14,999	10%
$15,000 to $29,999	16%
$30,000 to $49,999	23%
$50,000 to $69,999	20%
$70,000 to $99,999	14%
$100,000 or more	17%

11. Religion

Christian	87%
Muslim	1%
Other	7%
None	5%

12. Are you an active member of a church or religious group?

Yes	71%
No	28%

13. State and region (per the U.S. Census Bureau)

Northeast: Connecticut, Massachusetts, New Jersey, New York, Pennsylvania	11%
South: Alabama, Arkansas, Delaware, Florida, Georgia, Louisiana, Maryland, North Carolina, Oklahoma, Texas, Virginia, Washington, D.C.	38%
Midwest: Illinois, Michigan, Minnesota, and Ohio	8%
West: Arizona, California, Colorado, Washington	43%

Demographic Profile of the Interviewees

Following is demographic information on the 71 Black women who were interviewed.

1. Race/Ethnicity

   African American   94%

   Bi/multiracial   1%

   Caribbean   3%

   Other   1%

2. Were you born in the United States?

   Yes   96%

   No   4%

3. Age

   18 to 25 years   13%

   26 to 33 years   19%

   34 to 42 years   30%

   43 to 54 years   22%

   55 to 68 years   10%

   69 to 88 years   6%

4. Do you have children?

   Yes   51%

   No   49%

5. Employment status

    Employed   68%

    Student   11%

    Employed & student   10%

    Retired   6%

    Unemployed   6%

6. What is your current (or most recent) job position?

    Professional or technical   41%

    Manager or administrator   19%

    Sales   7%

    Clerical   21%

    Operative   2%

    Service worker   9%

    Private household worker   2%

7. Most of my work experiences have been in:

    Settings with very few Blacks   49%

    Settings which are very racially mixed   30%

    Settings which are mostly Black   14%

    Other   7%

8. Education

    Some high school   3%

    High school graduate   7%

    Technical school   1%

    Some college   32%

    Bachelor's degree   14%

    Graduate work or graduate degree   42%

9. Marital status

   Single, never married   52%

   Married   17%

   Separated   6%

   Divorced   16%

   Widowed   4%

   Living with partner   4%

10. Sexual orientation

   Heterosexual   96%

   Lesbian   3%

   Other   1%

11. Current household income (per year)

   Up to $14,999   20%

   $15,000 to $29,999   10%

   $30,000 to $49,999   25%

   $50,000 to $69,999   22%

   $70,000 to $99,999   6%

   $100,000 to $199,999   13%

   $200,000 or more   4%

12. Religion

   Christian   76%

   Buddhist   3%

   Other   11%

   None   10%

13. Are you an active member of a church or religious group?

Yes	59%
No	41%

14. State and region (per U.S. Census Bureau)

Northeast: New York, Pennsylvania	11%
South: Georgia, Kentucky, Maryland, Texas, Virginia, Washington, D.C.	49%
Midwest: Ohio	6%
West: California	34%

NOTES

Chapter 1: The Roots of Shifting

1. These figures are based on Census 2000. Available on-line at: www.census.gov/main/www/cen2000.html.

2. This Gallup Poll was conducted from June 3 to 9, 2002 with 1010 participants. The margin of error is 10 percentage points. This information is based on phone conversations with Mrs. Judith Keneman at the Gallup Organization in August 2002.

3. See bell hooks (1981). *Ain't I a Woman: Black Women and Feminism.* Boston, MA: South End Press. On the notion of "gendered racism," see Philomena Essed (1991). *Understanding Everyday Racism: An Interdisciplinary Theory.* Newbury Park, CA: Sage. Also see Yanick St. Jean & Joe R. Feagin (1998). *Double Burden: Black Women and Everyday Racism.* Armonk, NY: M. E. Sharpe.

4. During the years 2000 to 2002, seventeen hundred (1700) surveys were distributed and 333 were completed and returned, for a return rate of 20 percent. Women generally took from 15 to 35 minutes to complete the survey. A bookmark was included in each questionnaire packet as a token of appreciation.

5. As with the surveys, we aimed to recruit a diverse cross-section of women from varying walks of life. The interviews were conducted in eight dif-

ferent areas of the U.S., including the Northeast, South, Midwest, and West. Five interviews were conducted by phone. All others were face-to-face. We collected demographic and background information from each interviewee before beginning the interview, which generally lasted from 1½ to 2½ hours. All but two interviews were audiotaped. A semi-structured interview protocol that we developed for this study provided a framework for the interview, and the questions were similar to those on the survey. Five women participated in both the interview and the survey.

As a journalist and psychologist, we are guided by somewhat different professional codes and ethics in conducting research. Kumea and three research assistants/interviewers, who worked under her auspices, engaged in a recruitment and interviewing process that was approved by the Human Subjects Protection Committee at Alliant International University where Kumea is on the faculty. The women whom they interviewed were given $30 as a token of appreciation.

6. Many of the women we interviewed are highly educated professional women, sometimes with PhDs or advanced degrees. Others are currently or previously on welfare, and one woman, who was recently homeless, was living, at the time of the interview, with her children in one room in a family's home. Most of our interviewees are active in the work force; a number are in college, and some are retired. Most are heterosexual; however, two are lesbian, and one is bisexual. The interviewees represent all marital statuses—married, single, divorced, separated, widowed, and living with a partner. Two have husbands who were incarcerated at the time of the interview. Most are mothers, some are grandmothers, and one was a great-grandmother. Three-quarters are Christian; however, a couple of the interviewees are Buddhists or of other faiths, and a small number were not religious. The majority are active members of a church or religious group. A couple of our interviewees are physically challenged or chronically disabled. (See Appendix for additional information on the interviewees.)

7. Kumea Shorter-Gooden and two research assistants reviewed the surveys and developed a coding manual based on the responses. Then they each independently coded a sample of 30 surveys in order to determine if they could be coded reliably. All three coders agreed 95 percent of the time. Given that this is a very acceptable level of agreement, the remaining surveys were

each coded by one of the three researchers. Data were then input into SPSS 11.0 for Windows.

8. See (1) David G. Blanchflower & Andrew J. Oswald (Jan. 2000). Well-being over time in Britain and the USA. Working Paper 7487. National Bureau of Economic Research. Cambridge, MA; (2) Bruce S. Jonas & Ronald W. Wilson (March 6, 1997). Negative mood and urban versus rural residence: Using proximity to metropolitan statistical areas as an alternative measure of residence. Vital and Health Statistics of the Centers for Disease Control and Prevention, National Center for Health Statistics, No. 281. Available on-line at: www.cdc.gov/nchs/data/ad/ad281.pdf; and (3) Roy L. Austin & Hiroko Hayama Dodge (1992). Despair, distrust and dissatisfaction among Blacks and women, 1973–1987. *The Sociological Quarterly*, 33(4): 579–598.

9. This study was based on data from the 1991 National Health Interview Survey. See Bruce S. Jonas & Ronald W. Wilson (March 6, 1997). Negative mood and urban versus rural residence.

10. All of the clients and research participants are disguised so that they are not identifiable. Pseudonyms are used, ages are sometimes changed by a few years, locations are altered, and other identifying information, like occupation and family composition, is modified as necessary to protect the confidentiality of the women.

11. U.S. Census Bureau (2002). Table No. 216. Educational attainment, by race, Hispanic origin, and sex: 1960 to 2000. *Statistical Abstract of the United States*: 2001. Washington, D.C.

12. Bill Maxwell, "Blacks Caught in Education Gap," *Times Union*, August 8, 2000.

13. U.S. Census Bureau (2002). Table No. 216. Educational attainment.

14. Bill Maxwell, "Blacks Caught in Education Gap."

15. Martin C. Evans & Lauren Terrazzano, "The Faces of Tomorrow/ For Better and Worse/ It's a Paradox: Many Black Women are Making Gains while Others Fall Behind," *Newsday*, January 25, 1999.

16. Regina E. Romero (2000). The icon of the strong Black woman: The paradox of strength. In Leslie C. Jackson & Beverly Greene (Eds.), *Psychotherapy with African American Women: Innovations in Psychodynamic Perspectives and Practice* (pp. 225–238). New York: Guilford Press.

17. While there is evidence that Blacks are more involved in street crime

than Whites, Katheryn Russell reports that criminologists are not in agreement on whether this reflects an actual difference in criminal behavior or whether it reflects a disparity in the criminal justice system where "street" crime in contrast to "suite" crime is emphasized. See Katheryn Russell (2002). Development of a Black criminology and the role of the Black criminologist. In Shaun L. Gabbidon, Helen Taylor Greene, & Vernetta D. Young (Eds.), *African American Classics in Criminology and Criminal Justice* (pp. 281–292). Thousand Oaks, CA: Sage.

18. Fully 76 percent of Black women and 70 percent of Black men believed the rights of whites were being respected in the criminal justice system. See Note 2 for this chapter.

19. Bureau of Justice Statistics, Office of Justice Programs, U.S. Department of Justice. Characteristics of Drivers Stopped by Police, 1999. March 2002, NCJ 191548. Available on-line at: www.ojp.usdoj.gov/bjs/pub/pdf/cdsp99.pdf.

20. In a review of the impact of minority female status on treatment by the criminal justice system, Coramae Richey Mann reports that one study indicates that Black women are seven times more likely to be arrested for prostitution than women of other ethnic groups, yet it has not been established that there are a greater number of Black prostitutes. Mann also reports on a study that indicates that police are more likely to use their discretionary power not to arrest White rather than Black women. See Coramae Richey Mann (2002). Minority and female: A criminal justice double bind. In Gabbidon et al. (Eds.), *African American Classics* (pp. 263–277).

21. U.S. General Accounting Office (March 2000). U.S. Customs Service better targeting of airline passengers for personal searches could produce better results. Report to the Honorable Richard J. Durbin, United States Senate, Washington, D.C. In this horrifying report, the GAO states that in fiscal year 1998, Black women were significantly more likely to be strip-searched by customs inspectors than any other group of U.S. citizens. Black women were almost twice as likely as white men and women to be subjected to the invasive search, and nearly three times as likely as Black men. Yet Black women were about half as likely as Black men and only 1.4 times as likely as White women to be found carrying drugs or other illicit items during such examinations.

That same year, Black women were nine times more likely than White female U.S. citizens to be X-rayed after being searched or patted down. But, based on the X-ray results, Black women were less than half as likely to be carrying illegal goods as White women. Black women tended to be X-rayed more often than Black men when searched. Yet, among all citizens X-rayed for contraband, including Asians and Hispanics, Black women were least likely to be found carrying it.

22. Patricia Hill Collins (1991). *Black Feminist Thought: Knowledge, Consciousness, and the Politics of Empowerment* (chap. 4). New York: Routledge. Also see Chapter 2 in bell hooks (1981). *Ain't I a Woman: Black Women and Feminism.* Boston, MA: South End Press.

23. Kathleen H. Sparrow (2000). Dating and mating patterns. In N. J. Burgess & E. Brown (Eds.), *African American Women: An Ecological Perspective* (pp. 41–52). New York: Falmer Press.

24. The higher rate of teen pregnancy in Black girls is due in part to slightly higher rates of sexual activity and in part to less effective contraceptive use. See: (1) The Alan Guttmacher Institute. (1994). *Sex and America's Teenagers.* New York: The Alan Guttmacher Institute. (2) Robert Joseph Taylor, M. Belinda Tucker, Linda M. Chatters, & Rukmalie Jayakody (1997). Recent demographic trends in African American family structure. In Robert Joseph Taylor, James S. Jackson, & Linda M. Chatters (Eds.), *Family Life in Black America* (pp.14–62). Thousand Oaks, CA: Sage. (3) Gail E. Wyatt (1997) *Stolen Women: Reclaiming Our Sexuality, Taking Back Our Lives,* New York: John Wiley & Sons.

25. The teen birth rate has been decreasing in all ethnic groups. From 1991 to 1998, for girls ages 15 to 19 years, there was a 26 percent decrease for Blacks, a 19 percent decrease for non-Hispanic Whites, a 12 percent decrease for Hispanics, and a 16 percent decrease each for American Indians and Asian or Pacific Islanders. For 10 to 14 year olds, the birth rate decreased at an even higher rate. See: Number of births to women under 20 years by age, race, and Hispanic origin of mother: United States, 1998; birth rates, 1991–98; and percent change in rates, 1991–98, National Vital Statistics Reports, 47(26), October 25, 1999. Available on-line at: www.cdc.gov/nccd-php/drh/pdf/nvs47_26.pdf.

26. Gail E. Wyatt (1997). *Stolen Women.*

27. Jill A. Cermele, Sharon Daniels, & Kristin L. Anderson (2001). Defining normal: Constructions of race and gender in the DSM-IV Casebook. *Feminism & Psychology*, 11(2): 229–247.

Chapter 2: The Pain of Gender Silence

1. See Kumea Shorter-Gooden & N. Chanell Washington (1996). Young, Black, and female: The challenge of weaving an identity. *Journal of Adolescence*, 19: 465–475. Also see similar findings of the greater salience of race than gender for Black women from the 1984 and 1996 National Black Elections Studies as presented in: Claudine Gay & Katherine Tate (1998). Doubly bound: The impact of gender and race on the politics of Black women. *Political Psychology*, 19(1): 169–184.

2. Jessica Henderson Daniel (1995). The discourse on Thomas vs. Hill: A resource for perspectives on the Black woman and sexual trauma. *Journal of Feminist Family Therapy*, 7(1–2): 103–117. Also see Jessica Henderson Daniel (2000). African American women's memories of racial trauma. In Leslie C. Jackson & Beverly Greene (Eds.), *Psychotherapy with African American Women: Innovations in Psychodynamic Perspectives and Practice* (pp. 126–144). New York: Guilford Press.

Kimberlé Crenshaw introduced the term "gender silence." See Kimberlé Crenshaw (1992). Whose story is it, anyway? Feminist and antiracist appropriations of Anita Hill. In Toni Morrison (Ed.), *Race-ing Justice, En-gendering Power: Essays on Anita Hill, Clarence Thomas, and the Construction of Social Reality* (pp. 402–440). New York: Pantheon Books.

3. Paula Giddings (1992). The last taboo. In Toni Morrison (Ed.), *Race-ing Justice, En-gendering Power* (pp. 441–465). Also see Audre Lorde (1984). Age, race, class, and sex: Women redefining difference. *Sister Ousider* (pp. 114–123). Freedom, CA: The Crossing Press.

4. Frances Beale, a political activist, first coined the term "double jeopardy" to refer to the plight of Black women. See Frances Beale (1970). Double jeopardy: To be Black and female. In Toni Cade (Ed.), *The Black Woman: An Anthology* (pp. 90–100). New York: A Mentor Book.

5. Beverly Daniel Tatum (2000). Defining racism: "Can we talk?" In M.

Adams, W.J. Blumenfeld, R. Castañeda, H. W. Hackman, M. L. Peters, & X. Zúñiga (Eds.), *Readings for Diversity and Social Justice: An Anthology on Racism, Antisemitism, Sexism, Heterosexism, Ableism, and Classism* (pp. 79–82). New York: Routledge.

6. Current Population Survey, Bureau of Labor Statistics, Department of Labor (2002). Median weekly earnings of full-time wage and salary workers by selected characteristics. Available on-line at: www.bls.gov/cps/cpsaat37.pdf.

7. Jann Adams (1997). Sexual harassment and Black women: A historical perspective. In W. O'Donohue (Ed.), *Sexual Harassment: Theory, Research, and Treatment.* Needham Heights, Massachusetts: Allyn & Bacon.

8. Wyatt and Riederle also found that single, Black women were more likely to be sexually harassed at work than White women. See Gail E. Wyatt & Monika Riederle (1995). The prevalence and context of sexual harassment among African American and White American women. *Journal of Interpersonal Violence*, 10(3):309–321.

9. Gail E. Wyatt (1985). The sexual abuse of Afro-American and White-American women in childhood. *Child Abuse & Neglect*, 9: 507–519. In this research, which is one of the few studies of child sexual abuse with a random, representative, community sample, the rate of child sexual abuse was similar for Black and White women. Wyatt points out, however, that a number of studies have found that Blacks have a higher rate of child sexual abuse than Whites. Also see a follow-up study where there were similar findings: Gail E. Wyatt, Tamra Burns Loeb, Beatriz Solis, & Jennifer Vargas Carmona (1999). The prevalence and circumstances of child sexual abuse: Changes across a decade. *Child Abuse & Neglect*, 23(1): 45–60.

10. Common chant sung by some Black fraternities.

11. Nijole Benokraitis and other social scientists address the significance of "subtle sexism" in her edited anthology. See Nijole V. Benokraitis (Ed.) (1997). *Subtle Sexism: Current Practice and Prospects for Change.* Thousand Oaks, CA: Sage.

12. Beth Bonniwell Haslett & Susan Lipman (1997). Micro inequities: Up close and personal. In Nijole V. Benokraitis (Ed.), *Subtle Sexism* (pp. 34–53).

Chapter 3: The Many Shifts of Black Women

1. In addition to the research mentioned in the same paragraph, there are a couple of literature reviews which summarize the findings on the impact of racism and sexism on physical and mental health. For two excellent reviews, see Nancy Krieger, Diane L. Rowley, Allen A. Herman, Byllye Avery, & Mona T. Phillips (1993). Racism, sexism, and social class: Implications for studies of health, disease, and well-being. *American Journal of Preventive Medicine*, 9 (Suppl. 6): 82–122; and Rodney Clark, Norman B. Anderson, Vernessa R. Clark, & David R. Williams (1999). Racism as a stressor for African Americans: A biopsychosocial model. *American Psychologist*, 54(10): 805–816.

2. Elizabeth A. Klonoff, Hope Landrine, & Jodie B. Ullman (1999). Racial discrimination and psychiatric symptoms among Blacks. *Cultural Diversity and Ethnic Minority Psychology*, 5(4): 329–339.

3. Hope Landrine & Elizabeth A. Klonoff (1997). *Discrimination against Women: Prevalence, Consequences, Remedies*. Thousand Oaks, CA: Sage.

4. Carolyn M. Aldwin (1994). *Stress, Coping, and Development: An Integrative Perspective*. New York: Guilford Press.

5. Richard S. Lazarus & Susan Folkman (1984). *Stress, Appraisal, and Coping*. New York: Springer.

6. Clifford L. Broman (1996). Coping with personal problems. In Harold W. Neighbors & James S. Jackson (Eds.), *Mental Health in Black America* (pp. 117–129). Thousand Oaks, CA: Sage.

7. Cheryl Bernadette Leggon (1980). Black female professionals: Dilemmas and contradictions of status. In La Frances Rodgers-Rose (Ed.), *The Black Woman* (pp. 189–202). Beverly Hills, CA: Sage.

8. In 2000, 78 percent of African American women ages 25 and older had completed high school, and 17 percent had completed a bachelor's degree or more. The high school completion rate for Black men, White women, and White men is 79 percent, 85 percent, and 85 percent, respectively. The college completion rate for Black men, White women, and White men is 16 per-

cent, 24 percent, and 29 percent, respectively. See U.S. Census Bureau (2002). Table No. 216. Educational attainment, by race, Hispanic origin, and sex: 1960 to 2000. *Statistical Abstract of the United States: 2001.* Washington, D.C.

9. Janet K. Swim, Laurie L. Cohen, & Lauri L. Hyers (1998). Experiencing everyday prejudice and discrimination. In Janet K. Swim & Charles Stangor (Eds.), *Prejudice: The Target's Perspective* (pp. 37–60). San Diego: Academic Press.

10. Sherman A. James (1994). John Henryism and the health of African-Americans. *Culture, Medicine and Psychiatry,* 18: 163–182.

11. Ibid.

12. Brenda Major & Toni Schmader (1998). Coping with stigma through psychological disengagement. In Janet K. Swim & Charles Stangor (Eds.), *Prejudice: The Target's Perspective* (pp. 219–241).

13. Smyth and Yarandi administered the Ways of Coping Questionnaire to a sample of 656 African American women and completed a factor analysis of the responses. Factor analysis is a statistical method that informs the researcher which sets of items on a questionnaire or measure tend to yield similar responses and what underlying attitudes or beliefs are reflected in respondents' answers. Smyth and Yarandi identified three factors: *active coping,* efforts to change the situation; *avoidance coping,* wishful thinking and efforts to escape the problem through fantasy, overindulging, or taking it out on others; and *minimize the situation,* minimizing the problem and detaching oneself from the situation. See Kathleen Smyth & Hossein N. Yarandi (1996). Factor analysis of the Ways of Coping Questionnaire for African American women. *Nursing Research,* 45(1): 25–29.

14. Karen M. Ruggiero & Donald M. Taylor (1997). Why minority group members perceive or do not perceive the discrimination that confronts them: The role of self-esteem and perceived control. *Journal of Personality and Social Psychology,* 72(2): 373–389.

15. Karen M. Ruggiero & David M. Marx (1999). Less pain and more to gain: Why high-stai ; group members blame their failure on discrimination. *Journal of Personality and Social Psychology,* 77(4): 774–784.

16. Nancy Krieger (1990). Racial and gender discrimination: Risk factors for high blood pressure? *Social Science and Medicine,* 30(12): 1273–1281.

17. More than 81 percent of Black women in the National Survey of Black Americans reported that they used prayer as a way to cope with serious personal problems. The NSBA is a national survey conducted by the Program for Research on Black Americans at the University of Michigan. The findings derive from 2107 completed interviews conducted in 1979 and 1980. See Clifford L. Broman (1996). Coping with personal problems. In Harold W. Neighbors & James S. Jackson (Eds.), *Mental Health in Black America* (pp. 117–129). Thousand Oaks, CA: Sage. Also see Robert Hill's discussion of strong religious orientation as a core strength of Black families in Robert B. Hill (1999). *The Strengths of African American Families: Twenty-Five Years Later* (chapter 8). Lanham, MD: University Press of America.

18. Robert J. Taylor, Cheryl B. Hardison, & Linda M. Chatters (1996). Kin and nonkin as sources of informal assistance. In Harold W. Neighbors & James S. Jackson (Eds.), *Mental Health in Black America* (pp. 130–145). Also Robert J. Taylor, Linda M. Chatters, & James S. Jackson (1997). Changes over time in support network involvement among Black Americans. In Robert Joseph Taylor, James S. Jackson, & Linda M. Chatters (Eds.), *Family Life in Black America* (pp. 295–318). Thousand Oaks, CA: Sage.

Also see Robert Hill's discussion of kinship bonds as a core strength of Black families. Robert B. Hill (1999). *The Strengths of African American Families* (chap. 7).

19. Beverly Greene (1994). African American women. In Lillian Comas-Díaz & Beverly Greene (Eds.), *Women of Color: Integrating ethnic and Gender Identities in Psychotherapy* (pp. 10–29). New York: Guilford. See pp. 20–22 on internalized racism.

20. Virginia E. O'Leary & Jeannette R. Ickovics (1995). Resilience and thriving in response to challenge: An opportunity for a paradigm shift in women's health. *Women's Health: Research on Gender, Behavior, and Policy,* 1(2): 121–142.

Chapter 4: Seeking a Voice

1. John Russell Rickford & Russell John Rickford (2000). *Spoken Soul: The Story of Black English.* New York: John Wiley & Sons. Note that while the

term "Standard English" is often utilized, the term itself conveys the bias against other dialects or forms of English. Marilyn Lovett and Joneka Neely recommend the alternative term "Marketplace English," to denote the form of English that is expected to compete in the American marketplace. See Marilyn Lovett & Joneka Neely (1997). On becoming bilingual. *Journal of Black Psychology*, 23(3):242–244.

2. Rosina Lippi-Green (1997). *English with an Accent: Language, Ideology, and Discrimination in the United States*. London: Routledge.

3. Karla D. Scott (2000). Broadening the view of Black language use: Toward a better understanding of words and worlds. In Alberto González, Marsha Houston, & Victoria Chen (Eds.), *Our Voices: Essays in Culture, Ethnicity, and Communication* (3rd ed., pp. 164–170). Los Angeles: Roxbury.

4. RoseMarie Pérez Foster (1996). Assessing the psychodynamic function of language in the bilingual patient. In RoseMarie Pérez Foster, Michael Moskowitz, & Rafael Art. Javier (Eds.), *Reaching across Boundaries of Culture and Class—Widening the Scope of Psychotherapy* (pp. 243–263). New York: Jason Aronson.

5. For the perspective of linguists, see Rosina Lippi-Green (1997). *English with an Accent* (chap. 1). For the perspective of anthropologists, see Marvin Harris (1989). Primitive languages? *Our Kind: Who We Are, Where We Came From, Where We Are Going*. New York: Harper Perennial.

6. John Russell Rickford & Russell John Rickford (2000). *Spoken Soul*. This father-son team has written a moving account of the value and virtues of Black English.

7. Geneva Smitherman (1977). *Talkin and Testifyin: The Language of Black America*. Detroit, MI: Wayne State University Press.

8. Ibid.

9. Karla D. Scott (2002). Conceiving the language of Black women's everyday talk. In Marsha Houston & Olga Idriss Davis (Eds.), *Centering Ourselves: African American Feminist and Womanist Studies of Discourse* (pp. 53–73). Cresskill, NJ: Hampton Press.

10. Marsha Houston (2000). Multiple perspectives: African American women conceive their talk. *Women and Language*, 23(1): 11–17.

11. Rosina Lippi-Green (1997). *English with an Accent*.

12. For an in-depth history and analysis of African American Vernacular

English and of the 1996 Oakland School Board controversy, see John Russell Rickford & Russell John Rickford (2000). *Spoken Soul*. Also see Chapter 7 on the Oakland School Board controversy in Robin Tolmach Lakoff (2000). *The Language War*. Berkeley, CA: University of California Press.

13. Lisa M. Koch, Alan M. Gross, & Russell Kolts (2001). Attitudes toward Black English and code switching. *Journal of Black Psychology*, 27(1): 29–42.

14. Karla D. Scott (2002). Conceiving the language.

Chapter 5: *The Sisterella Complex*

1. There are several possible diagnoses of depression. Major depressive disorder is one of the more severe forms of depression. See American Psychiatric Association (2000). *Diagnostic and Statistical Manual of Mental Disorders—Fourth Edition, Text Revision* (DSM-IV-TR). Washington, D.C.

2. National Institute of Mental Health, The Numbers Count—Mental Disorders in America. NIH Publication No. 01–4584, 2001. Available on-line at: www.nimh.nih.gov/publicat/numbers.cfm.

3. Diane Robinson Brown. (1990). Depression among Blacks: An epidemiologic perspective. In Dorothy S. Ruiz (Ed.), *Handbook of Mental Health and Mental Disorder among Black Americans* (pp. 71–93). New York: Greenwood Press. Some but not all of the greater risk for depression of African Americans and African American women specifically has to do with the fact that they are disproportionately poor and that being poor adds risk.

4. In spite of high rates of depressive symptoms, Black women have very low rates of suicide compared to other groups. In the U.S. in 2000, the rates of completed suicides per 100,000 people was 1.8 for Black women, 9.8 for Black men, 4.5 for White women, and 19.1 for White men. See American Association of Suicidology (2000). Suicide Data Page: 2000. Available on-line at: www.suicidology.org/associations/1045/files/2000datapg.pdf.

5. Joan Berzoff & Michael Hayes (1996). Biopsychosocial aspects of depression. In Joan Berzoff, Laura Melano Flanagan, & Patricia Hertz (Eds.), *Inside Out and Outside In: Psychodynamic Clinical Theory and Practice in Con-*

temporary Multicultural Contexts (pp. 365–396). Northvale, NJ: Jason Aronson.

6. Diane Robinson Brown (1990). Depression among Blacks. Also see Harold W. Neighbors, James S. Jackson, Linn Campbell, & Donald Williams (1989). The influence of racial factors on psychiatric diagnosis: A review and suggestions for research. *Community Mental Health Journal*, 25(4): 301–311.

7. In a review of 11 studies of depression in Blacks, Diane Robinson Brown concludes that Blacks are more likely to have depressive symptoms than Whites, and Black women are especially at risk; however there are no racial differences in the prevalence rates of major depressive disorders. See Diane Robinson Brown (1990). Depression among Blacks.

8. Cheryl L. Thompson (2000). African American women and moral masochism—When there is too much of a good thing. In Leslie C. Jackson & Beverly Greene (Eds.), *Psychotherapy with African American Women—Innovations in Psychodynamic Perspectives and Practice* (pp. 239–250). New York: Guilford Press.

9. Daudi Ajani ya Azibo & Patricia Dixon (1998). The theoretical relationship between materialistic depression and depression: Preliminary data and implications for the Azibo nosology. *Journal of Black Psychology*, 24(2): 211–225.

10. Jeanne Spurlock (1985). Survival guilt and the Afro-American of achievement. *Journal of the National Medical Association*, 77(1): 29–32.

11. Dana Crowley Jack (1991). *Silencing the Self: Women and Depression*. New York: Harper Perennial.

12. Kevin W. Allison (1998). Stress and oppressed social category membership. In Janet K. Swim & Charles Stangor (Eds.), *Prejudice: The Target's Perspective* (pp. 145–170). San Diego: Academic Press.

13. Darielle Watts-Jones (1990). Toward a stress scale for African-American women. *Psychology of Women Quarterly*, 14: 271–275.

14. National Mental Health Association (NMHA) News Release, Depression in African Americans is *not* 'Just the Blues,' May 11, 1998. Available on-line at: www.nmha.org/newsroom/system/news.vs.cfm?do=vw& rid=43.

15. A major national study of the utilization of mental health services by Black, Hispanic, and White insured women found that even when differences

in education and salary were controlled, White women were more likely to use outpatient mental health services than Black and Hispanic women. See Deborah K. Padgett, Cathleen P. Harman, Barbara J. Burns, & Herbert J. Schlesinger (1998). Women and outpatient mental health services: Use by Black, Hispanic, and White women in a national insured population. In Bruce L. Levin, A. K. Blanch, & A. Jennings (Eds.), *Women's Mental Health Services: A Public Health Perspective* (pp. 34–54). Thousand Oaks, CA: Sage.

16. Charisse Jones, "More Blacks are Turning to Counselors for Help," *USA Today*, August 21, 1997.

17. These figures are for women ages 18 and older. The percentage of those who are overweight includes those who are obese. "Overweight" is defined as a BMI (body mass index) of 25 or above. "Obese" is defined as a BMI of 30 or above. See U.S. Census Bureau (2002). Table No. 197. Percent of U.S. adults who were overweight and percent who were obese: 1998. *Statistical Abstract of the United States: 2001*. Washington, D.C.

18. J. M. Siegel, A. K. Yancey, & W. J. McCarthy (2000). Overweight and depressive symptoms among African-American women. *Preventive Medicine*, 31(3): 232–240.

19. American Psychiatric Association (2000). *Diagnostic and Statistical Manual of Mental Disorders*.

20. The sample was randomly selected from women living in Connecticut and the Boston, Massachusetts area. It included 1628 Black women and 5741 White women. Recurrent binge eating was defined as a "minimum average of 2 binge eating episodes per week for a duration of 3 consecutive months." See Ruth H. Striegel-Moore, Denise E. Wilfley, Kathleen M. Pike, Faith-Anne Dohm, & Christopher G. Fairburn (2000). Recurrent binge eating in Black American women. *Archives of Family Medicine*, 9: 83–87.

21. Reports are that Black women spend four times as much on cosmetic and beauty products than White women. See "BeautyandSoul.com Finally Answers Needs of Largest Beauty Consumer—Black Women," *PR Newswire*, November 16, 1999, and "Myriad Opportunities in ethnic merchandising," *Business and Industry*, February 25, 2002, 19(4):28.

22. Regan Lester & Trent A. Petrie (1998). Physical, psychological, and

societal correlates of bulimic symptomatology among African American college women. *Journal of Counseling Psychology*, 45(3): 315–321.

23. Daudi Ajani ya Azibo & Patricia Dixon (1998). The theoretical relationship between materialistic depression and depression.

24. Somatoform disorders are described in: American Psychiatric Association (2000). *Diagnostic and Statistical Manual of Mental Disorders*.

25. The study included 2802 Black women. Black women had significantly higher rates of somatization disorder, a diagnosis based on a certain number of somatic symptoms, as well as somatization syndrome, which refers to the presence of somatic symptoms, but fewer than for a diagnosis of somatization disorder. See Marvin Swartz, Richard Landerman, Linda K. George, Dan G. Blazer, & Javier Escobar (1991). Somatization disorder. In Lee N. Robins & Darrel A. Regier (Eds.), *Psychiatric Disorders in America: The Epidemiologic Catchment Area Study* (pp. 220–257). New York: The Free Press.

26. Joan Berzoff & Michael Hayes (1996). Biopsychosocial aspects of depression. See discussion of self psychology.

Chapter 6: Doing Double Duty

1. The rates of labor force participation are as follows: Blacks, 73 percent, Hispanics, 84 percent, Whites, 77 percent. See Current Population Survey, Bureau of Labor Statistics. Employment status of major age-sex groups by race and Hispanic origin, 1994, 1999, and 2000 annual averages. In Stella Cromartie & Gloria P. Goings (2001). *Labor Force Characteristics of Blacks and Hispanics* (Table 1). Washington, D.C.: U.S. Bureau of Labor Statistics.

2. Full-time work is considered 35 hours or more per week. See Bureau of Labor Statistics, U. S. Department of Labor. "News"—Table 2. Work experience of the population during the year by race, Hispanic origin, and sex, 1999–2000. Available on-line at: www.bls.gov/news.release/work.t02.htm.

3. In 1999, 1.63 million Whites and .96 million Blacks were on public assistance. See U.S. Census Bureau (2002). Table No. 521. Number of persons with income by specified sources of income: 1999. *Statistical Abstract of the United States: 2001*. Washington, D.C.

4. Bureau of Labor Statistics, Department of Labor. Black Women in the Labor Force, No. 97–1, March 1997.

5. Median refers to the number in the middle of a series of numbers. Thus, half of the workers earned more than the median amount and half of the workers earned less. See Current Population Survey, Bureau of Labor Statistics, Department of Labor. Median weekly earnings of full-time wage and salary workers by selected characteristics. Available on-line at: www.bls.gov/cps/cpsaat37.pdf.

6. Catalyst (1997).*Women of Color in Corporate Management: A Statistical Picture.* New York.

7. Ella L. J. Edmondson Bell & Stella M. Nkomo (2001). *Our Separate Ways: Black and White Women and the Struggle for Professional Identity.* Boston: Harvard Business School Press.

8. Lynn Weber & Elizabeth Higginbotham (1997). Black and White professional-managerial women's perceptions of racism and sexism in the workplace. In Elizabeth Higginbotham & Mary Romero (Eds.), *Women and Work: Exploring Race, Ethnicity, and Class* (pp. 153–175). Thousand Oaks, CA: Sage.

9. Diane Hughes & Mark A. Dodge (1997). African American women in the workplace: Relationships between job conditions, racial bias at work, and perceived job quality. *American Journal of Community Psychology*, 25(5): 581–599.

10. Jennifer Tucker, Leslie R. Wolfe, Edna Amparo Viruell-Fuentes, & Wendy Smooth (1999). *No More 'Business as Usual': Women of Color in Corporate America—Report of the National Women of Color Work/Life Survey.* Center for Women Policy Studies, March 1999. This study was sponsored by CWPS, which describes itself as "the nation's first feminist policy research organization." The 1562 participants in the study were from 16 Fortune 1000 companies, and 52 percent of the participants were African American. The statistics on women who feel pressured to downplay their gender is from a phone conversation with Jennifer Tucker, Vice President, CWPS, on August 1, 2002.

11. Catalyst (1999). *Women of Color in Corporate Management : Opportunities and Barriers—Executive Summary.* New York.

12. Current Population Survey, Bureau of Labor Statistics, Department of

Labor. Unemployed persons by marital status, race, age, and sex. Available on-line at: www.bls.gov/cps/cpsaat24.pdf.

13. The official unemployment rate, per the federal government, includes persons without jobs who have looked for a job within the past four weeks or who were laid off and are expecting to return to their previous job. The hidden unemployed are those people who want to work but who have not actively sought a job in the past four weeks. Using data from the 1979–1980 National Survey of Black Americans, which included a representative sample of 2107 Black men and women, Bowman found a hidden unemployment rate of 24 percent for Black women, which was twice their official unemployment rate. See Phillip J. Bowman (1991). Joblessness. In James S. Jackson (Ed.), *Life in Black America* (pp. 156–178). Newbury Park, CA: Sage.

14. Diane Hughes & Mark A. Dodge (1997). African American women in the workplace.

15. This information is based on a conversation with Bernardo Carducci in March 2002. Dr. Carducci's ideas about salient objects have evolved from his work on the dynamics of shyness. See Bernardo Carducci (1999). *Shyness: A Bold New Approach*. New York: HarperCollins.

16. Barbara F. Reskin, Debra B. McBrier, & Julie A. Kmec (1999). The determinants and consequences of workplace sex and race composition. *Annual Review of Sociology*, 25: 335–361.

17. A.J. Franklin, & Nancy Boyd-Franklin (2000). Invisibility syndrome: A clinical model of the effects of racism on African-American males. *American Journal of Orthopsychiatry*, 70(1): 33–41.

18. This study included 101 African American and 262 European American women. No relationship was found between subtle mistreatment and cardiovascular reactivity in the Anglo women. See Max Guyll, Karen A. Matthews, & Joyce T. Bromberger (2001). Discrimination and unfair treatment: Relationship to cardiovascular reactivity among African American and European American women. *Health Psychology*, 20(5): 315–325.

19. Janis V. Sanchez-Hucles (1997). Jeopardy not bonus status for African American women in the work force: Why does the myth of advantage persist? *American Journal of Community Psychology*, 25(5): 565–580.

20. The percentage of Black men ages 20 years and older in the workforce in the year 2000 was 73 percent compared to 66 percent for Black women.

Current Population Survey, Bureau of Labor Statistics. Employment status of major age-sex groups by race and Hispanic origin, 1994, 1999, and 2000 annual averages. In Stella Cromartie & Gloria P. Goings (2001). *Labor Force Characteristics of Blacks and Hispanics* (Table 1). Washington, D. C.: U.S. Bureau of Labor Statistics.

21. In 2001 the median weekly earnings of a full-time Black woman worker was $451, compared to $518 for Black men, $521 for White women, and $694 for White men. Current Population Survey, Bureau of Labor Statistics, Department of Labor. Median weekly earnings of full-time wage and salary workers by selected characteristics. Available on-line at: www.bls.gov/cps/cpsaat37.pdf.

22. In a study of a representative sample of women in Los Angeles County, it was found that one-third of Black women reported at least one incident of sexual harassment at work and two-thirds of these had been directly and inappropriately propositioned in the workplace. See Gail E. Wyatt & Monika Riederle (1995). The prevalence and context of sexual harassment among African American and White American women. *Journal of Interpersonal Violence, 10*(3): 309–321.

23. Jennifer Tucker, Leslie R. Wolfe, Edna Amparo Viruell-Fuentes, & Wendy Smooth (1999). *No More 'Business as Usual.'*

24. Center for Women's Business Research (2001). African American Women-Owned Businesses in the United States, 2002: A Fact Sheet. Washington, D.C.

25. Ibid.

26. Ibid.

27. Karen Robinson-Jacobs, "Census Finds High Number of Black Female Entrepreneurs," *Los Angeles Times*, July 13, 2001. These findings are based on a survey by the U.S. Census Bureau in 1997. Notably, businesses owned by African American women had lower revenues (an average of $43,300 per year) than firms owned by any other group.

28. Three suggested readings on organizational diversity issues are: (1) R. Roosevelt Thomas, Jr. (1991). *Beyond Race and Gender: Unleashing the Power of Your Total Work Force by Managing Diversity.* New York: American Management Association. (2) J. Renae Norton & Ronald E. Fox (1997). *The Change Equation: Capitalizing on Diversity for Effective Organizational Change.* Wash-

ington, D. C.: American Psychological Association. (3) Katharine Esty, Richard Griffin, & Marcie Schorr Hirsch (1995). *Workplace Diversity: A Manager's Guide to Solving Problems and Turning Diversity into a Competitive Advantage*. Holbrook, Mass.: Adams Media Corporation.

Chapter 7: "Mirror, Mirror on the Wall"

1. Internalized oppression is a process where those who are victimized take in negative beliefs about themselves from the victimizers and incorporate them into their own belief system. In this case, the Black community at times takes in and perpetuates negative views about unprocessed hair or dark skin. See section on Internalized Racism in: Beverly Greene (1994). African American women. In Lillian Comas-Díaz & Beverly Greene (Eds.), *Women of Color: Integrating Ethnic and Gender Identities in Psychotherapy* (pp. 10–29). New York: Guilford Press.

2. Maxine S. Thompson & Verna M. Keith (2001). The blacker the berry: Gender, skin tone, self-esteem, and self-efficacy. *Gender & Society*, 15(3): 336–357. Also see Christine C. Iijima Hall (1995). Beauty is in the soul of the beholder: Psychological implications of beauty and African American women. *Cultural Diversity and Mental Health*, 1(2): 125–137.

3. Regan Lester & Trent A. Petrie (1998). Physical, psychological, and societal correlates of bulimic symptomatology among African American college women. *Journal of Counseling Psychology*, 45(3): 315–321.

4. See "Myriad Opportunities in Ethnic Merchandising," *Business and Industry*, February 25, 2002, 19(4): 28, and "BeautyandSoul.com Finally Answers Needs of Largest Beauty Consumer—Black Women," *PR Newswire*, November 16, 1999.

5. Darlene Clark Hine & Kathleen Thompson (1998). *A Shining Thread of Hope: The History of Black Women in America*. NY: Broadway Books.

6. Earlier studies indicate that body image is less central to Black women's view of themselves and that they are more accepting of themselves at higher body weights. See D. E. Smith, J. K. Thompson, J. M. Raczynski, & J. E. Hilner. (1999). Body image among men and women in a biracial cohort: The CARDIA study. *International Journal of Eating Disorders*, 25: 71–82.

The two official eating disorder diagnoses are anorexia nervosa and bulimia nervosa. Anorexia nervosa is characterized by a refusal to maintain a body weight at or above a minimal normal weight, (i.e., body weight is 85 percent or less of what is expected); a fear of gaining weight; and a distorted perception of the shape or size of one's body, (i.e. the person feels fat even when she is underweight). Bulimia nervosa is characterized by recurrent episodes of binge eating, where the person eats a large amount of food and loses control over the eating episode; repeated measures to prevent weight gain, through, for example, self-induced vomiting, abuse of laxatives or diuretics, or excessive exercise; and a perception of oneself that is excessively influenced by body weight and shape. Most bulimics are within the normal weight range and thus may not be obviously symptomatic to family members and friends. Binge-eating disorder is currently a provisional rather than an official diagnosis. It is characterized by recurrent episodes of binge eating with loss of control, the absence of compensatory measures (e.g., purging and fasting), and distress about the binge episodes and the impact on one's weight. People who meet certain provisional criteria for binge-eating disorder are currently diagnosed as "eating disorder not otherwise specified." Binge-eating disorder, which has been examined and researched much less than anorexia and bulimia, is generally not assumed to be a "White women's disease." See American Psychiatric Association (2000). *Diagnostic and Statistical Manual of Mental Disorders—Fourth Edition, Text Revision* (DSM-IV-TR). Washington, D.C.

Lisa Williamson (1998). Eating disorders and the cultural forces behind the drive for thinness: Are African American women really protected? *Social Work in Health Care, 28*(1): 61–73.

7. D.E. Smith, J. K. Thompson, J. M. Raczynski, & J. E.Hilner (1999). Body image among men and women.

8. In a survey of more than 7,000 women, conducted by Ruth Striegel-Moore of Wesleyan University in Connecticut and her colleagues, Black women were as likely as White women to report vomiting in the previous three months, and they were more likely to report recurrent binge eating, fasting, and the abuse of laxatives or diuretics. See R. H. Striegel-Moore, D. E. Wilfley, K. M. Pike, F. A. Dohm, & C. G. Fairburn (2000). Recurrent binge

eating in Black American women. *Archives of Family Medicine*, 9(1): 83–87.

In a survey of over 2000 Black women conducted in 1993 through *Essence*, researchers found that many Black women have abnormal eating attitudes and behaviors and that Black women's risk for eating disorders may be equal to that of White women. The *Essence* Eating Disorders Survey involved a questionnaire that was made available to readers. The sample was not random or representative; thus, the study doesn't provide us with national statistics on distorted body image and disordered eating attitudes and behaviors in African American women. See A. J. Pumariega, C. R. Gustavson, J. C. Gustavson, P. S. Motes, & S. Ayers (1994). Eating attitudes in African-American women: The *Essence* Eating Disorders Survey. *Eating Disorders: The Journal of Treatment and Prevention*, 2(1): 5–16.

9. Amy Mulholland & Laurie Mintz (2001). Prevalence of eating disorders among African American women. *Journal of Counseling Psychology*, 48(1): 111–116. Also see Regan Lester & Trent Petrie (1998). Physical, psychological, and societal correlates of bulimic symptomatology among African American college women.

10. Sharlene Hesse-Biber (1996). *Am I Thin Enough Yet? The Cult of Thinness and the Commercialization of Identity*. NY: Oxford University Press.

11. For an excellent in-depth discussion of the history and politics of skin color bias in the African American community, see Kathy Russell, Midge Wilson, & Ronald Hall (1992). *The Color Complex: The Politics of Skin Color among African Americans*. New York: Doubleday.

12. Mark E. Hill (2002). Skin color and the perception of attractiveness among African Americans: Does gender make a difference? *Social Psychology Quarterly*, 65(1): 77–91.

13. These data are from the National Survey of Black Americans conducted in 1979–1980. See Maxine S. Thompson & Verna M. Keith (2001). The blacker the berry.

14. Christine C. Iijima Hall (1995). Beauty is in the soul of the beholder.

15. The National Survey of Black Americans includes a representative, national sample of 2107 Black men and women who were interviewed in 1979–1980. See Verna M. Keith & Cedric Herring (1991). Skin tone and

stratification in the Black community. *American Journal of Sociology*, 97(3): 760–778.

16. Margaret L. Hunter (2002). "If you're light you're alright": Light skin color as social capital for women of color. *Gender & Society*, 16(2): 175–193. Hunter did the analysis using 1310 african American women participants in the 1979–1980 National Survey of Black Americans.

17. Naomi Wolf (1991). *The Beauty Myth: How Images of Beauty are Used Against Women*. New York: Anchor Books.

18. The percent who are overweight includes those who have a body mass index (BMI) of 25 or above. See U.S. Census Bureau (2002). Table No. 197. Percent of U.S. adults who were overweight and percent who were obese: 1998. *Statistical Abstract of the United States: 2001*. Washington, D.C.

19. Interview with Ndidi Moses.

20. This information is based on a telephone interview with Ruth Striegel-Moore.

21. This study concluded that "Women from minority groups who have eating disorders are underdiagnosed and typically not treated." In Fary M. Cachelin, Ramona Rebeck, Catherine Veisel, & Ruth H. Striegel-Moore (2001). Barriers to treatment for eating disorders among ethnically diverse women. *International Journal of Eating Disorders*, 30(3): 269–278.

22. Paulette M. Caldwell (2000). A hair piece: Perspective on the intersection of race and gender. In Anne Minas (Ed.), *Gender Basics: Feminist Perspectives on Men and Women* (2nd ed., pp. 98–105). Belmont, CA: Wadsworth.

23. It's estimated that 10 percent of women who are diagnosed with anorexia nervosa and who are admitted to university hospitals eventually die from the disorder, due to starvation, suicide, or a biochemical imbalance in the body. See American Psychiatric Association (2000). *Diagnostic and Statistical Manual of Mental Disorders*.

24. Naomi Wolf (1991). *The Beauty Myth*.

Chapter 8: Forging a Delicate Balance

1. For an excellent anthology that explores the reasons for and the implications of the decline in marriage among African Americans, see M. Belinda Tucker & Claudia Mitchell-Kernan (Eds.) (1995). *The Decline in Marriage among African Americans: Causes, Consequences, and Policy Implications.* New York: Russell Sage Foundation.

2. U.S. Census Bureau (2002). Table No. 49. Marital status of the population by sex, race, and Hispanic origin, 1980 to 2000. *Statistical Abstract of the United States*: 2001. Washington, D.C.

3. Ibid. In 2000, 13 percent of Black women ages 18 and older were divorced compared to 11 percent of White women and 9 percent of Hispanic women.

4. In 1998, the homicide rate for Black males was five times the rate for Black females and seven times the rate for White males. See U.S. Census Bureau (2002). Table No.115. Homicide rates by race, sex, and age: 1997 and 1998. *Statistical Abstract of the United States*: 2001. Washington, D.C.

In 1998, the suicide rate for Black males was almost six times the rate for Black females, though half the rate for White males. See U.S. Census Bureau (2002). Table No.113. Death rates from accidents and violence by race and sex: 1990 to 1998. *Statistical Abstract of the United States: 2001*. Washington, D.C.

In 2001, the number of Black males who were sentenced prisoners under state or federal jurisdiction was 585,000 as compared to 36,400 Black females. The rate of imprisonment per 100,000 persons in the population was 462 for White males and 3535 for Black males. See Bureau of Justice Statistics Bulletin, U.S. Department of Justice (July 2002). Prisoners in 2001. NCJ 195189. Available on-line at: www.ojp.usdoj.gov/bjs/pub/pdf/p01.pdf.

5. From the U.S. Census Bureau, Census 2000, available on-line at: www.census.gov/population/cen2000/phc-t1/tab01.txt. The population numbers are for "Blacks or African Americans alone or in combination with one or more other races," thus, these numbers include Blacks who identify as bi- or multiracial.

6. Donna L. Hoyert, Elizabeth Arias, Betty L. Smith, Sherry L. Murphy,

& Kenneth D. Kochanek. Deaths: Final Data for 1999, *National Vital Statistics Reports*, 49(8), September 21, 2001. Available on-line at: www.cdc.gov/nchs/data/nvsr/nvsr49/nvsr49_08.pdf.

7. Though the percentage of Black men, ages 20 and older in the labor force is greater than the percentage of Black women (73 percent vs. 66 percent), the actual number of men in the labor force is lower than the actual number of women (6,832,000 men vs. 7,774,000 women). See Current Population Survey, Bureau of Labor Statistics. Employment status of major age-sex groups by race and Hispanic origin, 1994, 1999, and 2000 annual averages. In Stella Cromartie & Gloria P. Goings (2001). *Labor Force Characteristics of Blacks and Hispanics* (Table 1). Washington, D.C.: U.S. Bureau of Labor Statistics.

8. Shirley Hatchett, Joseph Veroff, & Elizabeth Douvan (1995). Marital instability among Black and White couples in early marriage. In M. Belinda Tucker & Claudia Mitchell-Kernan (Eds.), The Decline in Marriage (pp. 177–218). Also see Robert J. Sampson (1995). Unemployment and imbalanced sex ratios: Race-specific consequences for family structure and crime. In M. Belinda Tucker & Claudia Mitchell-Kernan (Eds.). *The Decline in Marriage* (pp. 229–254).

9. In 2000, 35 percent of Black female-led families lived below the poverty level, in contrast to 6 percent of Black married-couple families. See Current Population Survey, U.S. Census Bureau (2000). Table A. People and families in poverty by selected characteristics: 1999 and 2000. Available online at: blue.census.gov/prod/2001pubs/p60–214.pdf.

10. This finding has been obtained in a number of studies, including a study based on the 1979–1980 National Survey of Black Americans, which included a representative national sample of more than 1700 Black participants. For a review of research in this area as well as results of this study, see Verna M. Keith (1997). Life stress and psychological well-being among married and unmarried Blacks. In Robert Joseph Taylor, James S. Jackson, & Linda M. Chatters (Eds.), *Family Life in Black America* (pp. 95–116). Thousand Oaks, CA: Sage.

In another study, based on the 1986 Americans' Changing Lives national survey, which included 534 Black and 836 White women, it was found that rates of depression were higher among unmarried in comparison to married

Black women. See J. A. Gazmararian, S. A. James, & J. M. Lepkowski (1995). Depression in Black and White women: The role of marriage and socioeconomic status. *Annals of Epidemiology*, 5(6): 455–463.

11. Verna M. Keith (1997). Life stress and psychological well-being among married and unmarried Blacks.

12. This finding is based on the 1986 Americans' Changing Lives Survey and included a national sample of 2059 married people. See Clifford L. Broman (1993). Race differences in marital well-being. *Journal of Marriage and the Family*, 55: 724–732.

13. J. A. Gazmararian, S. A. James, & J. M. Lepkowski (1995). Depression in Black and White women.

14. Robert B. Hill (1999). *The Strengths of African American Families: Twenty-five Years Later* (chap. 6). Lanham, MD: University Press of America.

15. See Haki R. Madhubuti (1990). *Black Men: Obsolete, Single, Dangerous? The Afrikan American Family in Transition: Essays in Discovery, Solution, and Hope*. Chicago: Third World Press. Also see Jawanza Kunjufu (1985). *Countering the Conspiracy to Destroy Black Boys*. Chicago: African American Images.

16. A report prepared by the Bureau of Justice Statistics based on statistics which were collected from victims, law enforcement agencies, and hospital emergency rooms reveals that between 1992 and 1996, an average of 7 Hispanic women, 8 White women, and 12 Black women per 1000 in the population experienced intimate partner violence each year. Black women were almost 6 times more likely to be victims of intimate partner violence than Black men. See Bureau of Justice Statistics, U.S. Department of Justice. (1998). Violence by Intimates: Analysis of Data on Crimes by Current or Former Spouses, Boyfriends, and Girlfriends. NCJ-167237. Available on-line at: www.ojp.usdoj.gov/bjs/pub/pdf/vi.pdf. For data on Asian women, see Bureau of Justice Statistics, U.S. Department of Justice (March 2001). Special Report: Violent Victimization and Race, 1993–1998. NCJ 176354.

There is evidence that the higher rate of partner violence against Black women is mostly due to the lower socioeconomic standing of Black women. In other words, when Black lower income women are compared to White lower income women, and when Black middle class women are compared to White middle class women, there are few differences in the rates of victimization. Yet, because of the disproportionate numbers of Black women who are stuck in poverty, the reality is that more Black women than women in the general population are suffering from partner violence. See a review of studies on spousal abuse of Black women in: Soraya M. Coley & Joyce O. Beckett (1988). Black battered women: A review of empirical literature. *Journal of Counseling and Development*, 66: 266–270. Also see a national study of violence in: Murray A. Straus & Richard J. Gelles (1990). *Physical Violence in American Families:Risk Factors and Adaptations to Violence in 8,145 Families*. New Brunswick, NJ: Transaction Publishers.

17. Odell Uzell & Wilma Peebles-Wilkins (1994). Black spouse abuse: A focus on relational factors and intervention strategies. In Robert Staples (Ed.), *The Black Family: Essays and Studies* (5th ed., pp. 104–111). Belmont, CA: Wadsworth.

18. Centers for Disease Control and Prevention fact sheet, July 2002.

19. Information obtained in a telephone interview with a spokeswoman for the Centers for Disease Control and Prevention in July 2002.

20. In the year 1998, of newly reported cases of AIDS among women in the U.S., 61 percent are Black women and more than 54 percent acquired AIDS through heterosexual sex. See Shannon L. Hader, Dawn K. Smith, Janet S. Moore, & Scott D. Holmberg (2001). HIV infection in women in the United States: Status at the millennium. *Journal of the American Medical Association*, 285(9): 1186–1192.

21. Gail E. Wyatt, Jennifer Vargas Carmona, Tamra Burns Loeb, Donald Guthrie, Dorothy Chin, & Gwen Gordon (2000). Factors affecting HIV contraceptive decision-making among women. *Sex Roles*, 42(7/8): 495–521.

22. Gina M. Wingood & Ralph J. DiClemente (1998). Partner influences and gender-related factors associated with noncondom use among young adult African American women. *American Journal of Community Psychology*, 26(1): 29–51.

23. Janet S. St. Lawrence, Gloria D. Eldridge, David Reitman, Connie E. Little, Millicent C. Shelby, & Ted L. Brasfield (1998). Factors influencing condom use among African American women: Implications for risk reduction interventions. *American Journal of Community Psychology*, 26(1): 7–28.

24. Hortensia Amaro & Anita Raj (2000). On the margin: Power and women's HIV risk reduction strategies. *Sex Roles*, 42(7/8): 723–749.

Chapter 9: The ABCs of Shifting

1. Current Population Reports, U.S. Bureau of Census. America's families and living arrangements: March 2000. Series P20-537. Available on-line at www.census.gov/population/socdemo/hh-fam/tabFM-2.txt. Internet release date: June 29, 2001.

2. Current Population Survey (2002). Table 1. Age, sex, household relationship, race and Hispanic origin: Poverty status of people by selected characteristics in 2001. Annual Demographic Survey: March Supplement. Available on-line at: ferret.bls.census.gov/macro/032002/pov/new01_001.htm.

3. In 2001, 47 percent of Black children under 18 years of age in single-parent female households were living below the poverty level. This is in contrast to 10 percent of Black children in married-couple families. See Current Population Survey (2002). Table 1. Age, sex, household relationship, race, and Hispanic origin.

4. See Current Population Survey, Bureau of Labor Statistics. Employment status by presence and age of youngest child, sex, race, and Hispanic origin, 1994, 1999, and 2000 annual averages. In Stella Cromartie & Gloria P. Goings (2001). *Labor Force Characteristics of Blacks and Hispanics.* (Table 11) Washington, D.C.: Bureau of Labor Statistics.

5. Carrie Allen McCray (1980). The Black woman and family roles. In LaFrances Rodgers-Rose (Ed.), *The Black Woman* (pp. 67–78). Beverly Hills, CA: Sage. Also see Beverly A. Greene (1990). What has gone before: The legacy of racism and sexism in the lives of Black mothers and daughters. *Women & Therapy,* 9(1–2): 207–230.

6. Michael C. Thornton (1997). Strategies of racial socialization among Black parents: Mainstream, minority, and cultural messages. In Robert J. Taylor, James S. Jackson, & Linda M. Chatters (Eds.), *Family Life in Black America* (pp. 201–215). Thousand Oaks, CA: Sage.

7. Michael C. Thornton, Linda M. Chatters, Robert J. Taylor, & Walter R. Allen (1990). Sociodemographic and environmental correlates of racial socialization by Black parents. *Child Development,* 61: 401–409.

8. Michael C. Thornton (1997). Strategies of racial socialization among Black parents.

9. Ella L.J. Edmondson Bell & Stella M. Nkomo (1998) Armoring: Learning to withstand racial oppression. *Journal of Comparative Family Studies*, 29(2): 285–295. Also see Beverly Greene (1994). African American women. In Lillian Comas-Díaz & Beverly Greene (Eds.), *Women of Color: Integrating Ethnic and Gender Identities in Psychotherapy* (pp. 10–29). New York: Guilford Press. Also see Beverly Greene (1990). Sturdy bridges: The role of African American mothers in the socialization of African American children. *Women & Therapy*, 10(1–2): 205–225.

10. Harold W. Stevenson, Chuansheng Chen, & David Uttal (1990). Beliefs and achievement: A study of Black, White, and Hispanic children. *Child Development*, 61(2): 508–523. For a review of the topic of Black parents' expectations of children's achievement, see Chapter 4 "Strong Achievement Orientation" in Robert B. Hill (1999). *The Strengths of African American Families: Twenty-Five Years Later*. Lanham, MD: University Press of America.

11. Chapter 7 "Strong Kinship Bonds" in Robert B. Hill (1999). *The Strengths of African American Families*.

12. Vetta L. Sanders Thompson (1994). Socialization to race and its relationship to racial identification among African Americans. *Journal of Black Psychology*, 20(2): 175–188.

13. Hillary Rodham Clinton (1996). *It Takes a Village: And Other Lessons Children Teach Us*. New York: Simon & Schuster.

14. Collins uses the term "othermother," which was coined by Rosalie Riegle Troester. See Patricia Hill Collins (1991). *Black Feminist Thought: Knowledge, Consciousness, and the Politics of Empowerment*. New York: Routledge. Also see Rosalie Riegle Troester (1991). Turbulence and tenderness: Mothers, daughters, and "othermothers" in Paule Marshall's *Brown Girl, Brownstones*. In Patricia Bell-Scott, Beverly Guy-Sheftall, Jacqueline Jones Royster, Janet Sims-Wood, Miriam DeCosta-Willis, & Lucie Fultz (Eds.), *Double Stitch: Black Women Write about Mothers and Daughters* (pp. 163–172). Boston: Beacon Press.

Chapter 10: "Can I Get a Witness?"

1. This finding is consistent with that of a number of other studies of religiosity. Taylor's study is based on data from five national data sets, including the Americans' Changing Lives Study which included 1174 Blacks, the General Social Survey which included 3610 Blacks, the Monitoring the Future Surveys which included 1760 Blacks, the National Black Election Study which included 1151 Blacks, and the National Survey of Black Americans which was comprised of 2107 Blacks. See Robert Joseph Taylor, Jacqueline Mattis, & Linda M. Chatters (1999). Subjective religiosity among African Americans: A synthesis of findings from five national samples. *Journal of Black Psychology, 25*(4): 524–543.

2. Robert Joseph Taylor & Linda M. Chatters (1991). Religious life. In James S. Jackson (Ed.), *Life in Black America* (pp. 105–123). Newbury Park, CA: Sage.

3. The most common strategy for coping with a stressful incident was to seek outside help and do something directly to confront the problem. The National Survey of Black Americans, which included a national representative sample of 2107 Blacks, was conducted in 1979–1980. See Clifford Broman (1996). Coping with personal problems. In Harold W. Neighbors & James S. Jackson (Eds.), *Mental Health in Black America* (pp. 117–129). Thousand Oaks, CA: Sage.

4. In the National Survey of Black Americans, 11 percent of respondents identified as being atheist, agnostic, or having no religious preference. Only slightly more than 1 percent identified as Muslim, Jewish, Buddhist, or Bahai. Robert Joseph Taylor & Linda M. Chatters (1991). Religious life.

5. In our survey of Black women, women identified as follows: Christian (86.7 percent), Muslim (1.2 percent), other religions (6.9 percent), and no religious identification (5.1 percent).

6. The seven historical Black churches, which compromise an estimated 80 percent of all Black Christians, include three Baptist denominations (National Baptist Convention, U.S.A., National Baptist Convention of America, Progressive National Baptist Convention); three Black Methodist denominations (African Methodist Episcopal Church, African Methodist Episcopal Zion Church, Christian Methodist Episcopal Church); and the

Church of God in Christ. An additional 6 percent of Black Christians are members of smaller historically Black denominations. See C. Eric Lincoln & Lawrence H. Mamiya (1990). *The Black Church in the African American Experience*. Durham, NC: Duke University Press.

7. C. Eric Lincoln & Lawrence H. Mamiya (1990). *The Black Church*. Also see Anthony B. Pinn. (2002). *The Black Church in the Post–Civil Rights Era*. Maryknoll, NY: Orbis Books.

8. See review of studies on religiosity, faith, and mental health in Black women in: Sherry L. Turner & Cherie A. Bagley (2000). The role of religion. In Norma J. Burgess & Eurnestine Brown (Eds.), *African American Women: An Ecological Perspective* (pp. 115–134). New York: Falmer Press. Also see discussion of studies on religiosity and mental health in Blacks in: Diane Robinson Brown (1990). Depression among Blacks: An epidemiologic perspective. In Dorothy S. Ruiz (Ed.), *Handbook of Mental Health and Mental Disorder among Black Americans* (pp. 71–93). New York: Greenwood Press.

9. This estimate is based on a national survey of 2150 churches in the seven major historical Black denominations. See C. Eric Lincoln & Lawrence H. Mamiya (1990). *The Black Church*.

10. Vashti M. McKenzie (1996). *Not Without a Struggle: Leadership Development for African American Women in Ministry*. Cleveland, Ohio: Pilgrim Press.

11 .C. Eric Lincoln & Lawrence H. Mamiya (1990). *The Black Church* (p. 304).

12. Anthony B. Pinn (2002). Sexism and church ministry. *The Black Church* (chap. 6).

13. The focus groups were conducted in St. Louis, Missouri at the church's annual meeting as well as in West Tennessee with women who were recruited from 20 churches in the area. See Marian H. Whitson (1997). Sexism and sexual harassment: Concerns of African American women of the Christian Methodist Episcopal Church. *Violence Against Women*, 3(4): 382–400.

14. For examples of womanist theology, developed by African American women theologians, see Jacquelyn Grant (1990). *White Women's Christ and Black Women's Jesus: Feminist Christology and Womanist Response*. Atlanta: American Academy of Religion. Also Renita J. Weems (1988). *Just a Sister*

Away: A Womanist Vision of Women's Relationships in the Bible. San Diego, CA: LuraMedia. For a sociological examination of Black women and the church, see Cheryl Townsend Gilkes (2001). *"If It Wasn't for the Women . . . ": Black Women's Experience and Womanist Culture in Church and Community*. Maryknoll, NY: Orbis Books.

A seminal anthology in the area of feminist spirituality is Carol P. Christ & Judith Plaskow (Eds.) (1979). *Womanspirit Rising: A Feminist Reader in Religion*. San Francisco: Harper & Row. A more recent anthology by the same editors is: Judith Plaskow & Carol P. Christ (Eds.) (1989). *Weaving the Visions: New Patterns in Feminist Spirituality*. San Francisco: Harper & Row.

15. Renita J. Weems (1988). *Just a Sister Away* (p. ix).

16. C. Eric Lincoln & Lawrence H. Mamiya (1990). *The Black Church*.

RECOMMENDED READING

Adams, Maurianne, Blumenfeld, Warren J., Castañeda, Rosie, Hackman, Heather W., Peters, Madeline L., & Zúñiga, Ximena (Eds.) (2000). *Readings for Diversity and Social Justice: An Anthology on Racism, Antisemitism, Sexism, Heterosexism, Ableism, and Classism.* New York: Routledge.

Bell, Ella L. J. Edmondson, & Nkomo, Stella M. (2001). *Our Separate Ways: Black and White Women and the Struggle for Professional Identity.* Boston: Harvard Business School Press.

Boyd, Julia A. (1993). *In the Company of My Sisters: Black Women and Self-Esteem.* New York: Plume/Penguin.

———. (1998). *Can I Get a Witness? Black Women and Depression.* New York: Plume/Penguin.

Boyd-Franklin, Nancy, & Franklin, A. J., with Pamela Toussaint (2000). *Boys into Men: Raising Our African American Teenage Sons.* New York: Dutton.

Cole, Johnnetta Betsch, & Guy-Sheftall, Beverly (2003). *Gender Talk: The Struggle for Women's Equality in African American Communities.* New York: Ballantine Books.

Giddings, Paula (1984). *When and Where I Enter: The Impact of Black Women on Race and Sex in America.* New York: William Morrow.

Gilkes, Cheryl Townsend (2001). *"If It Wasn't for the Women . . .": Black Women's Experience and Womanist Culture in Church and Community.* Maryknoll, NY: Orbis Books.

Hill, Robert B. (1999). *The Strengths of African American Families: Twenty-five Years Later.* Lanham, MD: University Press of America.

hooks, bell (1981). *Ain't I a Woman: Black Women and Feminism.* Boston: South End Press.

Hopson, Darlene Powell, & Hopson, Derek S. (1990). *Different and Wonderful: Raising Black Children in a Race-Conscious Society.* New York: Prentice Hall Press.

Hopson, Derek S., & Hopson, Darlene Powell (1995). *Friends, Lovers, and Soul Mates: A Guide to Better Relationships between Black Men and Women.* New York: Fireside.

Jackson, Leslie C., & Greene, Beverly (Eds.) (2000). *Psychotherapy with African American Women: Innovations in Psychodynamic Perspectives and Practice.* New York: Guilford.

Mitchell, Angela, with Kennise Herring (1998). *What the Blues is All About: Black Women Overcoming Stress and Depression.* New York: Perigree.

Morrison, Toni (Ed.) (1992). *Race-ing Justice, En-gendering Power: Essays on Anita Hill, Clarence Thomas, and the Construction of Social Reality.* New York: Pantheon.

Russell, Kathy, Wilson, Midge, & Hall, Ronald (1993). *The Color Complex: The Politics of Skin Color Among African Americans.* New York: Anchor Books.

Smitherman, Geneva (2000). *Black Talk: Words and Phrases from the Hood to the Amen Corner* (revised edition). Boston, New York: Houghton Mifflin.

St. Jean, Yanick, & Feagin, Joe R. (1998). *Double Burden: Black Women and Everyday Racism.* Armonk, NY: M.E. Sharpe.

Ward, Janie Victoria (2000). *The Skin We're In: Teaching Our Children to be Emotionally Strong, Socially Smart, Spiritually Connected.* New York: The Free Press.

Wyatt, Gail Elizabeth (1997). *Stolen Women: Reclaiming our Sexuality, Taking Back Our Lives.* New York: John Wiley & Sons.

INDEX

depression and, 128, 146
internalization of, 20
"paradox of strength," 20
psychological problems and, 19
relationships with Black men and,
211–13
Uzzell, Odell, 226, 318n. 17

Vanzant, Iyanla, 119

Walker, Madame C. J., 180, 312n. 5
Washington, Desiree, 51
Waters, Maxine, 99
Watts-Jones, Darielle, 130, 306n. 13
Weber, Lynn, 152, 309n. 8
Weems, Renita, 266, 324n. 15
Wek, Alex, 180
Whitson, Marian, 263, 324n. 13
Williams, Vanessa L., 192
Williams, Venus and Serena, 180
Winfrey, Oprah, 99
Wingood, Gina M., 228, 320n. 22
womanist theology, 266, 324n. 14
women, Black
dissatisfaction, statistics, 2, 8
education statistics, 13, 301n. 8
as entrepreneurs, 174
health and illnesses of, 5, 10,
64–65
labor statistics, salary, 150–51, 167
in managerial and professional
positions, 13–14, 151, 152–53,
155
marriage satisfaction, 209
marriage statistics, 208
as mothers, statistics, 238, 320n. 3
myths and stereotypes, 1, 2–4,
11–36

percentage of population, 2
shifting and, 6–10, 61–92
unemployment rates, 155, 309n.
13
welfare and, 151, 308n. 3
women's movement and, 41–42
See also depression; gender discrimination; language; race discrimination; sexual abuse and
harassment; workplace
women, White, Asian, and Hispanic
abusive relationships and, 225
body image and, 180–81
depression and, 209
dissatisfaction, statistics, 2, 8
eating disorders and, 180, 313n. 7
education statistics, 13, 301n. 8
labor statistics, salary, 150–51
in managerial and professional
positions, 13–14, 151
marriage satisfaction, 209
marriage statistics, 208, 316n. 1
sexual harassment vs. Black
women, 43
sexuality, 31
teen pregnancy, 31, 297n. 25
welfare and, 151, 308n. 3
women's movement and, 41–42
workplace, 9, 147–75
Black-owned businesses, 174,
311n. 27
Black single parents in, 238
Black women in managerial and
professional positions, 13–14,
151, 152–53, 155
Black women in labor force, 150,
308n. 1
diversity and, 167, 175, 311n. 28